CONTROL AND SUBVERSION

D1287088

Anthropology, Culture and Society

Series Editors:
Professor Thomas Hylland Eriksen, University of Oslo
Dr Jon P. Mitchell, University of Sussex

CONTROL
AND SUBVERSION

Gender Relations in Tajikistan

COLETTE HARRIS

Mehmet Kalyoncu
Maryland 2007

Pluto Press
LONDON • STERLING, VIRGINIA

First published 2004
by PLUTO PRESS
345 Archway Road, London N6 5AA
and 22883 Quicksilver Drive,
Sterling, VA 20166–2012, USA

www.plutobooks.com

Copyright © Colette Harris 2004

The right of Colette Harris to be identified as the author of this work
has been asserted by her in accordance with the Copyright,
Designs and Patents Act 1988.

British Library Cataloguing in Publication Data
A catalogue record for this book is available from
the British Library

ISBN 0 7453 2168 2 hardback
ISBN 0 7453 2167 4 paperback

Library of Congress Cataloging in Publication Data
Harris, Colette, 1948–
   Control and subversion : gender relations in Tajikistan / Colette Harris.
      p. cm. — (Anthropology, culture, and society)
Includes bibliographical references.
   ISBN 0–7453–2168–2 — ISBN 0–7453–2167–4 (Pbk.)
   1. Women—Tajikistan—Social conditions. 2. Sex customs—Tajikistan.
3. Social control—Tajikistan. 4. Post-communism—Tajikistan.
5. Tajikistan—Social conditions—1991– I. Title. II. Series.

HQ1735.25.H37 2004
305.42'09586—dc22

                                                      2003022869

10   9   8   7   6   5   4   3   2   1

Designed and produced for Pluto Press by
Chase Publishing Services, Fortescue, Sidmouth EX10 9QG
Typeset from disk by Stanford DTP Services, Northampton, England
Printed in the European Union by
Antony Rowe, Chippenham and Eastbourne, England

This book is dedicated to the memory of

Clif Dowell († 1992)
Michael Morrow († 1994)
Viktor Alekseevich Nechaev († 1995)
Karomat Isaeva († 1997)
Mikhail Mikhailovich Tajikov († 1997)
Ruth Liebrecht († 1998)

CONTENTS

ACKNOWLEDGEMENTS

Many people have helped and supported me in my study of Tajikistan, and without them my work would have been considerably more difficult and less pleasant. I shall try to remember them all here. However, if I have accidentally forgotten to name anyone, please do not think I am the less indebted.

My thanks to Greet Vink and the FUOS fund of the University of Amsterdam for providing me with two grants that allowed me to work on my research without taking a formal job. My thanks to Dave Hampson, Sjoerd van Schoneveld and the others who helped us with the first grants from Christian Aid for the Khatlon Women's Health Project. Thanks to Chris Buckley for his continued support, to Edith Wallmeier and the other CARE staff who enabled Ghamkhori (the Tajik NGO I was working with) to receive the EU/TACIS grant, and to the TACIS LIEN Fund whose support allowed me to continue working in Tajikistan until early 2001, and to carry on with our project to tackle some of the most critical problems of Tajik women.

My thanks also to Max Spoor for his comments on an earlier draft; to Natalya Kosmarskaya, Deniz Kandiyoti, and others for their useful material on topics related to Tajikistan, and their support of my research; and to Deniz also for her comments on an earlier draft. Thanks to Rayna Rapp, Paolo Possiedi, Rosalind Petchesky and my other New York friends for their support while I was doing my research there; to Ron Porta and Heather Mackay for welcoming me as a guest while I was reading in the British Library. Thanks also to the members of InDRA and AGIDS of the University of Amsterdam, and to many staff members of ISS for their support, especially to René Bekius for his bibliographical contributions. I am grateful to John Borstlap for his moral and practical support from the very beginning of this enterprise. I want to express particular thanks to Lorraine Nencel for her most helpful theoretical insights, suggestions on improving my approach and critiques of several drafts, as well as for introducing me to Pluto Press and thus facilitating the publication of this book.

Thanks to Gabrielle van den Berg, who gave me my first books in Tajik, and the benefit of her knowledge of Tajikistan. Thanks also to Janet Momsen for her belief in my work and to Margaret Merrill for helping me with the final manuscript. A very special thanks to Shirin Akiner, who applied her extraordinarily wide and deep knowledge of Central Asia to a critique of an earlier version, which helped me greatly to improve the political and historical sections of this text. I am grateful to her also for her strong support during the process of searching for a publisher.

Most heartfelt thanks to Joke Schrijvers, under whose guidance I wrote the original version of this book for my PhD dissertation, and whose sensitive oversight enabled me to develop my epistemological and methodological approaches. Her personal commitment and friendship, as well as her supervision, were invaluable. I owe much of what is good in it to her.

I wish to express my gratitude to Olga Dmitrieva, Natalya Kosmarskaya and my other friends in Moscow for their support during my visits, and for their introductions to people in Tajikistan at a time when I knew nobody there; to Larissa Dodkhudoeva for first inviting me to Tajikistan; to R.K. Rakhimov, Director of the Institute of World Economy and International Relations, for inviting me to become a guest researcher there in 1995; to Safro Isaeva for many things but especially for her introduction to her aunt Karomat; to Ayesha Homed whose support, comments and introductions were most useful; to Dr Sofia Hakimova for her help on matters relating to reproductive health; to the members of the ethnographic department of the Tajik Academy of Sciences for their bibliographical support; to the librarians of the Academy of Sciences library for their assistance; to Zoya Tajikova, Savely Dvorin, Zarrina Mirshakar, Zukhra Akhmedova, Volodya Savvateev and Margarita Voytova among many others, who helped me personally during my visits to Tajikistan. Thanks to all my friends from the international organizations in Tajikistan, especially those from CARE, Human Rights Watch, IFRC, Mission Øst, MSF Holland, Relief International, Save the Children Fund (UK), the Swiss Development Corporation, the UN's World Food Programme (WFP) and World Health Organisation (WHO). Especial thanks to the libraries of the Academy of Sciences, the Firdousi National Library of Tajikistan, ACCELS, and others for providing me with reading material outside my research topics.

Thanks to all those who kindly allowed me to print the stories they told me. They are individually acknowledged in the notes. In addition, I owe a great deal to the staff of Ghamkhori, who supported me, and continue to support me, and whose work has helped me learn so much about the culture of Tajikistan. And of course, a very, very special thanks to all those women (and men), who spent so many hours of their time with me recounting their (life) stories, and without whose friendship and openness this book would not have been possible. I hope one day to be able to publish it in Russian so they can read my conclusions for themselves.

Finally, I owe a great deal to the support of those persons, alas no longer with us, to whom I have dedicated this book. Clif and Michael died before I started my doctorate. Had they lived I am sure they would have done their best to support me in any way they could. Ruth helped me through many different phases of my life and was especially fascinated by the present one. I became friends with Viktor Alekseevich and Mikhail Mikhailovich on my first trip to Tajikistan. They spent the greatest part of their lives there and collected many useful books, some of which they passed on to me. Karomat was my daily companion during my first three trips to Tajikistan. Without her insights into Tajik life my understanding of the region would be much the poorer and so would this book.

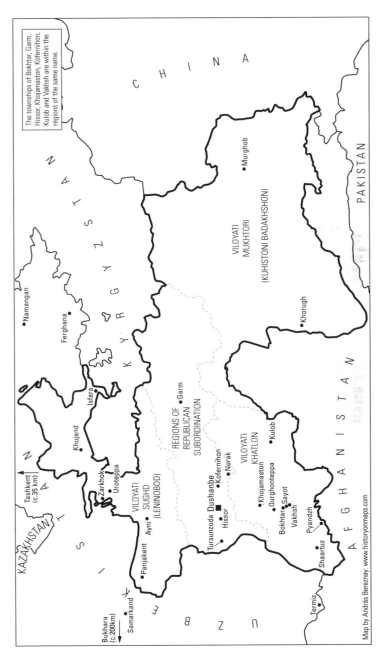

The townships of Bokhtar, Garm, Hissor, Khojamaston, Kofernihon, Kulob and Vakhsh are within the regions of the same name.

CHINA

KYRGYZSTAN

KAZAKHSTAN

UZBEKISTAN

AFGHANISTAN

PAKISTAN

• Namangan

Ferghana •

Istara

Khujand •

• Murghob

VILOYATI
MUKHTORI

(KUHISTONI BADAKHSHON)

• Khorugh

REGIONS OF
REPUBLICAN
SUBORDINATION

• Garm

Zarkhok •
Uroteppa •

VILOYATI
SUGHD
(LENINOBOD)

Tashkent
(c.35 km)

Panjakent •

Ayni •

Tursunzoda Dushanbe
Hissor • Kofernihon •
Norak •

Khojamaston •
Qurghonteppa •

Bokhtar • Sayot
Vakhsh •

Kulob •

VILOYATI
KHATLON

Pyandzh •

Shaartuz •

Termiz •

Bukhara
(c.200km)

Samarkand •

Tajikistan and surrounding region

Map by András Bereznay, www.historyonmaps.com

DRAMATIS PERSONAE

The main characters with their families. I have put in bold the names
of those who play an important role.

Family	Place of residence	Place of origin
Tillo	Dushanbe	Dushanbe
husband, **Chahonbek**	Dushanbe	Shaartuz
three daughters, two sons		
parents, grandparents		
Karomat (Isaeva)	Dushanbe	Zarkhok
husband, **Khudoydod**	Dushanbe	Dushanbe
niece, Safro Isaeva		
father, mother, sisters		
Jahongul	Dushanbe	Dushanbe
mother, **Nahdiya**		
brothers, Farhod and Farukh		
sister, **Tahmina**		
Tahmina's husband, **Rashid**	Dushanbe/Hissor	Dushanbe
Rustam	Dushanbe	Hissor
wife, **Jumbul**	Dushanbe	Dushanbe
four children		
girlfriend, **Zhenia**	Dushanbe/Russia	Dushanbe
father, **Malik;** mother, **Dilorom**	Dushanbe	Hissor
brother, Kurbon; Kurbon's wife,		
Mukhayo		
sisters, Khatiya and Sumangul		
Zora	Dushanbe	Uroteppa
husband, **Fayziddin**	Dushanbe	Khatlon
daughter, **Dila;** son, **Ali**	Dushanbe	Dushanbe

INTRODUCTION:
THE RESEARCH SETTING AND METHODOLOGY

It is a hot and sunny afternoon in the village of Sayot. A group of women are discussing the practical difficulties of attaining their rights and how complicated it is to control their lives when denied the use of direct action. In order to gain their husbands' approval they have to manipulate them without challenging the traditions that allow men unilateral rights of decision-making. Everyone is in fits of laughter as the women recount story after story of the clever ways in which they do this. The one that occasioned the most laughter was told by 30-year-old Zulfia:

My first two children were both girls. After the birth of the second I wanted a rest from pregnancy but my husband would not agree. He told me I would have to go on having children until I had a boy, however long this took. My third child was also a girl and I was becoming desperate.

I was pregnant for the fourth time in five years, exhausted, harried and dreading not only the birth of this child but the likelihood of having to face a fifth and perhaps even a sixth or seventh pregnancy, if the desired boy did not come along. I tried arguing that it would do no harm to wait a few years but my husband was adamant.

Lying awake at night trying to think of a way out, I eventually hit on a plan. When my labour pains started I sent for my husband. He immediately offered to fetch the midwife but I refused. I insisted on his preparing hot water, clean cloths and the other necessities. Then I called him to my side, took his hand, and held on to it.

Throughout my labour I did not let go, no matter how bad things got. When finally it was all over and my fourth daughter had been born he turned to me and said: 'That was ghastly! I can't let you go through it again. I will take you to get fitted with an IUD. It doesn't matter that we don't have a son. I can't face such horrors any more.' That was my last pregnancy and since then my husband has never again mentioned having a son.

We all laughed long at the vision of that poor man being forced to endure, if only at second hand, the pain that women go through every time they give birth. And we congratulated Zulfia on her clever tactics. Of course, she was lucky. Another man might have used violence to force her to let go, and walked away.

The Sayot women had come together through their participation in the health project I was helping to organise in their village and the neighbouring ones. I was present in my capacity as trainer of the educator but also as a researcher, using this as a golden opportunity to collect material for my work on gender relations in Tajikistan.

The memory of that afternoon and the roomful of merry women has remained with me ever since, an image of all that these women have to endure, but also of how they deal with their lives with ingenuity, imagination, strength and above all laughter.

After reading the manuscript of this book people have told me what a sad picture it presents. I can only say that, despite the sadness and the daily tragedies, the women at least still know how to enjoy themselves. Whenever a group of them gets together, no matter how many sorrows they have, they always manage to find something to joke about.

But indeed, over the last years Tajikistan has become a seriously depressing place. Twenty years ago it felt very secure, part of a system that would endure forever, where nothing much would ever change. The break-up of the Soviet Union and the civil war that followed put an end to even the remotest feeling of stability, leaving violence and economic collapse in their wake. The violence continues, although much reduced, and the threat of the imposition of a strict form of Islam, based on the *mujahaddin* model members of the opposition party brought back with them from their wartime exile in Afghanistan, has not completely disappeared.

Worst of all, however, are the serious economic problems that have closed state enterprises, caused massive layoffs and brought most people's monthly earnings down to considerably less than the lowest amount needed for survival. Although things have improved in the last few years, making ends meet remains a constant struggle for all but a fortunate few. It is clear to most inhabitants of Tajikistan that the secure past has vanished and nothing will ever be the same again. The belief that this means the end of the good times and that there is, therefore, little hope for the future, is very dispiriting.

But not all the problems in Tajikistan are due to the difficult political and economic situations. Many of the saddest and most tragic problems are the result of social pressures from within the communities themselves. This is in essence the subject of this book, in which I explore how social control in Tajikistan is exerted and subverted.[1] In order to do this I look at power relations, especially those based on gender and age, with – at their heart – control over (female) sexuality.

THE HEALTH PROJECT[2]

The Khatlon Women's Health Project is implemented by the Tajik NGO Ghamkhori. The project was conceived during discussions held in 1994–96 with women from Dushanbe and Khatlon. Financed by Christian Aid of London, it got off the ground in April 1997, with a small group of five staff. Since then, the number of staff has expanded considerably.[3]

The project serves inhabitants of villages in the Bokhtar, Khojamaston and Vakhsh regions of Khatlon province in southern Tajikistan, providing group discussions on health and social issues. Midwives provide basic services, including contraceptives, and train traditional birth attendants. Parents are helped to understand the early development of their children and the importance of nutrition. Sex education is provided for teenagers. The project also works on improving family relations and decreasing domestic violence through exploring gender identities and women's and children's rights. Village committees help guide the process and make the project sustainable long-term. In spring 2000 a women's centre was opened in the local urban centre, Qurghon-teppa, to aid victims of violence, and this provides psycho-social counselling, legal and sexological support.[4] The aim is to support participants in developing greater self-reliance and new visions, and perhaps even in moderating the strictness of their gender norms.

MY RESEARCH FOCUS

When I started this research in 1994, socialism and its relation to the lives of Tajik women were very much at the forefront of my mind. I diligently read through the collected works of Lenin and Stalin, dipped into Trotsky, and spent some months in libraries in Moscow, reading all the Soviet sources on Tajikistan and its women I could find. No doubt this, together with the time I spent studying life in Russia, stood me in good stead, by providing me with a sound background to the region. However, once I actually arrived in the republic, socialism as a topic in its own right started to seem less and less relevant and eventually came to take a back-seat in my work.

Therefore, this book dedicates little space to the successes and failures of Soviet socialism, but neither does it merely explore the lifestyles of women. Instead it has become an inquiry into the exercise of social control, and how this has been turned back on itself, resisted, evaded and suborned by both women and men. It is about the way power functions in intra- and inter-familial domination and repression, and the endeavours of the representatives of the state to control its Tajik citizens through inculcating Russo-Soviet gender norms. It deals with the oppression of women and of youth, but also with the secret subversion of the state by the Tajik people and their refusal of the gender identities the Soviet regime wished to impose on them, as well as about the subversion of, and resistance to, social control on the part of the community's (younger) members.

My inquiry into Tajik society centres round three interrelated points:

- The nature of the (gendered) power relations that produce and enable domination, and their function within the various layers of social relations. Here I have found the work of Michel Foucault, especially his work on power and on sexuality (1980a, 1990, 1992), to be invaluable in explaining the dynamics of communal power at the lowest levels of social interaction.
- The formation of human identity, that is the psychological development of the subject, the struggles around parental subjugation of children and their attempts to separate from their parents and attain agency. For this I have drawn on the work of Judith Butler (1997b).
- The way subjects form their (gender) identities and the significance of these for social control. Once again my theoretical basis is the work of Butler, this time her writing on gender and sexuality (1990, 1993, 1995a, 1995b, 1997a, 1999), most particularly her theory of performativity.[5]

My exploration starts at the level of state politics and ends at the marriage bed. Linking the two can be found that major institution of social organisation, the family. At each level I examine who exercises control, how this is done, and how far and in what way subversion and/or resistance follow. It may seem incongruous that an inquiry into the internal processes of Tajik society should start with an analysis of the relations of the Tajik community with the state. However, this is particularly important here, where the Soviet government's cultural engineering project discussed in Chapter 2 played a crucial role in the development of communal controls and gender identities. It may seem equally incongruous that it should end up in the marriage bed. However, the centre of gender power relations is control over female sexuality. Moreover, sex is at the heart of marriage, the foundational relationship of the family. This in turn reinforces the position of sex at the centre of social control.

RESEARCH AND SEX

At the start of this research project, I had a conversation on sex with several elite women from Dushanbe. They told me in no uncertain terms that I should leave the topic alone, since it was not a proper subject for study. 'Why do all [you feminists] find sex so important? Can't you find better things to look into?' they asked. My answer could only be a resounding 'No', because time and time again my fieldwork subjects themselves told me how important sex was in their lives.

As I hope to demonstrate, sex is the linchpin of correct gender performance in Tajikistan. As Foucault points out, it is a vital part of power relations at all levels of society and heavily regulated by public discourse as well as the state (1990: 103, 143). How then could I inquire into gender power relations and omit sex?

As I discovered, ignorance of sexual matters has to be one of the greatest causes of pain and suffering in the country. According to official statistics many divorces occurred because of young couples' sexual ignorance (Monogarova 1982: II, 61). How many girls could avoid unwanted pregnancies, how much personal unhappiness and even despair could be averted, how many fewer people would suffer from sexually transmitted diseases, if only there were appropriate sex education for all. Certainly, in the past Muslims believed in this. Mediaeval Muslim jurists produced extremely frank and open sex manuals (Chapter 6), where men are exhorted to satisfy their partners, and lovemaking is celebrated as bringing people nearer to God (Mernissi 1987: 41), in marked contrast to the Christian position that sexual pleasure was a sin (Musallam 1983).

The prudish attitude to sex on the part of educated Tajiks today is presumably largely due to the puritanical influence of the former Soviet Union, where from the mid-1920s all public mention of sex was banned. It was considered that for all practical purposes, presumably meaning for procreation, people knew what to do, so there was no point in wasting time and energy discussing the matter. The tremendous suffering caused by the resultant silence and consequent widespread ignorance was considered a purely private matter, which the Soviet regime always preferred to ignore (Gray 1991; Kon 1995; Shlapentokh 1984, 1989). The attitude fostered by this was for me typified by an incident from the live US–USSR television debates of 1986, when a middle-aged Russian woman stood up and pronounced with the utmost resolution: 'We have no sex in the Soviet Union' (see Kon 1995: 1).

It frequently happens in Tajikistan that two young and hitherto unacquainted people are forced to have intercourse on their wedding night,

without either having had the possibility of developing a personal relationship or knowing much, if anything, about the mechanics of the sex
act, let alone female sexuality. Male ignorance on such matters takes
much of the potential joy out of the marital relation. The ignorance girls
are kept in, first to prevent their becoming interested in sex before
marriage and later to prevent their running away petrified on their
wedding night, is conducive to making it difficult, and in some cases
impossible, for them even to tolerate sex.

I learned more of the sex-related suffering ordinary men and women
often endure from clients of the Qurghonteppa women's centre, who
made it clear how crucial sex is to the success of their marital relationships (Harris forthcoming).

LOVE

The vast majority of Tajik marriages are arranged by parents. This does
not prevent an ongoing debate, especially among women and girls, on
love within marriage, irrespective of whether or not the marriage is
arranged. Studies of other Muslim communities also show young women
yearning, usually in vain, to experience marital love (see Al-Khayyat
1990; Naamane-Guessous 1988). In Tajikistan love can be so important
that both men and women have been known to commit suicide rather
than face life without their beloved.[6] This is not a new phenomenon, as
is demonstrated by Karomat's story of pre-revolutionary life in Chapter
2, as well as by progressive Muslim fiction from the late nineteenth
century favouring romantic love as the preferred foundation for marital
relationships (Kamp 1998: 76).

Love was the favourite topic not only of the older girls participating in
the health project, who knew they would have no alternative but to
accept the husband of their parents' choice, but also of their mothers.
The latter seemed to delight in the chance to talk about the loves of their
youth, thoughts of whom had sustained them throughout the stresses
of life with the men their parents had saddled them with. It is revealing
to hear these nostalgic reminiscences on the part of women who, while
appearing to feel little positive emotion for their own spouses, nevertheless insist on the right to select their children's.

In considering love in relation to the stories in this book it should not
be forgotten that there are many different kinds. The romantic variety,
found in western novels and romances, as also in the soap operas and
films so many Tajik girls are devoted to, is only one of these, and not
necessarily what the characters in this book are referring to (Chapter 6).

THE SUBJECTS OF MY FIELDWORK

A question that frequently arises when one presents a body of ethnographic work is how far the researcher herself has influenced those whom she researched. It seems to me inevitable that the flow of information cannot be unidirectional but must to some extent represent an exchange. With most of the subjects of my book I had relatively little discussion of my own points of view, although I am sure they must have sensed my basically feminist standpoint and this must doubtless bear some responsibility for the ways in which they framed their stories.

I cannot know how much I influenced the people whom I met during my time in Tajikistan but my contacts with them certainly profoundly influenced the direction of my research. It was getting to know the women, especially the younger ones, which inspired me to change the focus of my work from an inquiry into socialism to an exploration of the inner workings of the Tajik community. It was seeing the constraints they lived under, especially the strong family pressures, that convinced me this was *the* major influence on their lives. Later, my friendship with the one man I got to know well, whom I call Rustam, greatly enriched my understanding of men's problems, enabling me to view issues of the relationships between the sexes from a very different angle, and realise that it is not only women who are oppressed.

Despite its geographical situation in Asia, Tajikistan is not a southern country in the pure sense of the term. Soviet colonisation provided its population with a solid material infrastructure. Moreover, exposure to Russian culture with its significant differences from their own traditions made Tajiks more conscious of these. The result was that they constantly talked of 'our customs', juxtaposing them to what they understood as the Russian way of life.

The most Russianised of all the Tajik actors in this book is Rustam. Son of an atheist Party official, Rustam went to school with Russians, read a great deal of Russian literature, and had intense emotional relationships with a series of Russian girlfriends. As a result, his outlook on male/female relationships resembles that of Europeans, so that it is not entirely coincidental that he was the one Tajik man with whom I was able to develop a close friendship. Even so, he has not been able to escape the constraints of Tajik society, particularly in his interactions with his own family. This makes his story particularly pertinent to this book.

Much of the ethnographic material I present consists of family histories. In each group I tried to interact with as many members as possible, although I usually had close contact with only one or two people from each. I must confess I find it almost impossible to interview people in depth if I do not feel drawn to them, so I spent relatively little time with those with whom I was unable to sympathise. Conversely, I developed emotional relationships with all those whose stories I tell at length, and even with some I met only briefly. This may in part account for the fact that so many people were open with me on such intimate subjects.

The strongest relationship I developed was with Karomat Isaeva, a very determined lady, almost 70 years of age, to whom I was introduced soon after my arrival in Tajikistan. At that time her nearly 94-year-old father was living with her, but unfortunately he died a few hours before I returned for my second visit, so that I walked right into the middle of the funeral ceremonies when I went round to say hello. My first flat in Dushanbe was near hers and while I lived there we frequently saw each other several times a day. We became so close that Karomat adopted me as her sister and would even introduce me as such to her friends. In fact, I was often taken to be her blood sister, at least by Russians, to whom I apparently resembled a Tajik.[7]

I owe a great deal of my understanding of Tajik life and society to Karomat, who devoted considerable time and effort to explaining it to me. Another debt I owe her is my fluency in Tajik. Although she was prepared to talk Russian with me when I first arrived, she was delighted I was learning her language and did all she could to encourage me. As soon as I was able to make myself understood she refused to talk Russian any more, no matter how many problems I had following the conversation in Tajik. This gave me invaluable practice, which was hard to get in Dushanbe, just because it was so much easier for people to speak with me in Russian.

Karomat was the one person who wanted me to use her real name in my work. She could not bear the idea that after her death she would vanish from the face of the earth as if she had never been. As she had neither children nor, as she put it, had produced any significant works of art that would keep her name alive, the solution she had chosen was to get her life story published. She had been thinking about this for some time before I met her and when she realised what I was doing in Tajikistan she decided to ask me to be the vehicle for this undertaking (see Harris 1998a).

I have done my best to conceal the identities of the remaining subjects of this book and to this end have given them assumed names, as well as changing many details of their lives. It is not too difficult to conceal the identity of people in urban areas but villages are too small. For this reason, as well as to avoid other complications, I have set the stories of the villagers from Bokhtar and Vakhsh, who all come from very similar surroundings, not in their real villages but rather in the invented village of Sayot, which I locate somewhere on the boundary line between the two regions. I conceive it as typical of the larger villages in the area, in being comprised of a number of different segments that function almost like separate entities.

One important question I have been faced with is how to reconcile the diverse subjects of my ethnographic inquiry. As noted in the history section of Chapter 1, there are well-demarcated regional groups within Tajikistan and less clear shades of difference also exist between small units such as villages, or even sections of villages. Such differences are noted by Tajiks themselves when they say '*they* have different customs from *ours*', although *they* may live less than half a kilometre away.

My problem is that each of the main group of families with whom I have had close links originated in different places, although they all ended up settled in Dushanbe, and some of the children were raised there entirely. My second group of families, those with whom the health project deals or whose stories are related by health-project staff, live in Khatlon. But most of their families are originally from Garm or nearby regions and today they still maintain strong cultural as well as social ties with their places of origin.

The extent of the regional differences might be considered to preclude these families from being regarded as belonging to the same cultural group. The question then arises whether it is even legitimate to put these persons all together in one book and deal with them as if they were culturally homogeneous. In other words, can they simply be lumped together as Tajiks?

I think the answer to this is both yes and no. It all depends on what exactly is under investigation, and which groups of Tajiks are being considered. While there are many differences in the rituals of daily life and domestic practices, for the mostly southern Tajiks I deal with here, regional variations in gender norms, the major cultural element explored in this book, are very minor. Indeed, they themselves suggest this when they preface every discussion pertaining to gender identities with the phrase 'We Tajiks ... ', while the rest of the time they reject the national label and insist on identifying themselves purely by locality. Therefore, I believe I am justified in grouping these families together under the single rubric 'Tajik' when dealing with gender relations, although perhaps this should be preceded by the adjective 'southern', since mountain Tajiks have somewhat more relaxed gender identities (see Tett 1994, 1995) and those from northern Tajikistan hold to somewhat more rigid social standards.[8]

TAJIKISTAN AND THE WEST[9]

When I arrived back in the west after my first visit to Tajikistan I spent a great deal of time trying to assimilate and make sense of my impressions. The most difficult points for me to come to terms with were the strong pressures towards conformity, the almost symbiotic, highly controlling parent/child relationships, and the lack of emotional ties between spouses.

I knew that in some western countries there were considerable pressures towards conformity, especially in Central Europe and parts of the United States. I knew also that people often consulted their families regarding major decisions, but having early on become self-reliant, as a result of my parents having died when I was very young, I had simply taken it for granted that in the west, or at least in north-western Europe and the United States, middle-class children at least left home around the age of 18, having already gained considerable psychological independence from their parents, and subsequently saw them relatively seldom.

With eyes fresh from Tajikistan I found to my shock how very many of the things I had found most difficult to grasp there were endemic in the west, and how much greater were the constraints that many westerners live under than I had previously realised.

An American friend told me how when she had become pregnant in the early 1960s, at age 17, her parents had sent her off to a hostel for single mothers-to-be, where the staff treated her as a criminal and removed her baby forcibly at birth. While she was away her parents made up some tale of her helping a sick aunt, in order for her 'wrongdoing' not to be made public and thus disgrace the entire family. The exact same thing happened with many middle-class English families around the same time. In the course of a BBC television broadcast one woman recounted how, when she became pregnant out of wedlock, her mother told her it would have been preferable had she committed murder![10]

With regard to young people in the west today I realised that their relative economic independence did not necessarily mean they were psychologically independent, and that many people had symbiotic relationships with their parents long after they were grown up, especially since many young people nowadays simply cannot afford to leave home at age 18.

Yet again, observing the often violent relationships between married couples and the lack of trust and communication between them, I started to wonder whether marriage in the west was based on significantly more open, honest relationships, psychological communication or even romantic love, than in Tajikistan. Moreover, considering the propensity of westerners – especially, but not only, men – for promiscuous behaviour, I also began to wonder how often they were able to focus on one specific object of passion (Chapter 6).

During the course of a BBC television inquiry into sexuality,[11] one young English woman recounted how a few years before, at age 17, she had participated in a discussion on the existence of the female orgasm. Not one of the women present had ever had one but they had all heard of it and were desperate to know if it really existed. Several men, including a married man aged 40, maintained that only they could experience orgasm, women could not.

This all sounded so much like Tajikistan that listening to it I felt as if these two worlds had suddenly been conflated and this, more than anything else, brought home to me how very many similarities there are between Britain and other western countries, and Tajikistan. How this came about was a question I kept asking myself throughout this research.

1 CONCEPTUAL BACKGROUND

Power relations

Zora is from the town of Uroteppa in the north, while her husband, Fayziddin, is from a village near Qurghonteppa in the south. They met and married at university and afterwards stayed on in Dushanbe. They have two children, a daughter Dila, and a son, Ali.

Although Fayziddin earned much less than Zora he considered himself the head of the family and insisted everyone obey him, so that, despite the fact that his wife held a taxing job, he always refused to help in the house. It was not his business to do 'women's' work. On the contrary Zora must wait on him. If she protested he would beat her. Zora was often very tired and could not cope with all the housework by herself. With only one daughter to help her she found herself forced to co-opt her son into assisting her.

Fayziddin, however, was concerned with the effect this was having on his children's upbringing and especially on the family image. It made him very nervous to imagine the neighbours' comments. Therefore, whenever he came home and found Ali helping his mother he would beat her and threaten to repeat this if he caught her encouraging his son to behave in 'womanly' ways again. 'Boys do not do housework', Fayziddin told Ali repeatedly, while also beating him for greater emphasis. Eventually Ali learned his lesson, so that even in his father's absence he would refuse to do any work in the home, including taking out the refuse, ignoring his mother's plaint that this was a man's job.

Fayziddin never laid a finger on Dila because her upbringing was her mother's responsibility. He did, however, check how Zora was fulfilling this task. He was a strict father and wanted his children to behave as he and his siblings had done in his native village. Although they lived in Dushanbe, he would have preferred Dila to dress in traditional clothes all the time, even at university. In Soviet times all students had to wear Russian dress. Dila had been allowed to comply with this but by the time she started university the Soviet Union had ended, and with it such rules. Fayziddin was determined his daughter would wear ezor to cover her legs. Dila wanted to protest, but she could not oppose her father directly. Instead she begged her mother to intercede for her.

Zora, herself raised in an urban culture, thought her husband was over-reacting and that his attitude reflected his village upbringing. She told him that dressing like that would make Dila a laughing stock. Reluctantly, Fayziddin agreed to allow Dila to wear Russian clothes, but he kept strict reins on her throughout her student days.

12

When Ali started college he found himself unable to concentrate or work hard. As a result his parents ended up paying for him to pass the exams he could not manage on his own. He has now graduated but since he did not gain much in the way of skills he cannot find a job, so he spends most of his time at home. Dila is also at home a lot and the two of them bicker constantly. Their parents, however, demand total obedience from the two of them, just as they did when they were little. Fayziddin no longer beats his son, who is too strong, but he will brook no opposition from either child. Ali can sulk, but, like his sister he does not dare answer his father back or refuse to obey him. He knows that it would be a serious offence to confront him directly.

Dila and Ali are neither materially nor psychologically able to free themselves from their parents. Ali, in particular, resents their authority over him but for the time being he is unable to relinquish his dependence on them. Without their help he could not have got through college and he is unlikely to obtain a job or be able to marry without their intervention. Dila too knows she has no option but to accept parental authority until such time as control over her is passed to her future husband and his family.

In the following chapters Zora, Fayziddin and their children, reappear, along with many others. Meanwhile, this story provides a context for the presentation of my theoretical framework, illustrating some dynamics of Tajik family relationships and how these are affected by interaction with the wider community.

As male head of the family, overall control is Fayziddin's responsibility, while Zora's task is to keep the household running. As Dila and Ali grow up they are expected to assimilate the appropriate gendered behaviour, at times coercively inculcated. The latters' resentment of their parents' dominion over them is tempered by their material and psychological dependence. However, Fayziddin's dominant stance does not mean that he holds all the power within the family while the others meekly assume positions of subordination. Even Dila, who as a young woman holds a very low position, is able to exert a certain degree of power. Moreover, it is notable that she behaves quite differently in front of the different members of her family. With her father she is the most submissive, living up to the prescribed behaviour for young girls. However, she exhibits less docility with her mother, while behaving anything but submissively with her younger brother. Thus, power circulates between the members of this family and each person is able to exert some degree of power over the others. Dila, for instance, can put pressure on her father, but only through her mother, not directly.

Foucault's theories on power (1980a, 1990) provide useful insights into such dynamics. According to him, all social intercourse is shot through with power relations (Foucault 1980a: 90). These are never one-sided, rather a dominant power position is met with a corresponding counter force, so that society functions by way of a multiplicity of points of pressure and resistance (Foucault 1990: 94–6), just as described above.

But the different family members exert power unequally. Dila cannot use speech to articulate her opinions to her father, which indicates her relative powerlessness, since the capacity to express oneself in words in front of others is an important measure of one's power position (Langton 1993: 314–15 in Butler 1997a: 86). Nevertheless, although she may have been silenced verbally she can show her resentment at her father's injunctions by, for instance, refusing to eat or do housework. These are strategies girls in Tajikistan traditionally use to articulate their feelings when they are culturally constrained from doing so through speech (Peshchereva 1976: 37).

In general, the ability to speak is not fixed but varies with circumstances. Almost everyone experiences both situations in which they are socially permitted to talk and others in which they are silenced. Thus, Dila may be silenced in front of her father but is able to scold her brother, since although male he is also younger.

At the same time, Fayziddin and his family do not live in a social vacuum. As head of the family he may be powerful at home but outside it he is vulnerable to community pressures, which censure fathers whose children do not conform. To avoid this he has to constrain his children. Foucault (1980a) explains that power is something that circulates, that it functions during everyday interactions at the level of the family, the community, and other basic units of society, through strategies of exclusion and surveillance he calls 'micro-mechanisms of power' (1980a: 96–102).

In my exploration of how these are used for the control of Tajik society I start at the lowest level of social organisation with gender norms and, following Foucault's concept of 'an *ascending* analysis of power' (1980a: 99, emphasis in original), work upwards to show how social control in Tajikistan is strongly organised around the dual entities of gender and age.

Gender norms

Gender is a much used term but one whose definition has never been completely agreed upon. It is commonly used by feminists to indicate the social construction of masculinity and femininity, as opposed to the biological male/female sexed bodies. My usage takes this a stage further. Starting from the ideas of Butler I define gender as: a culture-specific ideal, varying over time, that males and females are supposed to live up to in order to become intelligible to, and accepted members of, their own communities. It is an ideal that remains tenuous because it is never fully internalised, never quite lived up to (Butler 1995a: 31–2). The internalisation of gender ideals on its own is not sufficient. In order to become meaningful gender must be performed, not once but over and over (Butler 1993: 95).

This means that gender must be acted out, that it is rendered perceptible only through repeated patterns of behaviour, that Butler terms performance (1993: x). Each social group has its own ideas of how men and women should behave, and articulates its expectations accordingly (Butler 1995b: 34). In fact, when people say that someone is a 'real man' or a 'real woman' they essentially mean that his or her behaviour lives up to their society's expectations of gendered behaviour.

People do not, of course, mechanically follow behavioural prescriptions (Butler 1997b: 16) but rather are constrained within a range of norms that are slight variations on an underlying ideal that has been inculcated into them from birth until it forms an integral part of their psyche (Butler 1993: x). Moreover, the differing bodily experiences of men and women are intrinsically related to the way they convey their gender identities, including movements, gestures and styles, which together produce the illusion of a permanently gendered being (Butler 1990: 140).[1] In other words, when Dila behaves submissively towards her father she is correctly expressing her gender identity as a young girl, while Fayziddin considers Ali's helping in the kitchen inappropriate behaviour for a Tajik male, as it does not accord with the norms of masculinity.

Such norms are established '*through a stylized repetition of acts*' (Butler 1990: 140, emphasis in the original), sedimented into an effect of timelessness, generally called tradition. Reiteration gives such sedimentation the appearance of something normal and natural and once this stage has been reached it is only a small step before what seems natural acquires regulatory force (Butler 1990: 140). The more often each norm is reiterated, the more natural it appears and therefore the more important it becomes not to contravene it, as this will appear almost like going against nature. At that moment, maintaining such norms comes to seem essential for human survival, which may account for the strength with which communities cling to their traditions.

This appearance of timelessness is deceptive. What actually happens is that variations continually insinuate themselves, only to be apparently seamlessly resedimented and gradually accepted as tradition, as if no change had taken place, although, looking back in time it is possible to discern differences (Butler 1995b: 135).

The norms regulating Ali's and Dila's subordination are politically formed expressions of Tajik social ideals. The behavioural patterns that upon repetition form norms, are not a matter of arbitrary choice but are directly related to a society's hegemonic ideology (Gramsci 1971: 12), which, in effect, is 'the dominant material relationships grasped as ideas' (Marx 1846a: 64), so that changes in ideas are directly related to material transformations (Marx 1846b: 3). This does not mean that only the material counts, but rather that ideology and the material situation are not isolated phenomena but effects of the same cultural processes. Variations in gender norms are an inevitable concomitant of material change but can also be used for deliberate subversion of the norms.

When gender norms are well established it may not be necessary to articulate them. They may simply be taken for granted. It is only through tension around some aspect of them that they enter public discourse. The result is that they gain explicit definition, after which silent variation becomes considerably more difficult. Since they have been publicly defined everyone knows what they should be and their preservation may become a weapon in power struggles (see Foucault 1990: 101–2). Upholding the norms then becomes all the more vital since any change can be exploited as a weakness in a society's defences (Chapter 2).

Invaded and colonised by the culturally alien Russians, the Tajik people were forced to defend their culture when their homeland was incorporated into the Soviet Union, with the regime making a determined and organised onslaught on its values (Chapter 2). Withstanding this required an especially strong resistance, which took the form of hardening social norms (Chapter 3). Confronted with the alien values of the governing powers, the Tajik population could not afford to make changes in their own norms that would appear to be an acceptance of the conquerors' ideology. Probably for this reason, in Tajikistan behaviour that in other places might be considered modern is labelled 'Russian'. It is notable that it was gender identities, particularly feminine gender identities, that were central to the struggles around community values (see Anthias and Yuval-Davis 1992: 113ff).[2]

Gender identity and the theories of Butler

The work of Butler has been invaluable in helping me conceptualise a number of important aspects of the functioning of Tajik social norms for which I have been able to find no other convincing theoretical framework that makes sense of my observations. There are, however, several aspects of her work I find problematic.

The first of these is her discussion about the relationship of gender identities to such modalities as ethnicity, class and race. After stating that she finds them inextricably linked (1990: 3), she ignores them throughout the remainder of her discussions. This may well be intentional because Butler is exploring psychological categories, and at the level she is doing this, she may feel that the modalities of ethnicity, class and race do not possess overt meaning.

But in my view their influence is sufficiently important that we cannot afford to ignore them. As Moore states, gender discourse cannot exist outside discourse on these modalities (1994b: 20), since psychological subjects do not exist outside them. To assume otherwise is to perpetuate the hegemonic gaze of an elite. In this respect, and contrary to the universalistic approach of most psychoanalytical theory, including that posited by Butler (for instance, 1997b), I believe human psychological development to be culture dependent (see Ross and Rapp 1997). Thus, in those communities that prioritise group identity and conformity, it seems likely that individuals, and most especially the young, will be kept subjected to their parents as long as possible so that they develop agency much more slowly than the average middle-class white westerner.

In fact, Weyland notes it was traditional in rural Egypt for (male) heads of families to exert strict control over all family members, including adult sons. They did this partly through psychological pressures and partly through their control over economic resources, such as land (1994: 163–6). Although Dila and Ali are now in their 20s, they have no way of supporting themselves. Their parents expect them to remain financially as well as psychologically dependent, and their entire upbringing has been aimed at preventing them from wishing to break away. This is all the more vital since Tajik parents who cannot keep control over their offspring, irrespective of age, come under strong community censure.

In other words, ethnic differences produce highly significant distinctions in psychological development as also in gender identities (Chhachhi and Pittin 1996: 93ff; Cornwall and Lindisfarne 1994b: 40; Fraser 1995: 159) and in fact, gender performance is always mediated through the cultural norms of specific social groups (see Schrijvers 1999).

The struggle between Fayziddin and Dila over the clothes she should wear to university highlights the cultural differences between the Russo-Soviet identity privileged by the state and that of the Tajik community, differences symbolised by whether or not a woman should show her legs in public. Apparently trivial, this is fundamental to the different concepts of femininity in these communities. What is at stake here is not just the distinctive traits of each social group's specific gender norms, but also the strength of the pressure towards conformity, the range of variations in performance acceptable for each gender and the degree to which performances reflect internalised ideals. Each community is distinctive in respect of these values and they constitute some of the most important features that distinguish societies from one another; in other words, they form the essence of cultural identity.

I take issue again with Butler, or at least with Wittig's position as cited by Butler, on a further point. According to Wittig (heterosexual) men can be considered to constitute a universal from which all other types, being relative and particular, deviate. As a result there is only one sex, the female, since a condition of the existence of sex, and with it gender, is that it must be particular (Butler 1990: 115ff). In my opinion, however, (heterosexual) man cannot simply be considered as a universal. To do so is to follow the position taken by the elite classes, who consider that their ideals should form the norms to be accepted by the whole of society (see Gramsci 1971: 12; Marx 1846a: 64).

In practice, there are actually significant differences in masculine gender norms among men from varying ethnic groups and classes. Even within each one of these there may also be marked distinctions in masculine gender identities. For instance, in Tajikistan the constraints put upon Ali and other young men, and their subordinate relationships in respect of their fathers[3] would suggest that the young of both sexes are subordinated, not just women, so that neither can be said to be without compulsion to perform according to specific communal gender norms. I would therefore beg to differ from Wittig and say that although there may be a case for male heterosexuality constituting a universal,[4] the same cannot be said for masculine gender. The power differential between the hegemonic masculine gender identity (see Carrigan et al. 1987) of Fayziddin and the subordinate one (see Cornwall and Lindisfarne 1994a: 3) of his son make it difficult to conceive of men in Tajikistan as a universal ungendered category.

The formation of human identity

Something all communities have in common is pressure to conform to the norms, of which the most important are usually gender identities. Indeed, it might be said that those who do not conform may even be unintelligible to the community. In the vast majority of cases, the first criterion necessary for social intelligibility is a correctly sexed body, of which social norms generally permit only two types, the male and the female.[5] In most societies all bodies, whether or not they possess clearly categorisable genitalia at birth, have to be subsumed under one or other of these labels. While in the west the power to decide the sex of babies with indeterminate sexual organs is invested in the medical profession,[6] in the Muslim world this has long been the prerogative of jurists, who in the Middle Ages produced an immense literature on the subject (Sanders

1991). From mediaeval Islam to modern Europe, nowhere is there any suggestion that the opposite approach might be taken and the social categories expanded to include persons whose material bodies do not fit within the standard two. On the contrary, the material body has consistently been forced to fit into the limited categories of social acceptability.[7]

The second criterion for human intelligibility is that individuals must carry out gender performances as prescribed for their type of sexed body within their social group. Thus, the 'naming' of a baby's sex at birth (Butler 1997a: 49, 51) is the start of a process of gendering, whereby children learn to perform sex-appropriate characteristics. Fayziddin is preoccupied with his children's gender performances precisely because it is only by learning to perform correctly that they can become acceptable members of the Tajik community. Their failure to do so will not only bring down disgrace on *his* head, but also complicate *their* future lives.

When Fayziddin beats out of his son the notion that it is acceptable for males to do housework, he is endeavouring to inculcate in him those gender norms prevalent in Tajikistan. He has recourse to physical violence to counteract the influence of Zora and ensure that Ali learns to associate doing housework with negative consequences. As Butler states, children internalise gender identities through the reiteration of compulsion (1993: 94ff), although this is not necessarily physical. Usually constant repetition in itself is sufficient, and indeed more effective, since inducement functions better the less explicit it is (Butler 1997b: 21). When parents subjugate their children in this way, inculcating in them their community's regulatory norms, they are in essence making them recognisable (Butler 1995b: 134–6, 1997b: 7–12). Without this effect of subjugation, especially regarding gender identities, individuals would be as unintelligible to human society as Tarzan, or Romulus and Remus after being raised by the wolf.

Now, thanks to his father's pressures, Ali has internalised Tajik gender norms and thus behaves like a Tajik man. Although his internalisation of the norms was originally induced coercively he now thinks of them as just the way things are. This does not necessarily mean he has fully accepted them. His sister, Dila, certainly has not completely internalised the norms that maintain that girls should be silent and submissive, or she would neither try to contravene them by finding a way to get round her father's interdictions, nor be capable of standing up to her brother. This conforms to Butler's contention that norms are never wholeheartedly embraced, always being imbued with force and constraint (1993: 94ff). It is for this reason that parents always have to be on guard to see that, irrespective of the extent of internalisation, the norms are appropriately performed.

Just as Ali cannot entirely free himself psychologically from his parents, Butler's subjects can never completely liberate themselves from the subjugation that formed them; they develop a passionate attachment to their subjugators, which renders them vulnerable to subordination and exploitation (Butler 1997b: 7). It is this attachment that gives parents so much power over their children. The child that has not detached itself from its parents will not be able to give up its state of dependence on them and therefore its vulnerability to exploitation by them. Even when subjects have been freed from direct dependence, they will never be able completely to escape some level of conformity, witness Rustam's relationship with his father (Chapters 4–6).

As Ali and Dila grow up, they start to develop a sense of individuality and gradually learn to assert themselves as they start to assume agency. This occurs when individuals have internalised the power through which their parents first subjected them, which then becomes the basis for their own power. This will constitute the instrument of their learning to separate from their parents, and eventually to develop independently (Butler 1997b: 1–6).[8] Individual rates of development differ, and depend on many variables, including ethnicity, class, age and gender.[9]

Variant gender performances

Gender norms in Tajikistan are dependent on that ruling principle of Tajik society, the honour-and-shame system (Chapter 3). As a result of this system's influence, the most important masculine gender characteristics are those related to male honour – control over women and younger family members and virility, this last chiefly expressed through impregnation. The corresponding feminine characteristics are submission and virginity/chastity/fertility. Thus, male control is dependent on female submission, and virility contingent on female virginity before marriage and subsequent fertility and faithfulness. It is important to note here that what counts is *image*. To be acceptable, therefore, Dila must *visibly* display submission in front of her father.

Dila is not submissive in her behaviour with the less powerful members of her family, but only with her father, the male head of family.[10] The fact that she is capable of behaving non-submissively towards others proves she has not entirely internalised this. Thus, when she performs submissively in front of her father she is doing this *intentionally*.

I have not been able to find a theory that exactly covers this use of gender performance for the intentional projection of an image. Theorists of western society, including Butler, do not deal with this dimension of gender, although the suggestions by Riley (1988) and Moore (1994a), that there is a gap between discourse and practice in regard to the performance of gender, come close. There are also some relevant concepts in some recent work on Muslim societies, particularly on masculinities. Cornwall and Lindisfarne's notion that subordinate males respond to situations of dominance 'by creating variant masculinities and other gendered identities' (1994b: 24) is useful here, as is also the idea of different subjectivities embodied within one individual (Shire 1994: 152) and of the 'façade that hides profound ambiguities' (Kandiyoti 1994: 212). Cornwall and Lindisfarne raise similar questions to those I deal with here, in particular 'How do individuals present and negotiate a gendered identity?' and how do these 'change before different audiences and in different settings?' (1994a: 3).

Although situated within a somewhat different framework and in no way applied to gender identities,[11] Scott's conceptualisation of the way subordinates deal with the need for public display of submission as theatrical public performances in which their unacceptable and insubordinate real faces are carefully camouflaged behind stereotypically ritualistic mask-like expressions, 'the more menacing the power, the thicker the mask' (1990: 3) has provided a useful notion that I have drawn on for my analyses of subordinate gender performances in Tajikistan.[12] This comes close to my explanation of Dila's behaviour, when she assumes a thicker mask in front of her father than the one she uses in front of her mother.

Taken together, these concepts have led me to elaborate a theory of variant gender performances for both sexes that is enabled by the use of what, following Scott, I have labelled 'gender masks'. It is not only men to whom variant identity positions are open. Women can assume positions of dominance as well as ones of subordination. Moreover, variations exist within both dominant and subordinate gender positions. What I call variant gender performances are (semi-conscious) enactments of characteristics associated with the appropriate sexed body, varied by the actors according to situation and audience. This notion of gender masks has been further influenced by Butler's concepts of performativity and the impossibility of fully internalising gender (1995a: 31–2).

I conceive of these masks as closely resembling the use of the mask in classical Greek drama, that is, as a shorthand way of portraying stock characters. The masks have boldly delineated traits so that the audience can easily distinguish the characters they represent. Thus, in her portrayal of submission Dila uses a 'mask' to make her performance explicit to her father. Like the Greek masks the Tajik ones are assumed *intentionally*. Consider the remarks of an Azeri woman interviewed by Tohidi: 'Every day we [Azeri women] have to wear different masks and juggle multiple identities' (1997: 147). This suggests both consciousness and intention. What is more it shows that my concept of gender masks speaks to the lived experiences of women in such societies, the culture of (former Soviet) Azerbaijan bearing a close resemblance to that of Tajikistan, especially in regard to fundamental gender norms.

Tohidi (1996) explains how Azeri women understand themselves to have taken on a Sovietised gender identity in public, while retaining their Azeri identities in private. Their Soviet identity allows them to be strong, controlling, to take charge openly and even give orders to men. Their Azeri identities are more varied but generally much meeker, allowing these women to appear subservient to their menfolk, never overtly showing themselves strong or controlling but rather subtly manipulating them, while feigning powerlessness (Tohidi 1997: 160). The fact that they are conscious of their performances of variant identities to the point where they are able to discuss them, implies that *none* of these identities has been completely internalised, that the women are *deliberately* performing.

This contradicts Butler's position that gender performances cannot be assumed at will and can differ from the internalised ideal only by way of minute variations (1993: x). According to her the person carrying out the performance is unable to step outside the character being played, since individuals cannot step outside the social frameworks that have been instrumental in forming them. Performance is thus not so much akin to theatre as psychological. Butler considers that no-one can exist outside the act, since it is the performance that constitutes the person (1995b: 134–6).

It is my contention that this is only partially true. The power regimes that form human subjects (Butler 1995b: 134–6) may also force them into displays of characteristics other than or, perhaps more accurately, beyond those that have been internalised, in order to be accepted within their own communities. That is to say, people do not necessarily internalise everything that is supposed to constitute their (gender) identity. Examining the performances of Dila it can be seen that she projects different images depending on the necessity of the moment. Not all these images live up to the ideal of the submissive Tajik girl.

In most societies, and certainly in Tajikistan, gender norms are too narrow for people to internalise completely and too extreme to be accepted as corresponding to the way people really experience themselves. To do so would be tantamount to *becoming* the stock characters such norms appear to demand. What is important for the maintenance of social norms is not so much the rooting out of aberrations as their concealment. If people are willing to present themselves in the appropriate stock characterisation, what goes on beneath their gender masks becomes socially irrelevant. By displaying the appropriate surface, gender masks proclaim their wearers' willingness to conform. This is essentially what Dila is doing in enacting submission in front of her father. It is irrelevant whether she actually experiences herself as submissive.

Like the Azeri women Dila is capable of intentionally varying her gender performance. Thus, while at the deepest level of the psyche no doubt Butler's claim that there is no 'intentional subject behind the deed' (1995b: 136) is correct, this is not true at the level of social interaction. I would suggest that, like Dila, subjects can, and do, deliberately vary their gender performances according to their public. Of course, Dila's own self is inevitably always present and her performances are not merely assumed at whim but inevitably constrained not just by psychological, but also by external pressures. In fact, her enactments are likely always to consist of an admixture of the compulsory, the internalised and the intentional, but this last element is definitely present and it is this that allows her to assume the mask.

Although Butler talks about drag as the only conscious parody on gender performance (1993: 124ff) it could be said that Dila and the Azeri women consciously parody their gender identities as defined by the ruling discourse. Dila clearly does not experience herself as merely meek and submissive since she performs quite differently when with others, but she must portray such characteristics in order to be accepted by her father, and eventually by society at large. However, she is not just *pretending.* Nor is she simply trying to rebel when she behaves otherwise in different situations.

Moreover, it is clearly not possible freely to choose the identity one wishes to enact. Dila is severely constrained, not just by her father but also by the context she is performing in, as well as by her own internalised identity. Furthermore, even Ali has to behave submissively before his father, so he too learns to assume gender masks to protect himself.

It seems to me, therefore, that the theatrical analogy is more apt than Butler would like to admit. In this respect, perhaps that technique which in the United States theatre world is known as method acting might be a helpful metaphor.[13] Method acting stresses the impossibility of an actor giving a convincing performance without the character's identity first being internalised, in other words, without the actor's 'becoming' that character. In reality, of course, the actor and the character differ, and there will inevitably be inconsistencies between them.

Gender performance could be said to bear a strong resemblance to this, some performances being largely internalised and others more consciously enacted. As Dila's story demonstrates, the same individuals present variants on their gender performances at different times in front of different audiences, with varied levels of internalisation. But I would again stress that such performances are not enacted at whim but under constraint, in order to avoid the negative consequences of performing otherwise (Butler 1997b: 28). Thus, Dila might prefer to abandon her masks but if she were to do so the penalties would be too great. In order to remain acceptable she *must* wear them. This is vital to the preservation of social order. In fact, to some extent the gender masks assumed by Tajik women today are a symbolic version of the veils of pre-revolutionary times. The assumption of both demonstrates willingness to accept the norms, however their wearers experience themselves internally. At the same time, repeated assumptions of the masks influence their wearers psychologically, thus reinforcing their performances and to a certain extent also their internalisation of the norms.

THE RESEARCH SETTING

What must never be forgotten when addressing the subject of the performance of gender in Tajikistan is that people here can never be regarded simply as individuals standing before society as independent human beings. They are always subject to the controlling force of the family hierarchy. Even a head of family is constrained by this because his very position as the ultimate controller makes him vulnerable (see Gilmore 1987: 4). Should anything go wrong, he will be blamed. This not only shows why it was so crucial to Fayziddin that his children conform to gender norms but also proves Foucault's point that nobody, however powerful, can escape being pressured (1990: 92–7). Furthermore, in Tajikistan it must always be borne in mind that beyond all social norms stands Islam, the tenets of which are ultimately the arbiter of all community standards.

In order to grasp the dynamics of life in Tajikistan, therefore, it is necessary to know something of the country's history as also of the conceptual frameworks around Islam and the Tajik family, both in their socio-historical contexts and as regards their connection to gender relations.

A brief history of Tajikistan[14]

The Republic of Tajikistan is a small, mountainous country, geo-culturally divided into two. The majority speak Tajik, a Western Iranian language, and follow Sunni Islam. The Pamiri minority speak Eastern

Iranian dialects and are Ismaili.[15] This division is not clear-cut, some of the Sunni Tajik-speaking (semi-) mountainous peoples owing a great deal to Pamiri culture, as suggested by the differences mentioned in many pre-revolutionary sources between the plains Tajiks or *Sarts,* and mountain Tajiks (see Shishov 1904, 1910).

The question of ethnicity in Tajikistan is delicate, especially since the recent civil war. It is accepted that Pamiris[16] are ethnically distinct. However, it is unclear whether Tajik is a meaningful common label for the inhabitants of the remainder of the country and what the significance of the cultural differences among regions/localities – particularly Khujand, Hissor, Kulob and Garm – might be. While there are definite differences among these groupings it is hard to say how much these are indigenous and how much due to the specific relationship each had with the Soviet state. Top government officials were chosen from Khujandis, the majority of policemen were Kulobis, while the Garmis were the most religious and largely opted to remain isolated from the state. In addition, there are many Uzbeks in Tajikistan, the main difference between them and the plains Tajiks consisting of language rather than cultural practices.

There are certainly quite clear distinctions between the semi-mountainous population of the village Tett studied (1994, 1995) and the southern villages where I worked. The latter are largely inhabited by Garmis, while the former are heavily influenced by the more liberal culture of the mountain regions. These differences will be discussed further in later chapters. It should also be noted that large numbers of Tajiks live in the historically important areas of Uzbekistan: Bukhara and Samarkand. Moreover, there is also a significant Tajik minority in Afghanistan.

The Soviet system, and the purges of the elites during the revolutionary period and the 1930s, have left little social differentiation and no real class structure in Tajikistan. However, there exists an upper, generally highly educated social layer, which I refer to as the elite of today, who have somewhat Russianised gender identities. For the rest, even those with doctorates mostly live according to the same set of norms, despite some poorly defined indications of differential social groupings. The result is that groups that in other societies might belong to different classes, intermarry and lead very similar lifestyles. To a certain extent this is also true of urban/rural distinctions.

The population is somewhat over 6 million, roughly 64 per cent of which is Tajik, the rest Uzbek, Russian, Tatar, etc. The adult male literacy rate is 99 per cent, the female 96 per cent, with the teenage literacy rate dropping as the infrastructure deteriorates; 70 per cent of the population lives in rural areas and cotton is the country's main product. The largest industrial enterprise is the aluminium plant in Tursunzoda (Human Development Report 1997).

The area now known as Tajikistan was formerly part of Western or Russian Turkestan. Its oldest excavated settlements date from the fifth century BC, and in the fourth century it was incorporated into the empire of Alexander the Great. Starting in the seventh century AD, Islam slowly took hold in this formerly Zoroastrian and Buddhist region. Between the tenth and the thirteenth centuries the Tajik city of Bukhara, now in Uzbekistan, was the cultural capital of the world; its intellectual leader Ibn Sino (Avicenna) was one of the greatest mediaeval philosophers and scientists. In the twelfth century Genghis Khan and his Mongol hordes conquered the region. From the fourteenth to the seventeenth centuries the region was ruled by the Timurids and subsequently split into small khanates, which were vanquished by the Russian conquests of the 1860s–70s.

Bukhara lay on the silk route between China and the west, which no doubt accounted for the region's tremendous mediaeval flourishing. However, the development of alternative maritime routes in the late fifteenth century effectively destroyed its pre-eminence, around the same time that the Iranian adoption of Shiite Islam put a stop to that country's former easy interaction with the Sunni Muslims to the north. The result was the almost total isolation of Turkestan. For almost 400 years there were few foreign visitors and many of those who ventured into the region were either enslaved or killed (Adshead 1993).

In 1865 the Russians conquered Tashkent and in the following decades took over the entire region. Some of it, including Tashkent and the Ferghana Valley, came under direct Russian rule, most of the rest of the territory of modern Tajikistan remaining in the Emirate of Bukhara.

In the late nineteenth century the legal code of the Emirate was based on a strict version of *sharia* law, especially in the city of Bukhara itself. Women were discouraged from leaving their homes. Any found unaccompanied on the street could be punished. Men caught avoiding the mosque at prayer times were liable to be whipped. Stoning to death, or being thrown from the top of the Emir's tall towers was the punishment for many a crime (Meakin 1903: 65; Meyendorff 1870: 60).

Life expectancy was low. There were many serious health problems and epidemics, such as measles, scarlet fever, influenza and dropsy (Nalivkin and Nalivkina 1886: 180). Infant and maternal mortality rates were not improved by early marriage and frequent childbirth.

After the Russian Revolution, Turkestan came under Bolshevik rule and was reorganised into separate republics. In 1924 Tajikistan became an Autonomous Republic within the Union Republic of Uzbekistan, attaining full union status in 1929.

Stalin's policy was to permit each republic its own language, in the hope of forestalling nationalist insurrection (Stalin 1971: 90). In order to remove Central Asia from the influence of non-Soviet Muslim states, these languages were transcribed from their original Arabic scripts, first into Latin alphabets around 1930, and then some ten years later into Cyrillic (Fierman 1991: 45).

Despite this careful planning, all did not run smoothly in Central Asia. Soon after the revolution abuse of the local population sparked off a guerrilla resistance movement known as *basmachi*. Its mainstay was the conservative elite, backed up by tremendous popular support, fuelled by opposition to policies denying local peoples the right to freedom of worship. The movement was officially declared to have been defeated in 1926 but it continued sporadically in Tajikistan until the early 1930s (Caroe 1967: 114–30; Rakowska-Harmstone 1970: 20–36).

Dushanbe, originally a market village, became the capital in the mid-1920s and by the end of the Soviet era had a population of just over half a million. Although some traditional houses still exist, the majority of the town is Russian-built. Most people live in apartment blocks supplied with gas, electricity, indoor plumbing and central heating. The town centre is dominated by such monuments as the opera house, the university, the Academy of Sciences, the KGB building, the National Library, various theatres and the Supreme Soviet, most built after World War II.

Over the years increasing numbers of Russians and other nationalities – Ukrainians, Tatars, Germans, Jews – settled there in answer to the demand for industrial workers. Cultural differences, together with the incomers' racist attitudes, produced considerable friction with the local population. Dushanbe became so Russified that, according to Karomat, until 1990 for every local person one met walking down the street, one would meet 10–20 Russian-speakers, so that Russian was almost the only language heard. When a Dushanbe-born Russian friend returned in 1995 for her first visit since the civil war, she was shocked to hear mostly Tajik spoken in the streets; she said she had never noticed anyone at all speaking Tajik previously, it had been so rare.

While Russian-speakers dominated industry, most agricultural work was carried out by Central Asians, much of the latter by women (IMF 1992: 2, 40; Liebowitz 1992: 122; World Bank 1994), although Tajikistan had one of the lowest levels of formal female employment in the FSU (Human Development Report 1995: 44). Most children gained

access to schools. Hospitals, clinics, women's health centres and
maternity homes were built, and large villages had their own small
medical centres (Ministry of Health 1967). From the start of the 1960s,
in response to improved living conditions coupled with the government's
strong pronatalist policies, Tajikistan's population began to rise steeply
(Harris 2002). The surplus of un- and underemployed young men this
created was a significant contributory factor to the violence that dogged
the republic for much of the 1990s.

In August 1991 the Soviet Union disintegrated and on 9 September
Tajikistan declared its independence. The ensuing economic collapse pre-
cipitated struggles between, on the one hand a coalition of the newly
established democratic, nationalist and Islamic parties looking for
religious and intellectual freedom, and the Communist Party and their
followers on the other. The history of the demonstrations that took place
in Dushanbe in mid-1992 and the subsequent civil war that broke out
later that same year, has been told many times[17] and I will summarise
here only those points germane to the present work.

The protests started because the Khujand-based Communist Party
leaders wished to hold on to the power they had inherited from the Soviet
Union, refusing to make room for other parties, leaders and regions.
Popular feeling was the more strongly aroused because of the poor state
of the economy. The most serious fighting took place between mid-1992
and early 1993 and was at its fiercest in the Qurghonteppa area of
Khatlon.

Although it did not originate as a regional conflict, by 1993 the line-
up of forces was Khujandis, Hissoris and Kulobis on the winning
communist, or government, side and Garmis and Pamiris on the
opposition side, as the war aggravated long-standing regional tensions.

Tajikistan had never really integrated. The concept of Tajik nationality
was invented by Stalin and people took little notice of it, generally
preferring to refer to themselves by their locality or region. Tensions
between these were exacerbated by the unequal treatment meted out by
the Soviet government, which gave political leadership and economic
preference to the Khujandis (Tadjbakhsh 1996). Regional favouritism
has been continued under the current government of Emomali
Rakhmonov, whose members have been drawn largely from his native
region of Kulob,[18] which has also received a disproportionately large
share of development funding.

During and after the civil war, large numbers of Garmis and Pamiris
were forced to flee the country, along with the opposition leadership,
which remained in exile until mid-1997. With the signing of a peace
accord on 27 June that year, the last refugees started to return home,

until by mid-1999 most had been repatriated.[19] Meanwhile, Tajikistan was beset by political splinter groups, each of whose leaders was attempting to gain a slice of the power pie, usually by violent means. In fact everyday violence (see Schrijvers 1993) in the form of murders, brutal robberies, abductions and rapes, became for a time a way of life in Tajikistan. Although this has quietened down somewhat in the new millennium, such violence has now entered public consciousness, leaving behind a legacy of fear that continues to exert a powerful effect.

The post-war period has been difficult in many other ways also. A major food shortage occurred in the mid-1990s when the government could no longer afford to import grain. It did not reach famine proportions only because of help from international relief agencies but, for a long time, bread, the staple food of most Tajiks, was severely rationed and many people suffered significant hunger over a period of many months.

As a result of the previous integrated economic and productive system, Tajikistan is highly dependent on other former Soviet republics. Grain has to be imported from Kazakhstan and gas piped in from Uzbekistan. At times when Tajikistan's debt became too large, Uzbekistan shut off supplies, sometimes right in the middle of the worst cold spells of the winter, resulting in the death from hypothermia of many young children and old people.

Since the mid-1990s, there have been several major epidemics, most notably typhoid and malaria. In the immediate post-war years, infant and maternal mortality rose considerably. Poor nutritional levels additionally increased morbidity rates, just when the health system was deteriorating fast. Since 2000 there has been some improvement, thanks in part to foreign support in reorganising the health services, and improving access to food supplies.

After the Soviet Union collapsed the Tajik government did not have the means to provide raw materials, coordinate the production and distribution of goods, make up budget deficits nor continue paying employees a living wage. The downward turn that started with the economic policies of the *perestroika* period continued, until by 1992 the already low national *per capita* income had decreased by around 50 per cent; this tendency accelerated after independence. In 1997 the average pension fell to US $1.50 per month and many state wages were less than $10 a month. At the same time inflation was extremely high, in some years well over 1000 per cent (Human Development Report 1995: 16–17), and the introduction of the Tajik rouble in May 1995 did not lessen the pressures. For most people the post-war years have become a constant struggle to find ways to feed themselves and their families, many being reduced to one rather meagre meal a day, usually of watery vegetable soup with an occasional chunk of meat in it, with bread and tea at other times.

The economic situation was worsened by a major exodus of Russian-speakers, starting in 1990 and exacerbated by the war, which has left the country with a shortage of engineers and technicians. Many top professionals in every field have emigrated, including the best doctors and teachers. This exodus has been accompanied by a tremendous influx into Dushanbe of locals, largely from rural areas, at least doubling its population.

The economic situation has become so bad that a high proportion of men and a good few women now migrate regularly to other parts of the CIS, especially the Russian Federation, for work purposes. A small group of 'new' Tajiks, who earn a living through importing and selling foreign goods, including narcotics from Afghanistan, are growing steadily richer. The poorer people are still to some extent supported by the efforts of the UN, the Red Cross and international NGOs, and the Russian army continues to guard the Afghan border.

Islam in Tajikistan[20]

Notwithstanding Soviet religious bans and the fact that the closing of most *medressas* and mosques left Central Asians religiously illiterate, the populations of Tajikistan and the other Central Asian republics, never ceased to consider themselves Muslims, including non-believers who neither pray nor fast but have their sons circumcised.

Central Asians remained so attached to their religion that the Soviet government was periodically forced to relax its anti-religious stance in order to weaken opposition. The regime eventually learned how to manipulate the Central Asian peoples by allowing them greater religious freedom whenever their support was needed – such as during World War II.[21] In this way they were kept loyal. Meanwhile, the more pious, including a high proportion of Tajiks, managed discreetly to continue their religious practices.

Many people prayed at home. Those who did not hold formal jobs managed to fast during Ramadan. Islamic rites of passage continued secretly – boys were circumcised, *mullahs* officiated at weddings and Islamic funeral rites were carried out.

It was understood that many people, especially professional men, were obliged to transgress Islamic laws in order to keep their positions. Quite a common practice was for a man who wanted to build a career to forsake religious observance while looking for advancement and return to it at retirement. It was even not unknown for high-ranking Soviet officials to become *mullahs* in later life. Karomat's father's story was not uncommon:

Before the revolution had gained much of a hold on Central Asia, Karomat's father had been educated in a medressa *and subsequently became a cleric. In 1929 the Soviet government sent him to the army. During his service he joined the Communist Party. At first he worked in his local area but soon he and his wife were sent to Dushanbe to study. At this point, they stopped practising Islam and started to raise their family according to the new ideology. They often talked Russian at home, the daughters dressed in Russian-style clothes and wore their hair short, wine would be drunk at parties, and they didn't pray or fast. However, as soon as he ceased to be in the public eye, Karomat's father resumed his religious life, praying, fasting, wearing national dress and no longer consuming alcohol, and his wife followed suit. Karomat's father subsequently taught her and her sisters to pray, and one of his grandsons even became a mullah. Long before he died in December 1995 at the age of 94, he had completely abandoned socialism in favour of dedicating himself to Islam, even refusing to leave his flat for fear of laying eyes on a* kofir.

When the strictest controls over Soviet society were lifted during *glasnost*, the main demand in Tajikistan was for freedom of worship. Gorbachev was praised mainly for his role in allowing the open practice of Islam.[22] Since then, however, the relation of Tajiks to Islam has been complicated by the civil war and its aftermath. Islam was one of the issues the war was fought over and for some years afterwards it remained a hot issue. Many people, especially educated urban women, greatly feared being forced into an Islamic lifestyle similar to that of Iran or, worse still, Afghanistan. It is very possible that this was the ultimate aim of the opposition leaders. At any rate this could be inferred from their insistence in spring 1999 on trying to remove the clause in the Tajik Constitution that stipulates that the republic remain secular.

It is difficult to know how much support there might be for an Islamic Tajikistan. There has certainly been a significant increase in the public practice of Islam over the last few years. Religious schools have been re-opened. Many people are learning Arabic script to read the Qur'an, including otherwise illiterate village children. Even those who do not consider themselves particularly religious and who do not pray, are starting to fast during Ramadan due to strong social pressures. Despite increased interest, intellectual understanding of Islam in Tajikistan remains at a low level, owing to the lack of religious education coupled with an absence of intellectual discussion of Islam in the press.

As of late 2003, the post-communist government of Rakhmonov continues to take a strong stance against Islamisation and has joined with Uzbekistan and Russia to fight local radicals. The fear of attack from

Afghanistan meant that it was generally supportive of the US war on the Taliban.

Even the more religious men and women with whom I have discussed the idea of Tajikistan formally becoming an Islamic republic have been against it. They say the people are far from ready for such a step after the decades of secularisation.

The family and women's role in Islam

For Islam the family is of supreme importance, being considered the centre of life. The basis of Islam is its legal code, with at its core family law, which, of course, includes gender identities. This is no doubt why Islamic family law has been preserved by Muslim states that have otherwise adopted secular legal codes. Attempts to alter family law have generally been opposed by clergy and changes later overturned. For instance, Egypt's 1979 code, giving women greater rights in divorce, etc. was largely rescinded in 1985 (El Dawla et al. 1998: 74). Iranian family laws passed during the Shah's time were among the first to be abolished after Khomeini took power, although new laws more favourable to women have recently been adopted. The western powers see little importance in those aspects of law dealing with the family and so, as long as other segments of the law have been 'modernised', they have not pressured Muslim countries into changing family law (Dahl 1997: 61). However, as I discuss in the following chapter, the Soviet government (like the government of Atatürk) thought otherwise.

The Qur'an exhorts all single people to marry if they possibly can, and as soon as they can unless there are good reasons against it (Dahl 1997: 49–50,141).[23] According to the Qur'an the purpose of marriage is first and foremost to bring love and mercy (interpreted as passion, friendship and companionship plus understanding, tolerance and forgiveness) to the married couple.[24] Women should not be forced into marriage; their consent is always necessary. Where a minor has been married without this, she can ask for her marriage to be annulled on reaching the age of majority (Omran 1992: 15ff, 49ff). Nevertheless, most Muslim marriages today, in Tajikistan as elsewhere, have been contracted in contravention of these injunctions, as women, and even men, are frequently married off against their will.

It is believed that the Qur'an defines the female age of majority as nine, and that this may then be taken to be an acceptable age for girls to contract marriage. However, there is in fact no mention in the Qur'an of a specific marriage age. The statement that orphans should be married at an age when it might be expected for them to demonstrate sound judgement (*Sura* 4: 6) makes it unlikely that the marital age could have been anything like so young. The only texts that actually mention the age of nine are some of the *Fiqhs*, which, however, also talk of the dangers of young girls having sexual intercourse, as this is liable to tear the vaginal wall. They therefore do not recommend the practice. Although this was allowed in some Muslim societies in the nineteenth century, others were against it. For instance, Ottoman family law before 1914 decreed 18 as the minimum age of marriage for men and 17 for women (Omran 1992: 18–19).

Most Muslims are unaware that the Qur'an stresses the importance of the human side of the marital relationship. Instead they believe that the major purpose of marriage is for the benefit of the family, not the individual couple. Therefore, procreation and control over sexuality take precedence over all else (Dahl 1997: 54, 95, 103), and parents and other senior family members assume they have the right to decide on marital partners for the younger generation.

It is also widely believed that the Qur'an easily licenses both polygyny and divorce. Neither is true. Divorce is permissible, although the Prophet did not favour it, saying that marriage should not be abandoned lightly. There is nothing in the Qur'an to suggest that polygyny is unconditionally the entitlement of every man; it is permitted only according to very strict rules, mainly for the protection and support of women and children, for instance when there are not enough males to go round in times of war (Omran 1992: 18–22).

Widespread in the Islamic world is first-cousin marriage,[25] although the scriptures take the same point of view as modern medicine, that marriage between close relatives is likely to result in birth defects (Omran 1992: 22).

There is considerable confusion about the position of women in Islamic society. There is nothing in the scriptures to suggest that women should limit themselves to the roles of wives and mothers. Indeed, there is a great deal to suggest that women, as well as men, should be educated[26] and that they have the right to work, even if men hold the primary responsibility for the family's economic support. It is, therefore, contravening the scriptures to refuse girls and women the right to education and employment. In the early days of Islam, women appeared at public social functions, studied, took jobs and even served as council members and participated in battles (Omran 1992: 50).

The concept of veiling seems to have been adopted by Arabs from other cultures, and the Qur'an subsequently reinterpreted to read as if it were referring to this. In sixteenth-century Persia, women used often to dress more revealingly than western women. There is evidence that the coming of westerners to Muslim countries such as Egypt and Algeria, resulted in an increase in veiling as a protective mechanism (Keddie 1992: 47ff), and it is also a distinct possibility that the coming of the Russians to Turkestan produced the same result (Kamp 1998: 254–5). Whatever the origin of this custom, by the late nineteenth century *Sart* girls aged ten and over and all women would be expected to remain in seclusion, covering themselves completely when leaving the house and at any other time when in the presence of men not closely related to them. In the street they would wear a cloak, the *faranja*, essentially a stylised form of a man's coat with vestigial sleeves, worn over the head and body, and a coarse horse-hair face-veil without eyeholes, the *chachvan*. It is not clear exactly which women wore these garments, but it was probably largely the wealthier and/or urban and peri-urban women (Nalivkin and Nalivkina 1886: 92ff).

In the Qur'an it is stated that *immoral* woman are to be punished by being kept away from society. However, contrary to this, most Muslims believe that they are acting in accordance with the scriptures when they deny *respectable* (unveiled) women access to the world outside the family compound (Anonymous 1997: 61).

Popular Muslim belief maintains that men and women should inhabit separate worlds and that each sex has its own distinct functions. Within marriage a man's function is to provide for the family economically and to ensure order. A woman's function is to carry out domestic tasks, bear, breastfeed and rear her children, show obedience to her husband and fulfil all his needs, including sexual ones (Siddiqui 1996: 54). Women are supposed to be emotional rather than rational like men and it is this, together with their disturbing sexuality, that makes them appear dangerous to men and explains why the latter have been granted the right of control over them. The main function of a wife should be the provision of services for her husband, not companionship, since it is considered that women are liable to corrupt men who spend too much time with them (Dahl 1997: 139, 147, 179).

The above summary is not intended to imply that the whole community of Muslims worldwide hold exactly the same beliefs. However, the aspects I have noted here seem to be adhered to by and large by most of the dominant social groups in the majority of Muslim societies, from North Africa through the Middle East, Turkey and on into the Gulf States, Iran, the Indian sub-continent, Soviet Central Asia and Chinese Xinjiang, although they are considerably less relevant in Malaysia, Indonesia (except for Aceh), and the remaining Muslim regions of China and Africa.[27] This is most probably because, for the former group, their approach to everyday Islam is largely mediated through the honour-and-shame system, which has become intimately bound up with their local customary laws (Chapter 3). As a result, despite many significant variations among these societies, their basic gender norms tend to be very similar. However, this is not specific to Islam, since it originated in the Judeo-Christian Mediterranean region. In Central Asia the fact that such gender norms are not necessarily always and solely directly linked to Islam in people's minds is borne out by the fact that many of those who consider themselves atheists still believe it vital to adhere to them (such as Malik, Chapters 4–6).

As can be seen from this brief discussion, there is a significant gulf between the scriptures and the everyday beliefs of the average Muslim. At least as much as other Muslims, Tajiks tend to conflate Islamic and local customary laws, and many of the problems described in this book arise from this.

The Tajik family as institution

Tajiks tend to draw an analogy between the family and the state, insisting that a family needs the same kind of firm hand in its leader as a state, and that democracy is out of place in both. This leader is in both cases conceptualised as an adult male.[28] The strict hierarchy of the Soviet state is reflected in the family, or rather the other way round, since the latter long precedes the former. To Tajiks this hierarchy appears completely natural. It is, after all, dominated by a ruling 'class' that produced the ideology it is based on and to which it has been able to give the force of 'eternal laws' (see Marx 1846a: 64ff).

The 'ruling class' here consists of mature[29] males. Ideologically it is they alone who are eligible to become heads of family, to whom the remaining members are subordinated. While young men may eventually have the chance to join this ruling class, women cannot, nor can they ever become fully mature adults in the same sense as men in relation to public life. The fact that women heads of family exist, that women can and sometimes do earn more than their husbands, and that according to the Tajik Constitution they have equal rights with men, does not change the ideology that disenfranchises them. Nor does it prevent men from trying to stop women heading up enterprises, becoming members of parliament or assuming other high-ranking positions.

However, it is women who are largely responsible for carrying out the most critical family functions – the running of the home and the social reproduction of its members, that is to say, the production of intelligible social subjects from their boy or girl babies (Butler 1990: 16). Other than as breadwinners, men have relatively few functions in relation to their families, their main one being to act as the ultimate bearers of responsibility for control.

It is thus imperative for the survival of social norms, for women to be co-opted into maintaining them and, of course, they are not left to achieve this alone. They have the weight of their society's controlling mechanisms behind them, especially traditional law, which, as stated above, incorporates both the honour-and-shame system and popular interpretations of religious law (Chapter 3).

Central to Islam is submission to the will of God, and by extension to the will of parents. In pre-revolutionary days *mullahs*, *bibiotuns*, mosques and religious schools aided parents in imparting correct values to their children and this is once more the case today, especially in rural areas around Qurghonteppa and in the opposition-controlled areas of Garm, Tavildara, Karetegin and so on.

Before the revolution

The Tajik family is patrilineal and patrilocal. Soviet ethnographers identified three different types – the small or nuclear family, the large or extended family and the extended patriarchal family, where several married sons and even uncles/aunts lived in the same house/compound with a patriarchal family head, usually the oldest man. Before the revolution the local tax system made big families more advantageous (Kislyakov 1935: 121). Often 30 to 40, and at times as many as 60 people, lived in the same compound (Kislyakov 1959).[30] Family members would manage their finances jointly, all monies earned being placed together in one large pot,[31] controlled by the head of the family, with major spending decisions being taken in family council (see Kislyakov and Pisarchik 1976: 17; Monogarova 1982: I, 91–2).[32]

Parents chose their children's spouses. Girls might be betrothed at birth or married as young as nine, although the marriage usually would not be consummated before puberty (Peshchereva 1976: 34; Shishov 1904: 359; Yusufbekova 1989: 147–8). Only in the case of adult men or independent divorced or widowed women could they decide on their own partner, and even then the ban on social intercourse between the sexes made a go-between necessary and the couple often had not met before the wedding. Among wealthier Tajiks divorce and polygyny were frequent (Chapter 2). In some families, even after marriage, husbands and wives socialised relatively little (Schwarz 1900: 194). 'Not long since, when a wealthy citizen was asked how often he conversed with his wife, he replied – "About three or four times a year. Why should I talk to her? She is an uneducated and ignorant person"'[33] (Meakin 1903:

284). However, in the family where Nazaroff (1993: 51) took refuge from the Bolsheviks, husbands and wives spent considerable amounts of time together.

Infant mortality rates were so high that in the hope that at least one child would survive to reproductive age, women usually had large numbers of pregnancies – 10 to 20 were not uncommon (Harris 2002). In this setting it is not unreasonable to expect that parents would not invest much affection in the person of a child likely soon to be taken from them.[34]

In Soviet times

The birth rate in Tajikistan remained high until very recently even though, since the late 1950s, it has no longer been offset by high infant and child mortality rates. As a result it is now not uncommon for rural families to have 10–14 living children. This is in part due to a preference for large families and in part to Soviet policies rewarding 'heroine mothers'. According to a decree of 4 July 1944, the award of 'heroine mother' was given to women who had born and raised ten children or more to maturity. Mothers of seven to nine children received awards of 'motherhood glory', mothers of five and six children the 'motherhood medal'. The idea was that this would encourage Russian women to have large families to replace some of the almost 40 million lost to the Soviet Union through the purges of the 1930s and World War II. However, these incentives were not sufficient to compensate Russians for the difficult material conditions they lived under (Meek 1957: 204–5) and produced the desired results only in the Caucasus and Central Asia, areas that have traditionally favoured large families.

Before the revolution the nuclear family had been practically non-existent in Central Asia. The Soviet government wanted to establish there the type of family idealised in one of the main sources of Marxist-Leninist ideology, Engels's *The Origins of the Family* (1972). In effect, the ideal Soviet family was to be the bourgeois nuclear family beloved of capitalist states with, instead of a purely domesticated wife, one who took an equal part in 'social production' alongside her household and child-rearing duties.

Therefore, the government's policy was to encourage young Tajiks to relocate as nuclear families in separate households. The idea was that their resultant liberation from parental control would open them to persuasion to abandon their traditions in favour of a more 'rational', modernised and Sovietised way of life. Thus, the government wanted to force young people to live as far as possible from their parents, in the hope that geographical distance would lessen their influence (Bacon 1966:

168). The lack of housing available in the early Soviet period defeated this goal (Rakowska-Harmstone 1970: 62, 275), although eventually the policy of providing families with flats just large enough to hold one small family did oblige increasing numbers of young urban inhabitants to live neolocally.

Inevitably, this had some effect on the independence of the younger generation but, as I point out in Chapter 4, this very often remained slight. Furthermore, nuclear families are still in the minority even today and major decision-making for almost all families continues to be carried out in family council, not in individual nuclear units. Thus, senior family members retain a lifetime's veto power over the actions of younger members and always have a call on their children's resources, even when the latter keep their finances separate. In other words, the Soviet state clearly failed in its efforts to remove the younger generation from the influence of their elders and in this way to decrease the power of tradition.

After the October Revolution the new state established universal schooling, a major function of which was the Sovietisation of the nation's youngest generation (Heller 1988: 148ff). While appreciating some aspects of the school system, as members of a colonised nation Tajik parents found themselves fighting the alien values inculcated by it. The ensuing struggle between Tajik parents and the Soviet state over control of their children's minds may have made it necessary for parents to be more authoritarian than might otherwise have been the case. Furthermore, for most Tajik children their parents were also the sole source of their religious training.

As marriage in the Soviet Union was seen as a civil affair it had to be registered in the civil registry office (ZAGS). In Tajikistan this was one way the government tried to control both age at marriage and polygyny, although Tajik practices made a mockery of this. For a long time many families continued to marry their daughters below the legal age. In rural areas it was common to perform the religious ceremony (*nikoh*) first, after which a couple would begin to live together, and only register with ZAGS when the wife was old enough and had produced (male) children (Monogarova 1982: II, 78).[35] Some couples disregarded ZAGS altogether – Karomat's marriage was never registered, for instance. In the 1920s parents might simply take along an older sister or cousin to the marriage commission, registering her in the name of the younger one, who was the actual bride (Nukhrat 1930: 63). Later, birth certificates were introduced, which made marriage registration of under-age girls more difficult (Kislyakov and Pisarchik 1976: 33).

Polygynous wives would be married by *nikoh* and introduced in front of Soviet officials as relatives of the registered marital couple (Tett 1995: 111).

Civil registration was of little importance to Tajiks and valued mainly for providing access to resources, such as family allowances.

Today

The family remains the site where the 'ruling ideas' of Tajik society are internalised by children of both sexes, where they learn the appropriate gender performances. These depend not only on sex but also on age, defined not so much by calendar years as by generational positioning. This gives mature women an ambivalent position within the family, since their generational position gives them partial membership in the dominant group, while their sex places them in a subordinate position to the males. Moreover, struggles over the performance of gender are not limited to women but are basic to the conflicts between fathers and sons, as will be shown in Chapter 4.

For Tajiks the family circle is the centre of their lives. Most are unable to move outside it other than in a very transitory manner, for instance to attend school or to spend time with their friends. Until very recently the physical mobility of young men was rarely matched by psychological mobility and was usually subordinated to their obligations to behave correctly within the family, where they might have only the smallest room for negotiation. Moreover, in Tajikistan it has also been limited by lack of access to housing and nowadays to jobs as well. This makes it difficult for young men to establish independent households, although since the late 1990s they have increasingly managed to do this by migrating to work in the Russian Federation, from which more and more they are failing to return. Apart from this, by the time people have attained the age and position where they can make their own decisions, their parents will have long since ensnared them in a web of familial ties that virtually make mockery of their current options. In most cases, by then they will in any case have already forgotten the desire to rebel and will be chiefly concerned with reproducing conformity in their own children.

The above discussion should not be read as an indication that all children are simply only submissive to their parents, nor that all parents are equally autocratic. That the young can develop their own ideas and that they rarely acquiesce completely in their subordination can be seen in the stories narrated in this book. In some circumstances even girls may find a space in which to 'voice' their disagreement to their elders, although, as with Dila, this will rarely consist of verbal opposition. It remains rare for children explicitly to defy their parents. More drastically, it is common in Tajikistan, as in other countries of the region, for serious protest to take the form of attempted or actual suicide.[36]

The extent to which young Tajiks are able to have input into major life-decisions affecting them depends on many factors, including how their gender/ethnic performances interact with other modalities such as low/high educational levels and locality, as well as the dynamics within the individual family. This is, for instance, illustrated by the relatively greater freedom of the young people in the mountain village studied by Tett to choose their own marriage partners than even the young people from Dushanbe,[37] whose stories are narrated in this book (Tett 1995: 102).

Generation and sex are both integral to gender performance. In fact, even small age differences between siblings are important in power ranking. In Tajik, and culturally related languages, there are no words simply for brother or sister, there are only words for older or younger brother or sister.[38] That is to say, there is no word for sibling that does not bear the explicit power connotations of age relationship. Even when speaking Russian or other European languages Tajiks always differentiate by using terms such as older/younger brother/sister. As the eldest, Karomat expected deference from her younger sisters, even though she was by far the least educated. One of the reasons Dila was able to stand up to her brother was that, although a girl she was also the elder. This somewhat evened out the power relations between them.

Although men are supposed to be more dominant than women of their own age and generation, they are subordinate to both older men and women. Tajik men can usually exert control over older women only in the direct matter of the latter breaching the code of family honour (Chapter 3). For the rest, the superior power resides with the older person rather than with the dominant sex. From the books of Donish (1960) and the Nalivkins (see Chapter 2 this volume) it can be seen that before the revolution wealth and social position could make a very real contribution to the performance of gender, upsetting the usual male/female, older/younger dominant/subordinate positions. However, such differentials seem to have largely disappeared with the social equalising of the Soviet period.

CONCLUSION

In this chapter I have sketched the theoretical, conceptual and sociocultural environment of my work. Foucault's notions of power and resistance and the micro mechanisms of power utilised at the lowest level of the community, Butler's concepts of performativity and the psychological development of the human subject, and my own concepts of variant gender performances and masks form the theoretical basis of this book. All these mechanisms facilitate both social control and its subversion.

The stories I narrate in Chapters 3–6 take place against the background depicted in the present chapter. Their protagonists live in families such as those described above and their daily existence is shaped by the constraints of power relations between themselves and the other members of their families, as also among the network of families that constitutes Tajik society, in very much the same way as it is for Fayziddin and Zora, Dila and Ali. Above all, it is gender norms that are the key to the behaviour of the characters in this book, most of whose actions can be construed either as endeavouring to uphold or else secretly to subvert these norms.

Their lives have been further shaped by the constraints laid on them, and the institutions provided for them, by the Soviet state. Isolation from the world outside the borders of the Soviet Union also helped to keep the Tajik people out of contact with both Muslim and western societies, including social currents such as the movements towards Islamisation, feminism and civil rights.

Despite new influences in today's post-Soviet state, the social environment inhabited by the population of Tajikistan remains in many ways the result of the events set in train by the October Revolution, most especially those that took place between the mid-1920s and the early 1930s. This was the time of the Bolshevik attack on Central Asian gender identities (*hujum*), and of collectivisation.

2 THE BOLSHEVIKS ATTACK BUT THE TAJIKS RESIST

THE POWER OF THE STATE

The role of political power ... is perpetually to reinscribe [the] 'definite relation of forces that is established ... in war and by war', through a form of unspoken warfare; to re-inscribe it in social institutions ... and in language, in the bodies themselves of each and every one of us. (Foucault 1980a: 90)

The above passage might almost have been written with the Bolsheviks in mind, so well does it correspond to their policies in Central Asia.[1] In the early post-revolutionary days they had used the Red Army, first to fight the civil war, next to put down general local unrest and finally to suppress *basmachism*. But even before this had been achieved, the Bolsheviks were already substituting political for military warfare, making use of every one of the methods listed by Foucault.

This chapter explores the Bolsheviks' attempts to re-inscribe power relations in Central Asia in the 1920s in order to establish political hegemony, in particular through their manipulation of the position of women. It discusses Soviet endeavours not merely to ensure their ability to exercise control over the local peoples but also to demonstrate to the world their capacity to transform the social values of the many and diverse cultural groups living within the boundaries of the Soviet state. It also examines the response of the Tajik people and their struggles to retain if not political, then at least cultural, autonomy.

In their attempts at social engineering the Bolsheviks made laws, set up courts and a police service, established schools, literacy classes, crèches and women's clubs. They made much of language both in political discourse and in their specific linguistic policies for Central Asia. They even went so far as virtually to attack the bodies of Central Asians, particularly women, through their policy of forced unveiling. They did this with the aim of inscribing on these bodies the cultural values of the new regime – an amalgam of Russian cultural identity with Marxist theory –as well as from the economic necessity of including women in the socialist workforce.

It is no coincidence that the name the Bolsheviks gave to the most active thrust of their women's liberation policy was a military term – *hujum* (attack). However, the harder the Bolsheviks pressed, the more strongly the Tajiks resisted, and in so doing managed to subvert a good part of Soviet attempts at social transformation. In other words, the Bolsheviks' power did not go unopposed but met with a strong force from below (see Foucault 1990: 95). The attack and the resistance to it together transformed both the Soviet development project and Central Asian societies. Thus, to a large extent the *hujum* period determined the road that Tajik society followed during the rest of the Soviet era. The development framework and the terms of reference for relating to local populations and for Tajik–Soviet relations were established during those early years.

THE SETTLED POPULATION OF CENTRAL ASIA BEFORE THE REVOLUTION[2]

We have relatively little information on the pre-revolutionary Central Asian lifestyles the Bolsheviks wanted to destroy, and most of what we have comes from western travellers or Russian settlers in the region (see Harris 1996). We have only a very few accounts from locals (e.g. Donish 1960) and almost nothing from women, very few of whom could even write. The only oral history I was able to collect from the pre-revolutionary period came from Karomat, who with apparent ease could recall almost everything that had happened to her since her fifth birthday and even some things before that, including what her mother had told her about her early life before the revolution. What she could not remember her father filled in:

Karomat's mother was born of a well-to-do family in the northern Tajik village of Zarkhok. Her childhood had been happy. Life had seemed pretty good. Their family had their own farm, the land was fertile, and they had enough livestock to supply them with meat for festive occasions. But life was not always rosy. Girls and boys were not supposed to mix after the onset of puberty. If they did so it could spell disaster. An unmarried girl found to be pregnant would be stoned to death, although the boy would probably escape more or less unscathed. Young folk were not allowed to choose their own spouse. That was up to the older generation. Even if a girl loved a boy very much her parents would not necessarily allow her to marry him. If the girl felt very deeply about her friend, she might even go as far as to commit suicide rather than marry someone else. Once, when Karomat's mother was a teenager, she and her friends were present when one of their group deliberately drowned herself in the river to avoid an

unwanted marriage, and this upset them very much. They were also often sad because
of the death of a sibling. [3]

   At age 18, she married a young man from a well-to-do clerical family, who had
followed his forebears in also being educated at a medressa. Although she did not love
him at the time, afterwards she came to care for him very much. Karomat, their eldest
child, was born in 1925.

Karomat's stories about her childhood and that of her mother are
congruent with the stories told by other women in Tajikistan, as well as
with the accounts of westerners who travelled in the area in pre-revolutionary times (see Harris 1996). They show the lives of women in
Turkestan to have been very circumscribed, especially in the towns,
where, unlike in Karomat's village, women spent almost all their time
enclosed within the women's quarters of their houses. Their greatest
pleasure lay in receiving visits from relatives and friends, which provided
almost the only contact with the outside world (Meakin 1903). Few
women were educated. There were schools for boys, where most of the
study revolved around rote repetitions of the Qur'an and other holy
books. Similar learning for girls took place in the homes of *bibiotuns*.[4]
Even though most of the students were from the upper classes, few
became functionally literate (Kamp 1998: 129–30).

Karomat's family resembled the majority of those visited by western
travellers in being among the more privileged, but most people were
much less fortunate and many lived in circumstances of considerable
poverty. The Nalivkins' stories of poor families in the Ferghana Valley in
the late nineteenth century show how very tough their lives were,
especially during the harsh winter months, when the inside temperature
often dropped below freezing, making it impossible for women to
continue their income-generating activities, such as spinning or cleaning
cotton. Poverty might become so acute that children from poor families
would be given away to wealthy ones when their parents could no longer
afford to pay for their keep. Poverty was also a major cause of early
marriage for girls. At the same time as reducing the number of mouths
to feed, parents could earn *kalym* by giving a daughter in marriage to a
wealthier family. The poorer the family, the earlier the marriage
(Nalivkin and Nalivkina 1886: 113–14, 175).

   In fact, marriage age for both sexes was very much dependent on
financial circumstances. As wedding-related expenses were borne largely
by the groom and his family, inevitably the poorest families were likely to
find it advantageous to marry their daughters young but be hard pressed
to marry their sons until much later, while wealthier ones could afford to
marry both in their late teens. Census data from two provinces of
Turkestan in 1897 show a tiny number of boys and girls married before

age 10. While the majority of girls married between 17 and 20 most males were over 30 at first marriage (Kamp 1998: 81, 84–5). This age differentiation between the sexes is indicative of the high poverty levels.

After marriage many men were unable, or unwilling, to provide sufficient resources for their wives and children to live on. They might spend months or even years away from their families without providing adequately for them (Kamp 1998: 42–3). This was one of the few grounds for which women were allowed to sue for divorce (Nalivkin and Nalivkina 1886: 229):

A wife has the right to divorce in the following cases: if her husband has beaten her without reason and she still carries the marks on her body; if without her permission or agreement her husband takes a second wife; if her husband takes her further than three days' journey from her place of permanent residence without her permission; if he goes mad; if he becomes a leper.

A wife who is unsatisfied with her husband can go to the *qazi* and explain that her husband doesn't provide her food or satisfy her other material wants, and that she therefore does not wish to lie with him. The *qazi* sends an inspector to her home to check out the situation. If he finds no flour or other provision he will inform the *qazi*. Then the latter asks the husband whether he intends to feed his wife. If he refuses he is told to divorce her. If he will not do that he is forced to or the *qazi* does it for him. (Shishov 1904: 365, 418)

However, in order to be able to take such a step a woman would have to have an alternative refuge and source of income so that it is likely that someone from a poor family could only afford to ask for a divorce if she had already found another man willing to marry her afterwards. Women abandoned without financial support might have no recourse but prostitution (Kamp 1998: 43).

We have no information on how frequent divorce might have been before the revolution but, despite Nazaroff's suggestion that women moved from husband to husband as often and with about the same ease as a servant would move household in Europe (1993: 79–81), divorce is unlikely to have been common. It was probably a luxury affordable mainly by the wealthy.

According to *sharia*, men were permitted to repudiate their wives by saying *taloq* three times in front of witnesses. However, the expense was such that most men were hard pressed to afford even one wedding and, having saved for this, perhaps for years, it seems unlikely they would lightly end their marriage. Indeed it might be a tragedy for a poor man to lose his wife, as it would be very difficult for him to afford another (Schwarz 1900: 193). Moreover, divorce was in itself costly for men who initiated it since this entailed payment of the *mahr* that may only have been promised at marriage (Keller 2001: 75).

Polygyny, likewise, required considerable resources, as well as being a source of family disharmony. Stories of the jealousy of co-wives are legion. In the family where Nazaroff took refuge from the Bolsheviks the patriarch and his son each had two wives. This was the cause of a great deal of quarrelling and unhappiness. In the end the older man ended up divorcing his second wife since '[s]he is no use to me. She won't help with housekeeping, is lazy and now to have an extra wife is very expensive' (1980: 43). He sent for a *mullah* to witness the repudiation:

Next day at noon a mullah arrived. All the family was gathered round in a circle and the mullah read a prayer. They then sat down, ate pilau, drank tea and the divorce proceedings were over. An hour later the son took his father's divorced wife with her child and belongings back to her home in Tashkent. It was just as simple as the leave-taking of a domestic servant. (Nazaroff 1980: 43)

In many of the fights in this household, especially those started by the son's second wife, the youngest woman was the victor. However, it was unusual for young women to hold such power. More often they found themselves in a very menial position in their marital households. Women from poor families who had contracted polygynous marriages with wealthy men might be treated virtually as servants (Kamp 1998: 41). Or alternatively, their mother or some other poor relative might live with them in this capacity. 'Such servants have the same low position as any other servant. The daughter orders her servant mother about as if the only relation between them were that of mistress and servant' (Nalivkin and Nalivkina 1886: 111–12).

Women could also suffer considerable violence in the home. Forced into marriage as young children they might be severely abused in their new households:

A 14-year-old girl complains that she has been married nine weeks and wants to leave her husband. Being very poor and needing the money her mother sold her to an old man for 16 hammel. Her husband is a trader. He had had three other wives, all dead. This wife had gone to school for one year and wants to continue to study or at least to read. Her husband won't let her; he burnt her one book and beat her. He threatens to kills her if she as much as talks about unveiling. 'He does not allow me to go out, but I cannot sit on the ground the entire day twiddling my thumbs, so I ran away.' (paraphrased from Kisch 1932: 235)

In the remote village of Garash a holy ishan [*mullah*] whose wife was late in bringing in his tea, poured a cauldron of boiling water over her head, and gave her ... no medical treatment, only prayers and charms. When at last her flesh grew maggoty, the unfortunate creature was sent to a Soviet clinic in the township center. (Strong 1930: 151–2)

As the publication dates make clear these last few stories come from post-revolutionary times. I have included them here since they refer to traditional family situations. Being related by socialist sympathisers it is hardly surprising if these texts very much resemble those in the Bolshevik press and therefore they could be said to belong to the realm of propaganda. Nevertheless, through such accounts Central Asian women had the chance to make themselves heard more than at any previous time and the Sovietised stories offer important insights into the lives of the least fortunate women.

THE RUSSIANS CONQUER TURKESTAN[5]

After the Russian conquest of Turkestan in the late nineteenth century, the introduction of capitalism in the form of the production of cotton for export increased economic differentiation. This accentuated class distinctions and large numbers of the poorer peasants lost their land, ending up as sharecroppers (Sharma 1979). Incorporation into the Russian Empire also brought Central Asia into contact with government based on secular rather than religious authority and the rulings of Tsarist courts were often in conflict with those of traditional *qazi* courts based on *sharia* law. Those people living under direct Russian rule were no longer obliged by the state to obey the *sharia*, unlike those living in the Emirate of Bukhara, which covered much of what today forms southern Tajikistan. Nevertheless, in practice Tsarist courts rarely imposed their ruling on Central Asians and customary law remained the basis of everyday life all over the region, with Muslim clergy, both *mullahs* and *bibiotuns*, retaining their leading roles (Keller 2001: 10–11).

Conflicts between the Russian conquerors and their subjects occurred throughout the Tsarist years. The most serious, was the uprising of 1916 protesting the Russian army conscripting Turkestani men into semi-military positions. Interestingly enough, the protest was apparently started by *Sart* women furious at the threat of being deprived of their family breadwinners (Kamp 1998: 98–104). The fact that large crowds of normally secluded women were able to gather in the streets in the towns of Tashkent and Khujand, as well as in many villages, shouting and even throwing stones, shows a side of *Sart* women very different from the subservient portraits drawn of them in most of the historical literature.

Tsarist rule had been accompanied by the settlement not only of Russians and members of other European ethnicities but also of other Muslim peoples of the Russian Empire, notably the Tatars, who introduced to Turkestan the debates raging in such places as Turkey, Egypt and Iran over the terms on which the Muslim world should participate in the western project of modernisation (Kamp 1998: 24). The two main subjects of controversy were the importance and acceptability of secular education, and the status of women. At the centre of the discussions were female access to schooling and literacy, as well as their right to mobility and freedom from the *chachvan*, or veil.

Muslims from different parts of the Russian Empire joined in these debates, especially Tatar Jadidists and Central Asian Young Bukharans, including educated Tatar women, many of whom were schoolteachers. Thus, decades before the October Revolution, issues of veiling and female access to education were very much in the air in Central Asia. The fundamental question being asked was whether the Muslim world could participate in the modernisation project without a scientifically based education system, and with that half of the population whose time was largely devoted to the raising of (male and female) children hamstrung by illiteracy and seclusion (Kamp 1998: 26–63).

Both men and women contributed to the discussion, most of the latter, however, being Tatar. An exception was Khoqandli Ashraf ul-Banat Tajie, who in 1906 wrote a letter to the editor of a Turkic language women's journal *Alemi Nisvan* (Women's World) on this subject:

[W]e Sart ... Muslim women are regrettably in the condition of ... a sleep without ... awareness ... [in] ignorance and lack of rights ... [I]n our days scarcely one of a hundred Sart ... women knows how to read and write; and the other ninety-nine know no other skill than how to look at strangers while walking under a paranji. It is possible to say that in the world, there are no Muslim women so deprived of rights as we are. Our men treat us with ... oppression ... We have no free choice in anything ... [In our ignorance we] are causing our children to continue after us equally uneducated and deprived ... Let us ... struggle to reform our condition. Let us send our sons and daughters to the ... [new schools] to learn. (Kamp 1998: 27–8)

Even though, as Tajie herself suggests, she was an exception to the general state of *Sart* women, her letter, written over a decade before the Russian Revolution, shows that not all Central Asian women accepted their traditions uncritically. After 1917 Tajie may well have been among those few who welcomed the Bolsheviks' efforts to transform their society.

As this letter suggests, in 1906 only a small portion of the *Sart* population were in agreement with the ideas of the reformers. However, in the two decades following, increasing numbers of progressive schools with secular curricula were opened, introducing new types of knowledge and skills. By October 1917 then, Central Asians were already somewhat prepared for social reform.

THE BOLSHEVIKS ARRIVE IN CENTRAL ASIA[6]

When the Bolsheviks took over the government of the Russian Empire after the October Revolution, one of the challenges they faced was to find a way not only to control and manage all the very diverse peoples of the empire but also to incorporate them into a unified society (Keller 2001: 53). They would achieve this by inculcating into the multitude of heterogeneous groupings a new kind of consciousness, that inherent in socialist ideology. This objective was not so difficult to achieve in the Slavic regions. However, in the rest of the country their task was considerably more complicated, and nowhere more so than in Central Asia.

In fact, Central Asia presented considerable obstacles to Bolshevik ideological development. In Russia, Lenin and his followers had decided to privilege the industrial working class over the peasants, whom in many ways they treated almost as class enemies. However, in Central Asia there was too little industry to have produced a native proletariat. The largely rural environment consisted mainly of peasants led by secular and religious elites. Moreover, there was a strong cultural resistance to Russification, based to some extent on religious differences, and further complicated when the Bolsheviks substituted atheism for Christianity. But a significant part was also played by cultural norms, that is, by local gender identities and the associated family/community relationships. In addition, the dependence of the poorest families on the elite and the clergy for material support made them disinclined to aid the Bolsheviks in destroying them.

Despite this, while the majority of Central Asians remained hostile to Bolshevik ideology, a growing progressive minority looked to the new regime to collaborate with their project of reform and modernisation. This did not suit the Bolsheviks, however, who regarded them as more dangerous than the conservatives, since they threatened to co-opt Party principles to their own ends. Rather than collaboration with the ideas of others, what the new rulers demanded was unquestioning obedience to their own project and willingness to follow the flag of the Communist Party leadership. During the first post-revolutionary years, Bolshevik control over Central Asia was insufficient for them to impose their own ideas too strongly. As soon as this had strengthened, however, they decided to take compelling action to incorporate the region socially and culturally into the new state (Massell 1974).

THE BOLSHEVIKS AND THE WOMAN QUESTION IN CENTRAL ASIA

The project of social transformation, particularly in regard to the 'woman question', was one that occupied a great deal of the time and energy of the central planning apparatus of Lenin's government. Immediately after the October Revolution laws were passed reforming social and family life, removing control over marriage and other rites of passage from religious bodies and placing it firmly under the auspices of the civil authorities (Keller 2001: 50). This was a step on the path both to women's liberation and the disestablishment of the Church. However, the nation-wide legal measures taken in the early post-revolutionary years did little to effect change in Central Asia, where lifestyles derived from very different principles than in Russia. The particular situation of this region required its own special solution and, according to Bolshevik ideology, no part of this situation more insistently demanded transformation than the living conditions of its women. The problem was how to achieve this.

Unfortunately, there was little to be learned from Marxist sources on how to incorporate peoples from such cultural settings as Central Asia into a socialist state. Moreover, Lenin and his government saw religious belief as a major obstacle to socialist development. In January 1918 they removed the Russian Orthodox Church from its position as a state organ (Keller 2001: 50). However, the Hanafi Sunni Muslim sect, to which most Central Asians belonged, lacked any centralised institution that could be formally disestablished. The clergy were self-defining and answerable to no specific governing body, which made them extremely difficult to control or abolish.

At the same time the clerics of Central Asia held conflicting opinions on Bolshevism. While some upheld the old ways and believed that progressive ideas, and especially female emancipation, could only bring the peoples of Central Asia into immorality, others believed that backward traditions were responsible for moral corruption (Kamp 1998.67–70) and so supported the Bolsheviks' plans for liberating women (Keller 2001: 254).

Whatever their position, the clergy continued to be influential leaders. Before collectivisation the land farmed by the poorest peasants often belonged to that administered by the clergy under the *waqf* system. Most schools and medical establishments were also run by clerics, who thus played an important role in the daily life of most Central Asians.

Despite Lenin's opposition to religion, the relatively weak hold of the Bolsheviks on the region made him insist on going slowly on enforcing atheism there. Muslim supporters of socialism had their own ideas about how to wean their co-religionists away from Islam but they were ignored by the Bolshevik leaders, partly because the latter continued to operate according to the Tsarist model of treating non-Slavs as second-class citizens. At the same time, the majority of the Central Asian Party members were, of course, themselves Muslims and as such opposed to atheistic propaganda. An additional complication in the struggle to destroy adherence to religion was the way the population conflated their national and their religious identities. This was quite different from the attitude in Russia and the Bolsheviks' failure to grasp this greatly hampered their handling of the situation (Keller 2001: xvi, 51–9, 63–4).

The woman question played an important role in the fierce discussions of the 1920s on religious, legal and social issues, and the Bolsheviks were determined to implement major reforms to tackle it. To this end they drew up a set of laws especially for Central Asia, to deal with what they termed 'crimes based on customs'. These included the marriage of underage children, forced marriage, polygyny and the payment of *kalym* – conceived as bride purchase. Although no law was ever passed against wearing the veil it was made illegal to force anyone to do so. Mistreatment or insulting of women became a criminal offence (Northrop 2001: 119ff).

BOLSHEVIK NARRATIVES

Along with legislation, the Bolsheviks used propaganda as an integral part of their campaign to modernise Central Asia and justify their policies there. Their rhetoric blamed religion and local traditions for women's lowly position and suffering, as well as for the oppression of the population at large.[7]

Marrying off young girls, bride price, polygyny and many other customs, the circumstances of daily life among the Central Asian Muslims reduced the woman to the status of a thing ... The woman who had been bought through bride price became the full possession of her husband who had the right to punish her and even kill her for adultery. ... The woman in her husband's house became a dumb slave. She had to be the first to rise in the morning, serve the family and do the housework, look after her husband's parents, and she did not even have the right to eat at the main table. In the presence of others her husband did not talk to her, but with a threatening and stern glance would order her about. He would not defend her from the insults of his relatives or the older wives of the house. The woman submissively bore her heavy lot. All this was highly destructive for her health. By the age of thirty she was old and died young ... The Qur'an stipulated the obligatory wearing of the female ritual coverings – the *chachvan* and the *faranja* ... The women of Central Asia had neither rights nor the possibility of leaving their husbands. It was extremely difficult for them to divorce, while men could do so merely by pronouncing the magic word *taloq* three times ... the woman and all her possessions belonged to her husband. (Raskreproshchenie 1971: 4–7)

On the female toilers of the Muslim East, constituting the vast mass of the female population, lay heavy, hard work ... All domestic work lay on the shoulders of the women. They had to cook, sew, bring up the children ... The women did a great deal of work on the farm ... Shut up in the narrow circle of their households, isolated from society, the women of the East represented the most enslaved, sluggish, backward part of the population ... The basis of women's status specific to Central Asia, was the total, submissive dependence on men to whom they were considered inferior ... The Central Asian woman entered the twentieth century as the slave of her father, her husband, her father-in-law, her older brother, and even her son. The most prized characteristic of women was silence ... Seclusion, including the wearing of ritual clothing to cover the face, neck, and hands, was religiously observed in the daily life of the pre-revolutionary Central Asians ... Divorce was easily obtainable, but only on the initiative of the man. Divorced women did not even have rights to their children ... (Pal'vanova 1982: 5–7)

There was, of course, an escape from the monstrous fate described above – salvation by following the path of socialism, as represented by the institutions established by the Party, which enabled women to find freedom and happiness. For instance, Nasrulla, married at age 11 to an old man and so badly treated that she tried to commit suicide, was saved, left her husband, went to study in Moscow and subsequently became a member of the Uzbek government and editor of the largest Uzbek women's journal, all thanks to Bolshevism (Halle 1938: 312).

Nasrulla's story closely resembles those published in the Bolshevik women's press, such as the Uzbek-language journal *Yangi Yol*, which ran many stories portraying formerly oppressed women whose lives were radically transformed by contact with Bolshevism and incorporation into its new way of life (Kamp 1998: 214–16).

These stories paint traditional lifestyles in the blackest possible colours in order to heighten the contrast between the misery they represented and the bright future that awaited women under the new regime. Soviet discourse portrayed Central Asian women virtually as members of an oppressed class, similar in many ways to the proletariat in the European regions (Massell 1974: 96ff).

HUJUM

By 1926 it was clear to the Bolsheviks that their project to free women from the 'shackles' of tradition was not going according to plan. Attempts to enforce the laws against crimes based on customs did not have much effect in a setting where the local and even regional administrators were usually made up of men who followed these same customs in their own families. Moreover, in the absence of a proletariat, the Bolsheviks did not have a local support group and they were unable to make much headway in winning over the poorer peasants. It was in order to try to break this stalemate that the decision was made to reconstruct Central Asian women as a notional proletariat and to use them as a sort of battering ram with which to attack local cultures. Thus was conceived the major assault weapon on local traditions – *hujum* (Massell 1974: 35ff).

The main thrust of *hujum* was ending seclusion, to be expressed by the casting off of the veil and cloak (*chachvan* and *faranja*).[8] While the question of the veil had been raised by Muslim progressives before the revolution, it was never their major concern but to the Europeans meeting it for the first time, the *chachvan* appeared monstrous. It became a potent symbol of the lack of humanity with which these women appeared to be treated in their own society, as well as of the critical importance of freeing them from its shackles.

The first major event of *hujum* was to be the unveiling of local Party members' wives on International Women's Day – 8 March 1927 – when a mass unveiling campaign was organised in the cities of Tashkent, Samarkand, Ferghana, Namangan and others. Local Soviet officials were specifically ordered to attend, together with as many other local men as could be reached, and all were ordered to bring their wives and other female family members, with them.

Thousands of Muslim women went out into the squares of the old cities of Central Asia. There they cast off their *paranjas* and *chachvans* ... and they burned them on bonfires, whose huge flames, ascending towards the sky, announced the *hujum*. This started an attack on the centuries-old backwards, patriarchal-clannish way of life, seclusion. With this ceremony began a new era – that of the free Muslim women. (Pal'vanova 1982: 93)

In fact the effect was short-lived. Most of these women, including the majority of the wives of local Party members and government officials, resumed their garments soon afterwards, many on the following day, declaring they had understood the occasion to be merely symbolic – just for women's day (Halle 1938: 174), as a satirical verse of the time suggested:

> On the seventh of March I tore off my veil,
> But before I reached home
> I bought three new paranjas
> To veil myself more darkly.
> (Strong 1930: 273)

Although reactions to the unveiling campaign were mixed and a small number of Central Asian men supported it, including some of the progressive religious leaders, the majority experienced the campaign as an outrage. While they could not take direct action against the government, they could, and many did, retaliate against those involved in the campaign, killing both Soviet officials and unveiled women. The chief targets were men's own wives and sisters, the women who had caused them to suffer personal dishonour. There were even incidences of gang rapes and disembowelments, and it is estimated that several thousand men and women were killed or seriously injured during the course of the campaign. Less drastic measures to dissuade women from breaking with tradition included attacking unveiled women in the street, following them, jeering and shouting at them, knocking against them and pouring foul water on them (Massell 1974: 281–2).

Reactions were so strong that after 1929 *hujum* had to be abandoned. However, steady pressure to unveil continued over the succeeding decades until the numbers of veiled women on the streets dwindled to almost zero and, by the end of the Soviet period, the veil had disappeared altogether.

WOMEN'S OWN EXPERIENCES

As indicated above, women's stories usually entered the public domain in the shape of propaganda, always emphasising the negative elements in traditional lifestyles. The rhetoric of these stories suggests that women's lives had remained shrouded in darkness until the Bolsheviks brought salvation to the region. In reality, however, as we have seen, most of the elements the Bolsheviks distinguished as particularly conducive to backwardness were already being debated long before the revolution. Some decades before Tajie wrote her letter Marie Bourdon, a French woman who visited the region in the late 1870s, found that:

The Sart women in Tashkent are unhappy. They maintain that the Russian authorities did wrong in not passing a law allowing them to uncover their faces. This criticism was levelled at the government by the youth of both sexes but it was far from finding an echo among the older men who are quite intractable on this point. (Bourdon 1880: 151)

To acknowledge local movements towards emancipation would have weakened the Bolshevik position as the only legitimate force for social transformation. In order to ensure that control remained in their hands the Party dictated the terms of female liberation and ensured that women were never in a position to define their own needs or demands (Bobroff 1974). From the start, feminism was anathema to the Soviet rulers (Lenin 1972) and the rise of the second wave of feminism in the west only made them oppose it more strongly (Mamonova 1984). It is hardly surprising, therefore, that Soviet discourse insisted that the Soviets alone were responsible for the 'liberation' of Central Asian women. Thus, according to official sources, the women who unveiled in the late 1920s did so as a direct result of *hujum*. In reality, however, women did not all cast off their veils at once but rather did so gradually and in fits and starts, each having her own personal motivation and rhythm. For instance, some women left them off on Soviet-style occasions, while retaining them on more traditional ones, while others stopped wearing them for a time, only to resume them later before finally abandoning them altogether.[9]

In 1992–93 the American historian Marianne Kamp interviewed 34 women in Uzbekistan[10] about their memories of *hujum* and their own reasons for unveiling (1998: 19). She found this to have been a highly contested subject, and that women had unveiled in response not only to Bolshevik pressures but also to the arguments of the progressive Muslims.

Unveiling had supporters and opponents from every social class and group within Uzbek society: there were women who unveiled in opposition to their families, and women who remained veiled in opposition to their families; there were women from the families of *mullahs* who unveiled with their husbands' support, and those who remained veiled and strictly secluded. The communists did not agree among themselves what strategies to adopt on the matter of unveiling. Some advocated a very gradual approach in which women would unveil as a result of modern education, while others, notably a group of activist Uzbek women, sought to ban veiling outright (Kamp 1998: 250–1).

As suggested by Kamp, women's own responses to the call for unveiling depended on their personal circumstances. Those whose menfolk were progressive were in a very different situation from those living in conservative families. However, it was often outside stimuli that led to unveiling, such as travel outside Central Asia, or the chance to study or work in a setting that made veiling difficult. Regional reactions were also uneven. In some places local officials harassed and even fined women who remained veiled and young boys would tear their veils off, while in others men might torment unveiled women until they ended up resuming the garment (Kamp 1998: 311ff; Massell 1974: 302ff).

In theory, at least, the unveiling campaign and other Bolshevik policies provided women with a new range of choices considerably wider than any previously open to them, especially in urban areas, although these were not without their dangers. It must have been a highly confusing time for women. Should they unveil or not? What would their fate be if they did so? How would they live if they did not, since they could be excluded from literacy classes and jobs? Weighing up the pros and cons must have been tremendously difficult.

In any case, leaving off the veil after a lifetime of wearing it must often have been difficult and traumatic, especially when this was forced on women. An unveiled Tajik woman Egon Erwin Kisch met around 1930 on a trip to Central Asia told him that the first time she went out in the street unveiled her feelings were indescribable. She walked closely behind her husband with her face pressed to his back so that it could hardly be seen (1932: 355). Moreover, unveiled women were often treated as loose women by colleagues and other men with whom they came into contact, which placed them in difficult situations they did not always know how to deal with (see Kunitz 1936: 298–9).

The only one of my Tajik acquaintances who could give me any details about this period from personal experience was Karomat, who at the age of five witnessed her mother's unveiling:

Karomat's mother was one of those women forced by the Soviet authorities to abandon their faranjas. *This coincided with the start of collectivisation in her village and so with the need for women to work on the newly organised* kolkhoz. *Previously, the women had worked on their own homesteads, looking after their vegetable gardens and fruit trees, tending the livestock that lived near the house and carrying out domestic tasks, but not working in the fields. That was men's work. Under collectivisation all adults and many children were put to work on the farm.*

One day in early 1930 the whole village was informed that the following day there would be a great feast, which all the village women and those from several neighbouring ones would be expected to attend. Karomat and her sister went with their mother and her friends. A great fire was lit and all the women told to remove their faranjas *and* chachvans *and burn them. Karomat's father had already decided to support the Bolsheviks, regarding this as the only way to advancement under the new system, so his wife had her husband's agreement to abandon seclusion. Therefore, however traumatised she may have been at the idea of appearing 'unclothed' before men, at least she did not have to worry about what her menfolk would do. She was also young, without as many years invested in seclusion as the older women. So she complied with the instructions to throw her* faranja *on the flames with at least a show of acceptance.*

Not all of the women, however, were so lucky. Those whose menfolk had threatened them with dire consequences if they were to expose themselves and thus bring down dishonour on their families were particularly frightened. They had to have their faranjas *taken from them by force. Indeed, some of them clutched on to them so desperately they measured their lengths on the ground when the Bolsheviks wrenched them out of their hands.[11]*

These women crept away, trying to hide their faces, in a, perhaps vain, attempt to appease their menfolk. Karomat did not know what happened to them later, or how many, if any, from her village were actually killed on account of their unveiling. However, she distinctly remembered what it was like there immediately afterwards. The women did not resume their faranjas *and they looked so uncomfortable without them – like plucked chickens. At first they wore some garment or other draped over their heads, usually one of their husband's shirts, ready at any moment to pull the edges down to hide their faces from strange men. The older women never did get used to being* uncovered and many kept some form of covering for life. *The younger women, however, gradually became accustomed to the new ways and adopted the wearing of a kerchief, which has been maintained to this day.*

Soon after this Karomat's parents started Party school in Dushanbe. After graduation, they lived in a series of villages, mainly in what is now Khatlon province, where they frequently represented the first prolonged contact the local population had with Party organs and ideology. In this mostly rural region, women had never worn the *chachvan* and *faranja* and did not experience *hujum*. Nevertheless, they covered their bodies with flowing dresses worn over *ezor*, and concealed their faces with large headscarves, as the more religious still do today. Karomat's father and other officials started Party branches, while their wives showed an example by going out uncovered in public. Karomat's mother's job was to establish village schools in which the curricula were infused with Party ideology and to run literacy classes for the women, where they would be educated about the evils of seclusion and other traditional practices.

THE BOLSHEVIK–TAJIK CONFLICT AND GENDER IDENTITIES

At the most fundamental level the conflict between the Bolsheviks and the Central Asian peoples was a struggle over gender identities. This was made explicit by Ibrahim Beg, the last of the *basmachi* leaders, in his Proclamation of 1931:

This treacherous and horrid Government deprives its subjects of the right to be masters of their wives and property: the ZAGS (registry office) compels the wives of the *dechkans* to bare those parts of the body (face and hands) which it is, according to the Shariat, strictly forbidden a woman to display before other men ... The Bolsheviks are responsible for the undermining of the honor of women in Russian Turkestan. It is their doing that women go unveiled and are thereby converted into prostitutes. (Rakowska-Harmstone 1970: 296–8)

For Beg the masculinity of Central Asian men is under attack when they are deprived of control over their wives through *hujum* and of their material property through collectivisation. According to this view, by displaying even their faces and hands in public, women are rejecting male control and with it their claim to respectability, making them indistinguishable from prostitutes (see also Kunitz 1936: 298–9), and thus dishonouring their menfolk. In other words, if the veil symbolised women's acquiescence to male control, its absence logically symbolised their resistance, which amounted to emasculation of their menfolk.

This appears to be the rationale behind Beg's portrait of the way Central Asians were forced into abandoning their traditional gender performances as the Bolsheviks endeavoured to inscribe modernised concepts of femininity and masculinity on their bodies. It goes a long way to explain both the violence of the reaction to the *hujum* campaign and the long duration of female seclusion in the region. The fact that attacks on local traditions affected men and women at the deepest psychological level helps account for female reluctance to abandon veiling, to the surprise of the Bolsheviks who expected them wholeheartedly to welcome the chance to do so. Moreover, it was not only men whose gender identity was linked to control. Having undergone their time in the lowest power position as daughters(-in-law), older women were unwilling to relinquish their turn for greater control as mothers(-in-law). Finally, casting off the veil did not always result in greater freedom for women but could instead make it more difficult for them to leave home at all (Kamp 1998: 287, 295).

Insistence on maintaining traditional gender norms continued throughout the Soviet period in Tajikistan and was at the centre of resistance to Sovietisation. When political pressures made it difficult, if not impossible, to preserve the outward symbols of these norms, most notably in the case of seclusion and veiling, rather than abandoning them altogether they moved the goalposts. Novel ways of expressing appropriate Tajik femininity had to be contrived to fit the new circumstances. Most essential was for women to be *seen* to be submissive to their husbands. This was the more difficult to ensure, now that the overt material symbols of seclusion and veiling had been removed. Nowadays the symbol of women's willingness to comply with her husbands' dictates is rarely for her to wear a veil or remain in seclusion. Instead female gender performance has had to make up for the lack of a tangible mask by the assumption of a clear and well-delineated notional one (Chapter 1). Their submissive gestures have had to become larger and more obvious now they go out into public life and mix openly with men. Such gestures include women metaphorically bowing their heads and verbally acknowledging their husbands' rights over them, although in private they may behave quite differently.

The gradual substitution of the 'mask' for the veil did not happen overnight. Only very slowly did the social practices represented by material veiling give way to the virtual veiling of gender masks, which could only happen when the associated behaviour patterns had been repeated sufficiently for them to have assumed the feeling of tradition (Chapter 1). At the same time, despite the abandonment of the formal trappings of seclusion, women today, especially young women, are still unable to make use of the freedom of mobility granted them by law. They need explicit permission in order to leave the house to attend school, college or university, or to go out to work, and in many families there is great reluctance to allow them to leave home unaccompanied. Older women also may have constraints on their mobility. Until the end of her life Karomat's mother never left the house without telling her husband where she was going and when she would return. Karomat never went out on her own until she was in her 60s. Even when she went to work she would arrange with a woman friend to call for her and walk her home again. It was only after she retired that she started to go out by herself.

Although in Tajikistan they were never able to manipulate the Soviet system with quite the same panache or on quite the same scale as in Uzbekistan (see Lubin 1984), many men, especially those in positions of power, managed to squeeze considerable perks out of it. This gave them the best of both worlds. In public they were able to give the appearance of having accepted the 'modern' Russo-Soviet identity, while in private they quietly preserved their Tajik gender identities, the most potent symbol of which was the visible cultural and sexual purity of their womenfolk.

In Tajikistan resisting Sovietisation and refusal to abandon traditions became virtually synonymous. The chief tool of this resistance was the maintenance of masculine and feminine gender norms as near as possible to the ideals of the pre-revolutionary period so that the abandonment of seclusion was compensated for by changes in the details of gender performances, leaving the principles of masculine control and feminine virginity/chastity virtually untouched, and so making up for the lack of the previous material underpinnings.

Revolt by military means had failed with the *basmachi* defeat. The only defence left, therefore, was the turning back of the Soviets' own discourse upon them by making a bulwark of the traditions. But this very weapon that allowed the Tajik people to resist the Bolsheviks and remain psychologically unconquered within their own cultural boundaries despite their position as colonised subjects, ended up imprisoning them within their own society (Chapter 3).

At the same time, the very fact that urban women at least lived under a regime that actively encouraged social mobility opened up the possibility for escape from the narrowest confines of Tajik society for those willing to risk the consequences. Thus, throughout the Soviet era and since, there has been a constant renegotiation of the relationship between the government, socially relatively permissive in Central Asian terms but politically constraining, and the comparatively constrictive norms of Tajik society.

MODERNISATION OR TRADITION? THE CONTRADICTIONS OF
WOMEN'S LIVES IN SOVIET TAJIKISTAN

Government control of all public activities as well as all published
materials, allowed the state to define public discourse on the contested
terrain of cultural norms, such as those related to Muslim women's
domestic lives, but could not prevent private expressions of dissent or the
types of resistance discussed above, whereby the Central Asian peoples
did not simply submissively accept the rulers' terms but rather used
multiple modes of resistance to evade, rework and transform the terrain,
giving it a new meaning of their own. Karomat's life, which spanned
almost the entire existence of the Tajik Republic, exemplifies the way in
which the intermingling of Soviet and local Central Asian ideologies
formed new hybrid lifestyles.

*There was a good deal of Russian influence in Karomat's home life as a child (Chapter
1). The children even attended Russian schools when they lived near enough. On the
other hand, Karomat was taught all the Tajik customs, just as her mother had learned
them as a child. She was also taught complete submission to her parents; she had to do
her mother's bidding immediately and unquestioningly and see to her father's needs
and wishes before everything else, no matter what. Her father never relinquished one
jot of his right to dominate his womenfolk right up to the day he died. Each morning her
mother would inform her husband where she intended to go that day and for what
purpose, in order to get his approval. However, despite expecting to be waited on hand
and foot, he was never cruel or unkind. He was a good provider, a firm but not unreasonable husband and father, and a man of high moral principles.*

*Karomat attended school until the outbreak of World War II when she was 15. At
that point most schools in Tajikistan were closed down, as their teachers were sent to
the front and the older students drafted into the war effort, Karomat among them. She
worked in several different factories, and even spent some time as a street labourer,
helping to build post-war Dushanbe. Subsequently she spent 25 years working in the
Dushanbe textile factory, where she became one of the most highly skilled weavers,
with apprentices under her, one of the very few Tajik women to attain such a position.[12]
Although she thought life was better when women did not have to carry the burden of
responsibility for home and children as well as holding a job, Karomat also thought that
the only way to learn was to go out to work. 'Those women who stay at home all the
time are completely ignorant', she said.*

*Karomat half accepted and half resented the Russians. Some of her best friends were
Russian but she never really liked or trusted them. She spoke the language fluently and
reasonably grammatically, much to the surprise of most Russians she came across who
did not expect this in a Tajik woman of her age and educational level. Despite this she
believed that each society had its own culture and should stick to it. Russian culture
was for Russians, not for Tajiks, she maintained.*

*Soon after she married, her mother-in-law had persuaded her to stop dressing in the
Russian manner (Chapter 3) and she never returned to this. In the last years of her life*

Karomat turned increasingly to the old traditions. She prayed faithfully every day except when ill, and tried to stop her family from speaking Russian in her hearing.

Karomat kept all the old customs she had been taught by her mother and mother-in-law, believing in their absolute rightness. In following tradition she was rejecting not so much Soviet ideology, which she had never really grasped, as much as Russians and their way of life. At the same time she would not hear a word against 'that good man Stalin', had been very proud of being a Soviet citizen and deeply mourned the passing of the USSR, holding Gorbachev chiefly responsible for its collapse and for Tajikistan's enforced independence. On this last, and not on so much on the ending of the socialist system as such, Karomat blamed the ills of the post-Soviet period.

Karomat married a man of her own choosing but only because her father was absent at the front. Her wedding was celebrated by a mullah *and never registered with the civil authorities (see Harris 1998a). To the end of her life, her behaviour continued to reflect both Soviet and Central Asian ideologies, as she struggled to give meaning to a world poised between the two cultures. While she certainly felt more comfortable living by Tajik traditions than Russo-Soviet ones, she had learned enough of the latter for them to change her outlook in many ways. For instance, she was not only well aware of her rights under the law but also capable of making the system work for her. In order to do this she was not afraid to beard Soviet officials in their own offices and demand from them the benefits she believed she was legally entitled to, often surprising them with her knowledge of the system, and her forthrightness.*

The apparent contradictions of Karomat's life can be read as resistance to the sociocultural dominance of the Soviet state. She was able to gain real material benefit from it, such as making use of her position as a worker in the textile factory to procure for herself the flat she was living in when we met, while simultaneously maintaining an essentially Central Asian lifestyle that included many of the practices the Bolsheviks had been trying to encourage people to discard.

Karomat took advantage of her Russian-language education to read a great deal of literature, including Russian translations of western European classics. Although she found these fascinating, she did not consider the lifestyles they portrayed as relevant to her own, which she strongly believed should remain 'traditionally' Tajik. Nevertheless, she willingly supported the Soviet government, accepting much of its propaganda at face value.

Thus, on the one hand Karomat unquestioningly absorbed many Soviet concepts, while on the other she did not accept the right of the rulers to dictate to her how to think and live. Similar contradictions can be found in the lifestyles of large numbers of Central Asian men and women today, equally suspended between modernisation and tradition.

For some decades before the October Revolution the appeals for reform by the Jadidists and other progressive Muslims had called many customs into question. Once they entered public discourse they could never again be taken for granted, since this process had consciously defined and delineated them, and thus virtually codified them into customary law. This provided a yardstick against which to measure variations and thus facilitated conscious attempts to prevent change in order to preserve the status quo (see Foucault 1990: 101–2).

This process started in Turkestan long before 1917, but with the advent of the Bolsheviks the battle moved on to different terrain. No longer between two groups of Muslims contesting meanings and interpretations of their own cultural practices, the fight now pitted atheistic Russification against Asiatic Islam. Since the power advantage was firmly on the side of the former, overt rebellion by the latter could be very dangerous. Therefore, the Central Asians had to find other ways to handle the situation, such as silent refusal to change their customs. This covert resistance was supported by local officials, who sidestepped laws or stonewalled legal processes, often managing to keep cases of crimes against customs mired in bureaucracy for years (Northrop 2001).

In fact, at least in southern Tajikistan, the Soviet regime was never really effective in eliminating these 'crimes' and the struggles continue today, with President Rakhmonov's post-communist party rather uncomfortably positioned publicly to uphold modernistic values and fight religious extremism, while even its top officials simultaneously incorporate Muslim rites and traditional practices into their private lives.

In the 1960s the woman question was pronounced officially solved. The state was praised for having emancipated its women, particularly those of the Muslim East (Gafarova 1969). There had, of course, been significant changes in the 40 years since *hujum*. Nevertheless, in southern Tajikistan at least, the most conservative rural families continued virtually to seclude their women, withdrawing their daughters from school soon after puberty, especially if continuing to higher grades meant them attending educational establishments outside their immediate group of villages. To combat such practices the government made special provisions to encourage rural girls to attend establishments of higher education in Dushanbe and officials were sent into villages to persuade parents of promising youngsters to allow them to do so. Nevertheless, fears for loss of family honour if unmarried girls were permitted to live away from home, as well as a general preference for uneducated brides, kept the majority of parents from agreeing.[13]

The publications of the late Soviet period (for example, Gafarova 1969; Pal'vanova 1982) praised the accomplishments of the government. However, at the same time these books also exude a slight unease, a lack of conviction that the changes they discuss had really occurred, producing the impression that this literature was intended less to praise accomplishments than as a form of contemporary propaganda – proclaiming what they would like to be true in an effort to make it so.

Who reads these works and what effects did they and the emancipatory institutions they describe have on the communities of Central Asia? On the whole, the women I met in southern Tajikistan had had little contact either with the books or the institutions, neither of which appeared to have had as much effect on these areas as they had elsewhere. While the women Constantine interviewed in Uzbekistan claimed that their lives had been transformed by the institutions and, in at least one case, even by reading the Bolshevik literature on female emancipation (Constantine 2001: 2), I did not find anyone in Tajikistan outside Party circles who felt the same way. Karomat, who read Gafarova's book (1969) at the same time I did, commented that it was less true than a novel and much less interesting. On the other hand, perhaps it would have been different had she read it as a young woman with her life before her.

The women Constantine interviewed (2001) were either from urban areas or industrialised villages. She did not talk to those more isolated rural women whose only contact with the world outside their homes was work on the collective/state farm, such as those the health project works with in Khatlon. Our experiences have shown that this makes a big difference in outlook and this is backed up by research carried out by Karomat's niece, the socio-economist Safro Isaeva, who told me that her research in Tajikistan had demonstrated that those rural areas where large numbers of women had access to factory or other non-farm employment were much more progressive than those where they did not.

I certainly found that the rural women we worked with were relatively untouched by Soviet concepts. They spoke no Russian and barely understood it. They knew virtually nothing about the principles of socialism and were vehemently opposed to those Russian social values they were aware of. Meanwhile, their families continued to commit most of the crimes based on customs – forced and child marriage, polygyny, *kalym* and even female seclusion. For them the importance of the Soviet state had consisted in its provision of a reasonable level of material well-being, since they had certainly benefited from both the welfare provisions and the stable living conditions of the Soviet era, albeit without understanding that it was the Marxist underpinnings of the Soviet state that were responsible for these.

Despite their greater exposure to Soviet propaganda, most urban women I met still put more stress on the importance of behaving in line with local customs than on modernisation and emancipation. Indeed, except for the most highly educated, my Tajik acquaintances generally showed more of a tendency to resent Soviet cultural interference than to be grateful for what it had done for them. Karomat, for instance, insisted that life had been better in the 'old days' when women's work was largely limited to the household and the poor had been taken care of by Muslim charity.

Nevertheless, although Tajiks probably adopted Bolshevik values less than almost any other nationality in the former Soviet Union, they did not remain completely unaffected by Soviet rule. Whether or not they appreciate their gains, my more educated acquaintances in Dushanbe work in white-collar and professional jobs, some holding positions of great responsibility and superficially appearing quite modern, despite a comparatively traditional home life.

Other parts of Central Asia were somewhat less conservative, but Soviet rule in the region resulted in very uneven development and failed to produce the type of modernisation the leaders appeared to be aiming for. Nevertheless, looking back over the last century it can be seen that considerable changes did take place, even if their effect on gender identities, and thus on the position of women, was much less than the government liked to claim.

CONCLUSION

The importance of the 1920s for gender relations in Soviet Central Asia was the establishment of a normative framework for conceptualising the woman question, one that continued to be used with only minor changes throughout the period of Soviet rule (see Gafarova 1969; Pal'vanova 1982; Raskreproshchenie 1971; Tyurin 1962) and which still affects discourse in Tajikistan today.

During all this time the regime continued a more or less constant low-level bombardment on veiling, seclusion and crimes based on customs. Meanwhile, a modern infrastructure was gradually being put into place – roads were built, piped water systems constructed, communities electrified and provided with telephones, schools and medical centres. Libraries, universities and colleges, theatres and cinemas, newspapers and magazines, radio and television stations were established, and blocks of flats built in the urban centres. Inevitably, both the discourse and the material infrastructure have left their mark and have contributed to making Central Asian society today substantially different from what it was a hundred years ago.

Universal employment for both sexes was an important component of the Soviet value system and a fair proportion of urban Tajik women entered the formal workplace. But the vast majority of the 70 per cent of

Tajik women who lived in rural areas never did so, although many were employed as casual labour on the collective/state farms.

There has long been a debate over whether the Soviet Union fulfilled its avowed intent of modernising its women, and nowhere has this been as heated as over Central Asia (see Constantine 2001: 1ff). As far as southern Tajikistan is concerned at any rate, I believe the answer is that the women there did not fully modernise but neither did they remain the same as they would have been without Soviet influence. The women I met had absorbed certain Soviet values while rejecting (or not even being aware of) others, and retaining quite firmly the belief that it was important for Tajiks to keep to their own customs and not ape those of the freer and more sexually promiscuous Russians.

A recent survey showed that domestic violence continues to be a very serious issue in Tajikistan (WHO 2000), although one improvement over pre-revolutionary times is that the custom of honour killings mentioned by Karomat appears to have been abandoned, at least in the regions where I have worked. In contrast to studies of family life across the southern border, in Iran, for instance, where violence appears to be considered a norm (Friedl 1989; Hegland 1992) the Soviet legal system, which punishes domestic violence by prison terms, suggests that it is unacceptable. Discussions with both men and women in Sayot revealed that, despite a belief in the right of elders to control youth, they are ultimately not at all sure that the use of (physical) violence is an acceptable way of doing this – a major step on the way to reducing it. The result is that family violence in Tajikistan, while still at very high levels, appears to be less all-pervasive and vicious than in Iran. This is another example of the positive contribution of the Soviet system.

So, yes, unequivocally and inevitably, the decades of Soviet rule produced major and often positive changes at all levels in both the lifestyle and the outlook of Tajik women (and men). Nevertheless, the underlying gender identities that privilege male control and allow elders complete power of decision over their children's fate appear not to have changed much over the last 50 or even 100 years, although they are now expressed somewhat differently. It is the maintenance of these gender ideals that has allowed polygyny, child marriage, forced marriage, *kalym* and the practice of seclusion to continue covertly and, in the decade since independence, increasingly overtly.

This chapter has discussed the salient issues that entered Soviet Central Asian discourse during the *hujum* period, in order to clarify the context of the sociocultural setting of the contemporary characters whose stories are central to the chapters following. When Tillo and Jahongul, for instance, talk about 'our Tajik traditions' they are speaking within the framework of reference established in the struggles of the 1920s and passed down from generation to generation, as well as placing their own lifestyles firmly in opposition to those of the Russians, with differences in gender identities being the most important aspect of this.

Thus the 1920s was a formative era in Soviet history, when the terms were set that would guide the treatment of Central Asian populations and particularly of Central Asian women for the following six decades, both in regard to legislative practices and to discourse, and its terms are constantly referred to by both population and government.

3 COMMUNITY CONTROL

AUTO-SURVEILLANCE, AUTO-REPRESSION

The prison the Tajiks created for themselves was bounded by the community, and its members kept under control by means of the micro-mechanisms of power discussed by Foucault (1980a: 96–102). Two of the most important tools of repression – innate to and at the potential disposal of *all* societies – are auto-surveillance, that is surveillance *of* members, *by* members and its twin, auto-repression. Together they form the most effective, neat, efficient and powerful method of control ever devised, one run largely, although certainly not entirely, by women, who are at once the most repressed and the most repressing community members. It is the women who have the most to conform to, as their gender identities are the most stringent. It is the women who therefore have to be put under the strongest pressure, and who could do this better than other women, who have good opportunities to police each other since they inhabit the same world.

Women's role in preserving communal norms does not consist only of policing their neighbours. As they are the ones who spend most time with their young children, they are also the ones who first subjugate them to social and thus gender norms (Butler 1997b: 8).

Feminists have considered the way women pressure each other to conform to gender identities that appear essentially to benefit men as a sort of false consciousness, where women have been persuaded to be complicit with the 'enemy' against what are seen as their own best interests (see Firestone 1971: 249ff; Gardner 1970; Peslikis 1970). However, I do not believe this is necessarily so. Given the situations most women live in, compliance may bring them real benefits: for older women in the form of status and power from their position as arbiters of social mores, and for younger women through being publicly labelled as 'good'. This no doubt accounts for Central Asian women's lack of cooperation with the Bolsheviks, as well as for why it took so long for them to abandon their veils.

THE TAJIK COMMUNITY

Once unveiling had become general, people in Tajikistan were left in a state of vulnerability to external penetration, a little like a tortoise without a shell. The intense male reaction to unveiling shows how important that carapace had been to masculine identity. Now the Soviet state presented a threat to the masculinity of the entire nation. This made *each* woman's correct behaviour the business of *all* men. This is why rape is practised as an instrument of war precisely in those cultures where men's personal honour is heavily dependent on their womenfolk's purity, such as Pakistan, Bosnia and pre-revolutionary Cuba. This was also why Tajik men reacted *en masse* to the Bolsheviks' attempts to force unveiling. It was a national dishonour.

Threats to groups inevitably cause their members to close ranks. In this case, the threat being to male honour via the females, any circumstances where males and females come together in a group can lead men to react in this way. One such place is the integrated school system, which provides easy opportunities for the violation of feminine gender norms by placing girls and boys in close proximity in the classroom. The result is that young men in educational facilities feel it particularly necessary to ensure their comrades do not violate their appropriate feminine identities. It is as if the class had become a sort of extended family so that the men come to regard themselves as honorary brothers, responsible for the good names of their sisters:

Jahongul[1] was 16 years old, in her last year at high school, and living with her widowed mother, younger brother and sister in Dushanbe. One afternoon after school Jahongul went to her aunt's office to practise on her typewriter. By the time she arrived home it was almost 5 o'clock. One of the boys from her class who also lives in her building was standing near the entrance to her flat. He looked surprised to see Jahongul and immediately asked whom she had been out with and why she was coming home so late still in her school clothes. Jahongul said she had been practising her typing. The boy said 'I hope you have not been out with a boy. You are our neighbour and you should not do things like that.'

Jahongul said all the boys in her class seemed to feel responsible for her, as if they had appointed themselves her keepers, and that they always kept a look out for her. For instance, when once a boy from another class started to bother her, her classmates immediately rushed to throw him out of the room. Those boys in her class who live in the same block of flats as Jahongul feel doubly connected to her, and thus doubly possessive of her good name.

Because masculine identities are dependent on female purity, the honour of the Tajik people came to appear to rest on social vigilance in helping ensure its preservation. Here, the concepts of honour and shame were, and still are, used by Tajiks to differentiate themselves from the non-Muslim Russians, and thus they play an important role in preserving their gender identities.

HONOUR AND SHAME

Tillo was born in Dushanbe in 1961, the only daughter in a family of four children. They lived with her paternal grandparents, who did not support the Soviet regime. They told her that to be a communist – especially a Party member – was a sin. It was also wicked to join the Komsomol. All Russians are kofirs. Kofirs *are non-Muslims and basically not nice people. However, in school they learned that Islam was bad and communism good.*

Tillo remembers her childhood as very boring. Although, as the only daughter, she was spoiled and not forced to help in the house, she was rarely allowed to go anywhere except to school. She does not remember what television programmes she liked to watch, or even if she watched at all. Her chief memory of those days is of persistent boredom.

As a young girl Tillo only ever wanted one thing – to be a singer – and she wanted that with all her might. However, although most of the men in her family are musicians, they consider it a disgrace for their womenfolk to have anything to do with professional music-making. It is a sin for a woman to be a musician. In fact, a woman should not study at all. Her future could lie only in marriage.

Tillo was never close to her mother and they never discussed anything important or interesting. They never had any sort of heart-to-heart conversation, never discussed her mother's life, marriage or anything. Tillo's only confidantes were her girlfriends at school. But one thing they never talked about was the future. Although they all knew they would have to get married they never discussed it. It simply didn't occur to Tillo to think what life might have in store for her. She was too young and ignorant. She never thought about what her future husband might be like or indeed much about anything at all beyond her desire to sing.

Soon after she left school at age 17 Tillo's parents told her they had arranged a marriage for her and she accepted this unquestioningly. She didn't see the boy until the wedding day and then she didn't like him at all. But she had no choice. Everything was arranged and it would not have occurred to her, or indeed to anyone, that she might refuse to marry him.

Tillo knew nothing at all either about marriage or about housework. She and her husband lived with her parents-in-law. Her mother-in-law had to teach her how to do everything. She just obeyed her and did what she was told.

Her husband was revolting. She not only did not love him, she could not stand him. He was unpleasant to her and sometimes beat her. After a while she realised he was a drug addict and eventually he was caught and put in prison. In all he went to prison three times. Then he went mad. At this point she couldn't stand it any more, so she moved back in with her parents.

But they did not want her and her three children living with them so they insisted she remarry. At least this time they allowed her some say. They came to a compromise between her parent's wishes and her own. Her second husband's mother was Russian, his father Tajik. He was a sculptor who held some sort of high-up political function as head of some committee or other, which she did not really understand. However, it brought them in enough money so that they were able to buy the large house in which she now lives.

Tillo did not love either of her husbands, but she claims that neither was she especially submissive towards them. She obeyed her first mother-in-law in whose house she lived but did not take that much notice of her husband. She fought a lot with her second husband, who used to drink a lot and beat her. But in general their relationship was not too bad. Although she could not love him, she respected him because he was good looking. Although Tillo already had three children when she married him he insisted on her having two more, so that by the time Tillo was 29 she had five.

However, when things got really bad in Tajikistan her husband decided to make use of his dual nationality and move to Russia. He offered to take Tillo with him but she did not want to leave her homeland. He decided to go anyway, so he just abandoned her and their two children, although he said three taloqs before he left so that she was free of him as far as religion is concerned. In Russia he married again. However, she is not sure on what terms, since his marriage to Tillo was registered at ZAGS and they never divorced. Russian women don't do nikoh, so she figures they are just living together informally.

Tillo scarcely ever hears from this husband. He doesn't send her even one kopeck to pay any of the expenses of his children, nor does he even ask after them. After all his insistence on having children he has now abandoned them. 'So much for them being important to him', she says.

Tillo was furious when he left her and she threw out all his things, including his books, of which he had a lot. She stayed on in their house and determined to figure out a way to keep herself and her children without any outside help.

After Tillo had divorced her first husband she went to work in a sewing factory on the administrative side. She loved it there, especially since there were always lots of people to chat to and she was never bored. Most of her colleagues in her department were men, since women mostly did the sewing. Tillo preferred working with men because she said they were less nasty. 'Women's conversation is mostly spiteful gossip, although it can be nice talking to them too', she said.

Tillo was able to support herself and her children, and she continued to do so throughout her second marriage. However, by the time her husband left things were very different. The Soviet Union had collapsed. Financially, it became impossible to make ends meet, as the factory management first found it could no longer pay a living wage and later was forced to lay off most of the workers. Also, after her second husband left her, Tillo had two more children to support and a large house to take care of.

So she decided to start her own trading business, buying abroad and selling at home. She had a couple of women friends also in the business and they always travelled together. Tillo concentrated her business largely on cloth, something she knew well both from her time in the factory and from her own interest in clothes. She ran her business for two years, during which time she travelled to Iran, Moscow and Tashkent. In this way she was able to see something of the world, which was great.

When Tillo brought her goods back to Tajikistan she had to deal with Kulobis, since by then they owned most of the stores and dominated business. She hated this, as they gave her so many problems. Several of them tried to pressure her into becoming their lover and when she refused they threatened to kill her. She was very frightened but she needed to deal with them to keep her business. So she tried her best to work out a way of doing this while not sleeping with any of them.

Meanwhile, her two younger brothers decided that Tillo's actions in running her own business and dealing with Kulobis were disgracing the family. They particularly hated her dressing up when she went into town, especially her wearing Russian clothes, including long boots, which they considered showed off her legs. When she wouldn't stop they beat her up and did all they could to make her life miserable.

For two years Tillo stayed alone. Two husbands whom she did not love were more than enough so she did not plan to remarry. However, two things happened that made her change her mind. The first was her brothers' harassment. Tillo said that although publicly they claimed to beat her to stop her dishonouring the family she believed the real reason was that they wanted her house. They were not well off and had small, not very nice homes so they had decided their sister and her children did not need such a large house and were trying to force her to give it to one of them. They offered to buy her a three-room flat, not nearly as nice as her house, nor worth anything like as much. Tillo did not know how long she could resist them and she was tired of the beatings and wanted protection from them.

The second reason she changed her mind was that she was being pursued by a man called Chahonbek, who wanted to marry her so much he would follow her all over the place, even to work. Sometimes he would even jump over her fence at night and ring her bell. At first she asked him to leave her alone but eventually she gave in and in February 1995 she agreed to marry him.

Her brothers objected even more strenuously to this than to anything she had done before. After all, once she had a husband they could hardly expropriate her house. They claimed that by custom Tajik women may not marry three times. Furthermore, Chahonbek was not an ethnic Tajik but an Arab.[2] They were furious that neither husband their sister chose for herself was a proper Tajik. The final straw was that Chahonbek was already married so that Tillo would become his secondary wife. Moreover, his primary wife lived just a few houses away. This was disgrace indeed. This deserved a real beating.

Thus, when Tillo insisted on marrying, her brothers beat her again, so severely she almost died. She went through with the wedding but her family has never forgiven her. Since her marriage they have refused to speak to her; even when her mother lay dying and begged to see her daughter, her father would not allow her to visit.

Before I first met Tillo I had already heard a lot about her. She was the talk of the neighbourhood. She was the one who had her own business, travelling all over, consorting with Kulobis, dressing shamelessly in Russian clothes, and finally and most scandalously marrying polygynously. She was also the one whose brothers had beat her up so severely that for a while it seemed as if she might not survive. The story of the beating was told at all gatherings of the neighbourhood women, accompanied by many sighs and shakes of the head. Tillo's brothers, it seems, always administered their beatings publicly and the last time she was left lying on the ground at the gate to her house in full view, unable to move.

As soon as it became known that Tillo had agreed to become Chahonbek's secondary wife tongues started wagging in earnest. All up and down her street Tillo formed the main topic of conversation. To defend herself she insisted that she had accepted the marriage in order to improve her financial position, as her new husband was a wealthy man.

The neighbourhood women decided to test this, to see if they could catch her out and shame her, annoyed that she seemed to consider herself superior to them. They got together and went over to Tillo's place en masse, and just sat there, so she would be bound by the laws of hospitality to feed them. Would she really put before them all the expensive meat dishes and other delicacies that wealthy persons gave their guests as a matter of course? They did not believe she could do this. They were sure she was too poor to have anything of the sort in the house, and they hoped that this would shame her into admitting she was no better than the rest of them. When they told me about it afterwards they were really laughing. They said they had gone along and sat there for several hours waiting to be served. Tillo had done her best with the little she had but it had been very inadequate, so they felt they had made their point and that she would never put on airs with them again and pretend she was rich.

The neighbours also amused themselves telling many stories of Tillo's husband's supposed infidelity. I could never figure out whether these had any basis in fact or whether they were just fabricated to make their point.

While the women went for Tillo the men attacked her sons. For months 5-year-old Aziz, Tillo's younger son, could hardly bear to leave the house because of their mockery. They would always find something nasty to say about his new 'father' that would send him running home in tears.

I was taken to meet Tillo soon after she recovered from her last beating. Despite her bruises it was clear she was a good-looking woman. At 35 she had a bloom on her that made all the other women look drab and worn out. In fact, she looked just like the famous Tajik singers one sees on the stage or on television. She was beautifully made up and exquisitely dressed in traditional Tajik clothes made out of expensive-looking material. Her house was decorated so as to further enhance her looks. It was spotlessly clean, with curtains that harmonised with her clothes.

Tillo and I got on well and she agreed to allow me to interview her. At our first private meeting she immediately set out to ensure I didn't believe the bad things she was sure I would have heard from her neighbours, for instance, that she slept round during the two years she lived without a husband, and that she stole Chahonbek from his wife and married him purely for money, because with five children and no husband she could not make ends meet.

'None of this is true', she assured me. 'I had no lover at all, no sex life whatsoever, during the time I was on my own. It is also untrue that I stole Chahonbek from his first wife. It was he who chased me. He was so determined and declared his love for me so passionately I couldn't help myself. I just had to accept him. I know everyone hates me for it, not just the neighbours but my whole family. You see Tajik women are not supposed to marry three times. That looks like excess, as if we could not live without a man. I should have been resigned to my fate and stayed single. But it is very hard today to do that. The men will not leave such a woman alone.'

What Tillo did not say, and I only found out later from the neighbours, was that Chahonbek's primary wife lived so near her home. They said that no-one would have made much fuss had she lived on the other side of town but that to live a few houses away from her new husband's primary wife was to bring the latter into ridicule and make her life hell.

The neighbourhood women have not ostracised Tillo but they mock her, sometimes mercilessly, especially because of her boasting about her new husband's riches. However, when things became really tough after Chahonbek lost his job and Tillo had no choice but to admit to poverty as she needed to borrow food in order to survive, they helped her out. Nevertheless, most of them have never completely forgiven her, not only for transgressing the norms but also for what they see as the airs she put on when she remarried. [3]

The vigilance of the Tajik community, in attempting to prevent women like Tillo from besmirching the nation, is mediated through the honour-and-shame system (*nomus* and *ayb* in Tajik), which I introduced in Chapter 1, and which is the major reason why popular Islam is so constraining for women.

The existence of such a system was posited in the 1960s by the anthropologist Peristiany, who perceived it as naturalising a static relationship between male dominance and female chastity (1966). More recent scholarship examines the way this system reifies male–female power relations while actually permitting considerable flexibility, including variations in gender identities, within the behavioural patterns of each of the sexes, which even allows an apparently disempowering system for women actually to serve those capable of its successful manipulation (Lindisfarne 1994: 82ff). This is certainly true in Tajikistan, where the very word *ayb* can be wielded like a sword to keep order.

It is the honour-and-shame system that bears the chief responsibility for the similarity of social norms, and thus for many resemblances in lifestyle, across a wide geographic region, where it has been a vital factor in the way gender norms are defined, at least as regards their most elemental characteristics. These are those directly related to female virginity and chastity, and male control over women.

Nevertheless, the boundaries differ widely among communities and social groups, each of which imposes its own limitations of the acceptable along with its own definitions of the shameful. What is crucial here is to understand how men and, by extension, the family, can be shamed by even the hint of female non-compliance. Masculine gender identities and with them men's honour are highly dependent on the visible demonstration of their ability to control their womenfolk. This makes men extraordinarily vulnerable, since their honour can be destroyed by a single deed or even word (see Gilmore 1987: 4) and this is what allows gossip to play such a vital role in social control.

The popular image of Muslim societies depicts women as powerless, completely under the control of their menfolk. However, the reality is much more complex. Men fall within a hierarchy, from hegemonic to subordinate and the honour-and-shame system in practice works to support the honour of the hegemonic. Typically in these societies age is a major component of hegemony. That is to say, like Fayziddin (Chapter 1), it is male family heads who have the privilege of domination but who are simultaneously given public responsibility for controlling *all* family members, not just women, and thus whose honour is most at risk.

The result is that younger men find themselves in an ambivalent position. In Tajikistan at least, they have control over women of their own age and younger while being subject to the control of their elders *of both sexes*. Unlike women they are not restricted in their mobility and are even applauded for having multiple sexual relations, which can only improve their masculine image. However, they must *visibly* comply with their fathers' orders. A rebellious son, such as Rustam (Chapter 4), can be as harmful for a father's and his family's honour as a recalcitrant woman, but control over sons usually becomes a problem only at crucial moments, such as when important decisions have to be taken, while women's purity is a matter of daily consideration, at least while they are young. As they age they represent less a risk than a support in controlling the younger generation (see Hegland 1992: 205). In other words, the masculine and feminine norms legitimised by discourse are at opposite ends of a continuum, which situates mature men at one extreme, young women at the other, and the rest in between. Class, wealth and other social differences also play a role in the way the honour-and-shame system is used to manipulate behaviour (Lindisfarne 1994).

For young women, almost more important than *being* pure is being *seen* to be so. The slightest scandal can destroy their reputations and by extension that of their families. As Warnock puts it:

Since honour was a matter of external appearance, it had to be constantly open to inspection and to be proved by contact with the external environment. Honour consisted precisely of what other people said ... The slightest deviation would arouse comment which would be, in itself, dishonour. (1990: 25)

What is at stake, therefore, is not so much a woman's sexual behaviour as the perception of her behaviour, the *image* projected. This is something *all* societies dominated by the honour-and-shame system have in common. Since above all it is *image* that is important, punishment will follow not so much the actual violation of the norms as the violation being made public. In fact, since the very infliction of punishment would be a sign that something was wrong, it can only take place once a violation has been made public. However, if this happens castigation *must* follow for honour to be vindicated, even when this may take the form of a girl's execution. Ginat, for instance, mentions a case in Palestine, where a girl who had had a secret abortion was put to death by her family many months later because a woman feuding with the family insisted on making the matter public, thus forcing them to act (1982: 180). He points out that community pressures do not affect all families equally, but depend on social standing. The lower a family's place in the community, the more important is their demonstration of control (1982: 180).

In Tajikistan the honour-and-shame system is as important as anywhere else in the Muslim world, although killing is no longer a punishment for causing *ayb*, as in this Palestinian case, or over the border in Afghanistan. The conflict between Tillo and her brothers should be read in the light of this system. It is a struggle between Tillo's wish to live in her own way and the demands of family and the community. Tillo's brothers had to show willing in front of the neighbours to take action to control their sister. If Tillo looks as if she can get away unscathed with such terrible deviations another woman might copy her, and then another, and who knows where this might end.

The neighbours used spying, gossiping and tale-bearing – that is, a selection of Foucault's micro-instruments of power (1980a: 101) – to ensure that Tillo's brothers knew exactly what was going on. It was clear that, as soon as her second husband left, she had become a target of communal scrutiny, which had increased when she started her business and her travelling. The clothes she wore, the places she went to, and the people she met there were all relayed back to her brothers. Thus they were not only kept informed of everything their sister did; they knew she was the focus of gossip and, moreover, that everyone realised they knew. This meant they had to act or else lose *nomus* in a big way. The public beatings, then, were intended as demonstrations that they were doing their best to salvage family honour.

When Tillo was young she had automatically complied with her parents' wishes, not thinking she could have any say in her fate. After her first husband went mad she took some measure of control by leaving him. By the time her second husband abandoned her she was ready to take full charge of her life and she did this openly. Here was a woman who seriously challenged gender norms. She was beautiful, knew how to present herself attractively and took great pride and pleasure in doing so. She travelled abroad, even though always in the company of women friends. She openly consorted with men in her business, and with Kulobis at that, a regional group at present heartily disliked in Tajikistan because of their crude and unpleasant behaviour since taking over the government. Although she never brought a man home, nor was ever seen doing anything specifically bad, no-one could tell for sure what was going on when she was out of sight.

Tillo was thus a challenge to the norms. Her beauty was a threat to her neighbours whose husbands saw her every day in the street and knew she was on her own. She dared to do what other women did not – to live on her own with her children, to travel, to earn money through her own initiative, in short to behave like a man. The more Tillo defied the conventions, the more the neighbours tried to pressure her into conforming, by means of the only weapon they had, the pressure on her family's *nomus,* and her brothers took this very much to heart.

The fact that all concerned lived within a few streets of one another heightened the neighbours' potential for interference, since Tillo's neighbours were also her family's. The men would congregate in the street and talk for hours, from time to time sending loaded glances towards Tillo's house as they did so. I could never get close enough to overhear, but it was clear even from a distance that it was about her, and that it was not complimentary. The women also sometimes gathered outside to gossip about her, reinforcing the pressures and making it hard for *anyone* to miss the fact that something untoward was going on.

Tillo's brothers may also have felt shamed by the fact that she, a woman on her own with five children, was visibly living more prosperously than they were. Once she remarried they would not only be unable to get their hands on her property, but would no longer be able to chastise her. Thus they would still suffer the shame of her bad behaviour without being able to exert the slightest control over her. Their father was too old to be able to punish her physically so his public reproof consisted of refusing her permission to see her dying mother, something the whole neighbourhood was made aware of. The fact that his wife was denied her dying wish, appeared less important than their neighbours' opinions.

Tillo's story shows the power of gossip. Along with its companions, spying and tale-bearing, gossip is used not just in communities based on the honour-and-shame system but in all communities where the preservation of social norms, most particularly, of course, the appropriate performance of gender, is a paramount consideration.

Melanie Tebbutt, who studied gossip in working-class English neighbourhoods from the late nineteenth through the mid-twentieth centuries shows it was used there in the same way and to the same ends as in Tajikistan, especially by older women intent on preventing deviation by younger ones. Gossip was particularly aimed at the preservation of female chastity (Tebbutt 1995: 9, 49ff). Al-Khayyat, who studied her own Iraqi community claims that there '[g]ossip operates as one of the strongest forms of social control, particularly in policing women. [Girls] are very conscious of gossip' (1990: 23).

Roger Abrahams claims that gossip is a necessary tool for the maintenance of *any* community's social system, that in general it is gender norms that are the main focus of gossip, and that gossip is important in providing active ways to guarantee a certain level of homogeneity of ideals and social practices. He suggests that there is an ongoing tension between the interests of the community, which are served by gossip, and those of individual families, who are always under threat of becoming focuses of gossip (1970: 297ff).

Moreover, gossip provides a way of channelling group discussions into paths chosen by community leaders, who tend to be older men and women. This is another way to control youth. Regulating the range of acceptable subjects and the attitude to be taken to them, is used by elders to groom young people to tread the same well-worn paths in their own discussions and thus to prevent them developing new and independent viewpoints.

Gossip also provides a way of uniting a community, of letting people feel they are part of a group with common interests. Anyone who does not identify with those interests and is not willing to participate is not a true community member. For people everywhere the opinions of their neighbours and fitting into their community are vitally important. In Tajikistan there is little that is more important, at least that is the impression I got when I heard repeated over and over again: 'I can't do that. What would the neighbours say?' Once, when I was really tired of hearing this, I asked Jahongul, 'Does it really matter what they say?' She replied, 'It matters to *us*. We are simply not in a position to ignore it.' The neighbours are clearly only too ready to 'condemn and distort' (Wikan 1984: 636).

Gossip is reinforced by the concept of *ayb*, a tiny word that carries a gigantic force. Everything and anything can be *ayb*, from loss of virginity before marriage to the length of girls' sleeves but it usually has to do with some aspect of gender performance. For this reason, although *ayb* tends to be aimed at women it can also be directed towards (younger) men, towards anyone, in fact, whose gender performance can come under pressure from a controlling individual, whether this is the older generation subjugating the younger, males dominating females, or even men exerting pressure on each other.

Tillo's activities had enormous potential to cause *ayb* – her wearing long boots, Russian clothes, talking to men and especially to Kulobis, daring to go abroad at all,[4] and especially without an accompanying male with jurisdiction over her, her presumption in marrying for a third time and above all in becoming a secondary wife to a man whose principal wife lived nearby. In short, it was hard to find any aspect of her behaviour that was not shameful. Nevertheless, Tillo did not appear to allow either this, or her neighbours' opinions of her, to deflect her from her path.

How is it that Tillo was able to take so little notice of her neighbours and refuse to let their condemnation deter her, while other people, such as Jahongul, are petrified of putting a foot wrong, of doing anything the neighbours might comment on adversely? The chief reason may be that Tillo is in her 30s. She is no longer financially dependent and has her own home. Although she cares about her eldest brother and her mother, she cares more about her own life. She has learned that if she does not take control of it she will be forced to live in a way she finds unpleasant and she feels she has been doing this for long enough. She regrets not having had the strength to make her own decisions when she was younger. Now she has decided to live as she wants, openly prioritising her own needs, not a particularly acceptable trait in a Tajik woman. Perhaps she has learned this strength from living without a husband or other constraining figure.

Having spent several years as her own boss and, what is more, travelling widely as well as becoming a successful businesswoman, Tillo now knows what she wants out of life. In other words, after the end of her second marriage Tillo was gradually able to develop agency, since at that point she had nobody directly demanding her submission. This does not mean she has abandoned Tajik customs, merely that she now has ideas of her own. Nevertheless, in her general lifestyle she lives very much the same way as other Tajik women and most of the time is as controlling of, and watchful over, her daughters as any of her neighbours. Moreover, upon marriage to Chahonbek she found herself forced to relinquish her newfound agency, at least in front of her husband, and allow herself to be subjected to his will, unable to bring herself to defy him outright, as her story later shows (Chapter 6).

Jahongul was in a very different situation. She was 16, unmarried, living at home with her mother and subject to her control and that of her brothers. Furthermore, the whole family was in a vulnerable position owing to the lack of a father, who could have simultaneously ensured conformity with social mores and protected them from harm. Any stain on her reputation might have made it impossible for her to make a good marriage. Her reputation was the only resource she had, and it was important to take good care to preserve it (Chapter 5). A girl has to be careful of almost everything she does in public, it is so easy for her to bring shame on her family. Moreover, she may do so completely involuntarily and through no fault of her own, such as by being raped, something that was only too frequent during the war years. This forces young women and their families to be doubly vigilant.

MALE HONOUR

A man is not disgraced by committing rape, any more than Tillo's first husband was disgraced because of his drug-taking and his prison record, since these do not negatively affect *nomus*, which is concerned only with things that negatively impact male gender identity. Rape may even enhance a man's reputation by demonstrating his power over women and ability to engage in extra-marital sex.

Men are pressured into upholding their *nomus* by the threat of mockery or the worst possible accusation, that of being womanlike. This last is so potent it compels men to buy into the desirability of living up to the dominant gender norms because to do otherwise is to risk 'becoming' the inferior (see Moore 1994a: 145). Thus, male failure to conform presents a greater psychological risk than female failure to conform. However, since men do not fully internalise the norms either, they may also assume gender masks in the hope of avoiding accusations of *ayb* because of inappropriate gender performances, which may range from doing housework to failing to enforce control over unmarried daughters. If they do not cover this up, other men are quick to pressure them into conforming. One of the health project's male staff recounted how he was mocked for helping his wife:

One Sunday morning my wife and I carried our rugs down into the communal courtyard for cleaning. We had just started on this when I noticed several of my [male] neighbours standing round staring. When they saw what I was doing they started jeering – 'Are you a woman to do such work?' I stood it for about 15 minutes but then I couldn't bear it any longer. Throwing a quick excuse at my wife I rushed off, leaving the rest to her. After this I decided to restrict my help to chores inside the flat, where no-one could see me and, if a visitor came, I would always pretend to have been doing something else.[5]

Mockery appears to be very effective in controlling men. It is even more important for getting them to control their womenfolk, especially when applied to boys who are not yet sure of their masculinity. Jahongul's younger brother, Farukh, for instance, was very sensitive to any gossip about his sister and would immediately confront her if he heard any. He is not alone in this:

When Ibrohim was 12 years old, his mother Basgul, a widow in Khujand, decided to remarry. However, her new husband took drugs and would become violent when under the influence. He would come home night after night stoned and desperate for sex,[6] *to the point that if Basgul did not immediately acquiesce he would beat her, or rape her at knife point. To escape his violence she spent many a night huddled in fear on the staircase outside her flat and it was clear to everyone that things were not going well. Ibrohim was scared his mother would get a divorce and then later would wish to marry again. Women who have had more than two husbands are considered immodest. Ibrohim had heard his school friends jeering at other boys whose mothers had done this; indeed, he had joined in. He was scared that he might now end up as the butt of their ridicule. So he told his mother that she must just endure her situation. He would not accept her divorcing this man; somehow she had to learn to live with him. Basgul eventually did find a way to get her husband to stop taking drugs, and their marriage has since become more bearable. She admits that Ibrohim's fears definitely influenced her decision to try to make the most of it.[7]*

Men can be extremely harsh to and unforgiving of one another when they consider that serious infringements of *nomus* have taken place. The men in Tillo's street were quite hard on Chahonbek for marrying a secondary wife living so near his first one. They made it very clear what a disgraceful action that was, although they probably would not have said a word had Tillo lived further away, so that no-one would have seen them.

Hamid lives in a village in Kofernihon. Shortly before the civil war his unmarried daughter became pregnant. Immediately they learned of this the men of his village got together and decided to take action. They felt that if they were not careful their village might become a laughing stock in the region. They decided the most effective punishment was ostracism. They hoped this would show Hamid that his lack of control over his daughter's behaviour had dishonoured the whole village.

The ostracism continued for some months. Hamid was very upset by his fellow villagers' behaviour but he did not know how to make amends. One day he decided to see if he could force the men to accept him again. There was a tui at a neighbour's house and Hamid decided to attend. He sat down at the dastarkhon with the other men. Immediately they all moved away from him, leaving him by himself. Hamid had still not been able to get the men to change their attitude towards him when the war broke out and the villagers scattered in exile.[8]

The ostracism of men who are felt to have violated gender norms or *nomus* serves not just as punishment and pressure to rectify this but also as a warning to others. It is notable that committing such acts as robbery with violence or even murder seems less shameful than an unmarried daughter getting pregnant.[9]

AYB AND RELIGION

I went to Khojamaston together with my colleagues to interview potential new staff for the health project. One of the things we wanted to find out was the candidates' attitudes towards Tajik traditions, as we needed staff open to the possibility of change. We asked 50-year-old Yusuf what he would do if a man came to him and said, 'My wife has taken a lover, what should I do?' What advice would Yusuf give him? Yusuf was horrified, and said firmly that he believed in all the Islamic teachings and that marital fidelity was obligated to women under Islamic law. A wife who had taken a lover would be polluted and her husband should immediately divorce her. Meanwhile, the man himself would be dirty and no other men could have anything to do with him. 'A man has the right to have more than one wife, so he may take another whenever he wishes. But a woman can't have more than one husband at a time. Her husband first has to say taloq *and only then can she remarry, so it's always a sin for a woman to have sex with another man while she is still married. There is nothing that can change this law. It is so written.' Needless to say, we did not hire Yusuf. Instead we found other men who, while believing it to be undesirable for women to have extra-marital sex, do not condemn either party.*

Khojamaston is a very religious region. Yusuf was not the only man there to hold such views nor to make use of religion both as a potent weapon for control over women and as a very handy justification for men's rights to a more hedonistic lifestyle, while legitimising the right to exert control over other men by insisting they enforce the norms within their own families. They ignore or, more likely, are unaware of the fact that the Qur'an condemns men who marry secondary wives without their primary wives' permission (Chapter 1). Thus, religion lends itself to being used as one of Foucault's micro-mechanisms of power and it is very easy for people to (re)interpret the scriptures to their own ends.

The use of religion as a mechanism for social control is not limited to men. For instance, when Karomat was in agreement with a plan she would be happy discussing it. However, when she was not in favour or was in a bad mood she would say, 'You should not plan for the future. That is in God's hands.' Again, at some times she would say that one should put all one's trust in God, while at others she would go haring off to her doctor for help.

The name of God is often invoked in Tajikistan in the sort of situation where in the west the word 'natural' might be applied. For instance, a westerner might say that it is not natural to fly and that had human beings been meant to do this we would have been born with wings. That same person may not have anything against trains, although we were not born with wheels. More commonly the word 'unnatural' is applied to things people find morally reprehensible, especially in regard to sex. The arguments are not based on logic but rather serve to impose social control, since the word 'natural' holds a regulatory force that prevents its being queried. In Tajikistan evoking the name of God is even more potent, as it is that much more difficult to question.

Lutfia lives in the village of Sayot. She had an IUD inserted some time ago, when she felt she had completed her family. However, one of her children has recently died and Lutfia is now trying to have another. So far she has been unable to conceive, since her IUD has left her with gynaecological problems. A group of women were sitting round discussing this. The younger ones were commiserating with her but several older ones condemned her for having used contraceptives, insisting that the death of her child and her current infertility were God's punishment.

Ailsa is a widow also from Sayot. She is extremely poor and has started trading in the market in order to feed herself and her children. Few men from her mahalla *of Sayot were killed in the war so that Ailsa is one of only a handful of widows there and most of the others have some sort of support. Although many women from other* mahallas, *where the number of widows is higher, have been trading for some time, where Ailsa lives the number of women in dire straits is insufficient to have forced a consensus that this is permissible. Thus her neighbours are extremely upset with her behaviour.*

Feeling ill one day, Ailsa went to see the village doctor. While she was waiting in the queue several older neighbours started muttering. Finally they turned to her and asked why she was there. She said she was not feeling well and had come for treatment. 'Of course, you are not well', they said. 'God is punishing you. Your illness is a direct result of your immorality. All you have to do to become well is to stop trading. God cannot be for you when you behave like that.' Ailsa became very upset and started shouting that she had no other way of feeding her children and did they expect them to starve. The reply was: 'That isn't important; you must not contravene God's laws.'

In both these examples God's name is being invoked to enforce community values that may actually be the opposite of the teachings of the Qur'an. There is no justification in the scriptures for not using contraceptives. These are permitted by the mediaeval jurists; the Central Asian Ibn Sino mentions 20 different forms (Musallam 1983: 67) and the Prophet Himself mentions *coitus interruptus* (withdrawal) as perfectly acceptable. There is also nothing in the scriptures to suggest that women are forbidden to trade or earn a living (Chapter 1).

COMMUNITY RELATIONS

Safarmo is a war widow in her mid-30s, from the same mahalla *of Sayot as Ailsa. After her husband was killed Safarmo was left with seven mouths to support. Except for her older son who lives in Kazakhstan and occasionally sends her money, her children are too young to help. Safarmo has no special skills, so she decided to trade the produce from her plot of land in the town market. However, the neighbours took the same attitude with her as with Ailsa. After she had been trading for a short time a deputation of older women came to her and asked her to stop, saying it was not appropriate and that she was shaming both herself and the village. Safarmo weighed up the consequences and decided she could not afford to get herself a bad name, so she agreed to give up trading, although she was now so poor she and her family could barely afford to eat. She was also very preoccupied by the fact that she had no money to buy her children school exercise books and pencils. Nevertheless, Safarmo did not feel strong enough to defy village tradition.*

A year later she had to rethink her situation. Her son in Kazakhstan had stopped sending her money and without it they could not survive. She absolutely had to earn something. She started baking non *and selling it in the market, telling the neighbours that if they wanted her to stop they would have to feed her and her children.*

Because she has neither a mother-in-law nor any adult men in her household, Safarmo has become an object of suspicion. Old women will turn up to sit with her to check that all is in order and the village boys spy on her constantly. Things became so bad, Safarmo confided, that she could no longer meet her women friends openly; the boys would not leave them alone, even crouching down outside the windows to listen to what was going on inside, thus preventing the women from talking freely. For this reason they have taken to meeting at night. Around midnight, when they hope everyone else in the village is asleep, Safarmo's friends, shoes in hand, tiptoe down the paths of their homes and out into the night, trying not to waken the dogs. They gather at her house, have their conversations in peace and, around 3 a.m., return home in the same way. So far they have not been caught.

Each village *mahalla* is small enough that everyone can easily manage to get to know everyone else's business and they all do their best to discover each other's secrets. On a number of occasions when a woman set out for our clinic the boys were already telling everyone where she was going and why, long before she had left her own neighbourhood. This spying and the ensuing gossip acts as a strong deterrent to any woman looking to keep her visit, or at least the reason for it, private.

Safarmo and her friends go to quite extraordinary lengths to evade community vigilance in order to be able to meet in peace. However, they clearly find the opportunity to get together important enough to make the effort. All these women were extremely enthusiastic attendees at the health project's classes and this may have been a contributory factor to their desire to have private discussions. Perhaps they are learning to be subversive in ways that alarm the community, and this may also be why there is so much pressure on them.

However, it is not any emancipatory effect of the health project but sheer necessity that drives both Ailsa and Safarmo into defying convention and trading in the market. Their options are to do this or starve to death, along with their children. They are in a far more drastic situation than Tillo, who could probably have found some way to exist without starting her own business. She defied convention because she wanted to live above the mere survival line. Ailsa and Safarmo have not managed to raise themselves more than a tiny fraction above this even with their trading, which is on a very much smaller scale and thus very much less lucrative than that of Tillo, but at least they are managing to keep their heads above water.

It is difficult to know whether their critics would really have preferred these families to starve to death rather than contravene the norms, or whether the pressure is just a way of reminding everyone of the punishments for transgression, while not necessarily being intended to prevent them. In other words, a woman who is really desperate might trade, if this is what it takes to stay alive, but other women should not think this gives them the right to trade just to improve their living standards.

There is, thus, obvious and visible tension between communities and the individual families of which they are composed. In Tajikistan, just as in other societies based on the honour-and-shame system, it is almost impossible to avoid considering what people will say about virtually everything one does (see Wikan 1984: 636). If people publicly transgress social norms, especially if they dare to challenge accepted gender performances, there will be a concerted effort on the part of other community members to squash this, to ferret out wrongdoing and to reveal it where the disclosure can have most disciplinary force.[10] Through their spying the village boys act to support the senior community members in retaining their power base, and thus they play a significant role in the preservation of community norms.

The tension between families and the communities they live in is occasioned largely by the former trying to preserve their secrets, while everyone else tries hard to discover anything discreditable. Winning families are able to preserve their own secrets, while taking a high moral stance over the aberrations of others. Thus family dramas are played out against the background of community observation, with the constant threat of exposure and its consequences hanging over everybody's heads.

Although in Tajikistan these consequences may not be as negative as for Ginat's (1982) Palestinian girl discussed above, they may still be very bad. This accounts for the sometimes quite extraordinary lengths that people may go to in order to preserve their secrets intact from public gaze, enveloping them in a maze of intricate lies and deceits. Such cover-ups are clearly especially important when a girl's reputation is at stake. For instance, mothers who find out their unmarried daughters are pregnant will rush them off to a distant region in order to get them abortions somewhere they hope no-one will recognise them.

In fact, in Tajikistan female neighbours often do have some idea of what is going on. Whether they will reveal their knowledge depends partly on the esteem the family is held in but most especially on whether its members are perceived to be trying to remedy the situation. Where it is clear they are doing their best to maintain gender norms and that they acknowledge the shame of their wrongdoing, the community may leave them in peace. It is as if a supreme effort at covering up suffices to demonstrate that the family respects the norms and that its women will be controlled without the necessity for public exposure.

In other words, a community's older women, who are very often the arbiters of its morals and actions, may not always be malicious. It seems that at times they may be content to leave a family unexposed in order not to cause irreparable damage, as long as it is clear all round that the norms are not going to be violated and that it is unlikely that particular person will soon transgress again. But their knowledge of the transgression is something they can if necessary use in the future and a family may be very aware of this, without anything overt having been said.

The women of the community, for instance, may be aware that those of a certain family have conspired to cover up some transgression on the part of a daughter without their menfolk finding out. It is not infrequent in the case of girls' infringement of *nomus*, resulting for instance in clandestine abortions, that the women keep this secret from the men. The community women may tacitly agree that the men need never find out. In this way they may gain great power over the women of an offending family because there is always the unspoken threat hanging over them that they might make the transgression public.

Thus, although *nomus* may be far from beneficial to women they are certainly not just passive victims of it. On the contrary, they play a very active role, as guardians of *nomus* or its (deliberate) transgressors, as concealers of violations within their own families or revealers of the infringements of others. Older women derive power from their position as controllers of young women's honour as well as being able to manipulate family honour to their own advantage, which gives them the incentive to initiate cover-ups rather than have their own inadequacies exposed to the public gaze. But when senior community members see that families are permitting 'shameful' behaviour to continue, they apply pressure until the situation has been rectified.

Zora, whom I introduced in Chapter 1, was very aware that she and her family were the focus of considerable gossip, because her daughter Dila was still unmarried at the ripe old age of 23. Zora had decided to allow Dila to wait to get married until she finished her physics degree at Dushanbe University, as she had great hopes of an academic career for her. However, keeping to this resolution was getting very hard. Dila was now by far the oldest unmarried girl in her circle. Her situation, together with much speculation as to the reason for it, was becoming a major topic of conversation among all their friends and acquaintances.

Even Jahongul, herself only too aware of how difficult it can be to tread the minefield of gossip, could not refrain from adding her mite. 'How extraordinary that Dila is not yet married. They must move in very different circles from ours. We could never get away with being unmarried at such a late age. Someone would be bound to start insinuating there was something wrong with us', she concluded. Zora did her best to take no notice but she got really tired of greetings that increasingly consisted mainly of the question, 'Have you married your daughter yet?' Things got so bad that she would go out of her way to avoid meeting acquaintances she had not seen for a while.

Dila's brother, Ali, was most upset when his friends jeered at him about it, insinuating that his sister was afraid to marry because she was no longer a virgin. Almost every day he would come home and beg his mother to marry his sister, as he couldn't stand the pressure any more.

Finally, Dila finished her degree and registered for postgraduate studies. A fellow student had had his eye on her for some time and his family offered for her shortly before graduation. Thus, she finally married. A year later she had a baby, demonstrating that after all there was nothing wrong and she was well able to conform to social norms.

The friends and acquaintances of each family member all exerted tremendous pressure to force this family to conform to the norms they were too visibly defying. In a society where practically all girls are married before the age of 20 a girl of 23 is virtually on the shelf. As Jahongul said:

Here in Tajikistan a girl who has reached the age of 18 without her hand being asked in marriage is considered an old maid. I want to marry as late as possible, perhaps between 20 and 22. Only, brides over 20 look so old and awful!

So, a girl unmarried at the age of 23 must have something wrong with her. If nothing is obviously amiss, people's first thought, like that of Ali's friends, is that she is frightened to get married because she is no longer a virgin. It is inconceivable to most people in Tajikistan that a girl might postpone marriage in order to be able to concentrate better on her studies. I have even known Tajik women studying in Moscow come home to give birth, leave their new baby with their mothers, and return to Moscow to finish their studies, perhaps not seeing the child again for several years. Most girls in Tajikistan today get married on leaving high school and study afterwards. Luckily, for Dila it all came right in the end and she is now working on her master's degree.

On her first workday after her marriage, Karomat dressed in her Russian clothes. All the women in the street stared at her and began to talk loudly, so loudly it reached Karomat's ears. They were asking, 'How can she go around without ezor? She must be a shameless hussy. Karomat wanted to lift her skirt and show that she was wearing Russian-style knickers underneath and was not naked. But she decided this might not be a good idea.

Day after day she would go to the factory dressed in European clothes, and day after day the women would gather in the street and stare at her, muttering their disapprobation. Karomat hated running this gauntlet but she carried on with it. Meanwhile, the women went to her mother-in-law and said to her, 'How can you let your daughter-in-law dress like that? It is absolutely disgraceful. Who are her father and mother? Why does she wear such clothes?' Karomat's mother-in-law replied that her son had promised his bride before they were married that he would allow her to wear Russian clothes and so nothing could be done at present. However, she agreed to talk to her daughter-in-law after she had had time to settle in.

A couple of months later, Karomat's mother-in-law said to her, 'Come and sit down with me, I want to talk to you.' Karomat protested that there was too much housework, but her mother-in-law said she would help her later. Then she said, 'Sweetie, lovey, pet, I am an old woman – I am now 45 and have borne 12 children and buried 10 – in a few years I'll be dead. When I am in my grave you can do as you please, but right now I beg of you to do as I ask.' Karomat asked, 'What? What do you want me to do?' Her mother-in-law said, 'No-one will invite me to their homes, everyone says we are shamed because we have a daughter-in-law in the family who dresses like a Russian and doesn't wear ezor. They ask, "Where are her parents from?"' Karomat replied heatedly, 'My parents are from the north and they are Tajiks, just as I am.' Her mother-in-law begged, 'Please, just for my sake and just for the few years I have left to live, please wear Tajik clothes.'

Karomat told me she was 'somewhat stupid in those days' and really believed that probably her mother-in-law was so old she would soon die. So she agreed. The following day she went to work wearing ezor and a rumol, in other words Tajik traditional dress. All the Tajik women looked approvingly on as she walked down the road. When she got to the factory the Russian women all crowded round her and said 'Clara,[11] what is it, what happened? Why are you dressed like that?' Karomat explained, adding, 'My mother-in-law is like a mother to me and her word is law. What can I do?' Then the Russian women said, 'You see, you were promised you could wear Russian clothes, but now he has got you under his thumb you see what has happened, you are doing what he says and he is not sticking to his promise.' They went on like this for a long time. Karomat continued to turn up to work in Tajik clothes and every day her co-workers would discuss them.

Finally, she got fed up and told them that she worked with them for eight hours a day but then went home and lived her life outside the factory. She was Tajik, her family was Tajik, and her mother-in-law and husband too, and they were more important to her than her co-workers, who should shut up and leave her alone. So they did and never bothered her again on the subject.

In Sayot there lives Tojiddin, an older man who delights in manipulating his fellow villagers. He spends much of his time on the look out for things to criticise. The young people, especially the teenage girls, go in terror of him and do their best to avoid drawing his attention. One day Tojiddin decided the sleeves on many of the girls' dresses were too short. In the mosque that evening he told their fathers their daughters were shaming them by wearing their sleeves so short. The men returned home and punished the girls, who then had even more reason for fear. This is a fear that constantly hangs over them. I have heard them discuss whether or not to do something and decide against it because they were frightened Tojiddin might see them.

In both these cases the community's self-appointed representatives were able to force individuals to change their behaviour, even though in neither case had a major transgression occurred. To make so much fuss over mere clothes might seem trivial, but it is far from insignificant in the context of an opportunity for society's self-proclaimed leaders to demonstrate their power. Moreover, the issue of whether to wear Russian or Tajik clothes directly impinges on gender norms, as was discussed in relation to Dila in Chapter 1.

The terror that the Sayot girls feel in front of Tojiddin is very real. Even their fathers fear this man because they never know what shortcomings he will expose next. But because gossip and spying give power, because men feel themselves helpless in a situation that could publicly expose them as unmanly, they feel compelled to pay attention to Tojiddin.

Men are weaker where such things are concerned than older women. While Tillo and especially the 70-year-old Karomat can say, to hell with what the neighbours think, men rarely appear able to shrug off public derision. In fact, especially since they are the group most impervious to gossip, older women use this as a weapon in power struggles not only against women but also against men.

But when she was 17 and newly wed Karomat was not in a position to be able to ignore the neighbours. The threat to her relations with her mother-in-law, and perhaps also her husband, seemed very real. It is also possible that her mother-in-law had her own objections to Karomat's wearing Russian clothes and was using the excuse of their neighbours' disapprobation to impose her wishes in a non-conflictive manner.

MEN AND *AYB*

Paradoxically, the men who spend so much time and energy on ensuring their sisters and daughters are never touched by a strange man even in gossip, may also spend inordinate time and energy trying to get other men's womenfolk into compromising situations. This is because masculine gender performance depends on proving virility and one way of doing this is to have large numbers of sexual partners, as I discuss in greater detail in Chapter 6. In fact many men feel that any other man's womenfolk are fair game.

Such an attitude towards sexuality is not restricted to Tajikistan, nor to Muslim countries but is common to *all* countries whose moral system is based on the honour-and-shame system, such as Cuba[12] and Spain, which is why female seclusion was practised in all of these. That is to say, seclusion is not peculiar to Muslim societies, it is rather that Islam is a juridical religion, which can adjudicate on how people should lead their lives. As such it has the authority not only to interpret the scriptures in line with prevalent morality but also to use them to enforce compliance. It is this that allows female seclusion and veiling to be incorporated into religious practices, legitimising them in a way unavailable to Christianity today. However, it is not so long since Spanish men expected to keep control of their wives' mobility. I remember that when I was living in

Spain in the mid-1980s the husbands of some of my older women friends expected their permission to be sought before their wives might participate in activities outside the home.

Before the revolution large numbers of Cuban men secluded their wives. One of the chief reasons men who emigrated to Cuba in the 1960s gave for leaving, was that they had felt themselves dishonoured by the new laws that brought women out of their homes and into the workforce. These men felt the necessity of secluding their wives most strongly because they believed that it was impossible that a 'real man' could be contented with only one woman. Their status among their men friends was dependent on their success in seducing other men's womenfolk, while their honour was dependent on their wives' being kept from contact with other men (Fox 1973: 275–8).

Men in the Arab countries have the same basic approach, which is the major reason why both men and women in Cairo feel more relaxed when the latter wear the *hijab* to work, as it makes them symbolically untouchable (MacLeod 1991), something that clearly does not exist in the less structured conditions of Christian societies. Use of the *hijab* gives Egyptian women the freedom to leave home while remaining protected. In both societies men aim to have (sexual) contact with as many women as they can, while simultaneously endeavouring to keep their own women pure. According to Abu-Odeh, in Egypt this struggle between men for each other's womenfolk is so strong that some even make (silent) pacts with their best friends that they will not touch each other's women but will help each other seduce other men's. However, most Egyptian families do manage to protect their womenfolk and as a result most Arab men are still virgins at marriage (1996: 152–3, 179).

In Tajikistan the same tensions between families apply. On the one hand, the community exerts pressure on its families to ensure its females preserve their chastity, while on the other, men from the community do their best to get them to violate it. This even happened during the period of *hujum*, when Central Asian men felt their collective manhood to be at stake. It was not merely that men attacked women who unveiled in order to force them to resume their veils (Chapter 2) but also Central Asian communist officials would use their position to expropriate the unveiled wives of the poorest men (Massell 1974: 305).

This accounts for a great deal of men's unease at the thought of their womenfolk being exposed to strange men and explains why they try so hard to keep track of all their movements outside the home.

CONCLUSION

Foucault's micro-mechanisms of power are made the more potent in Tajikistan by the honour-and-shame system, especially through its influence on the formation of both masculine and feminine gender identities. *Nomus* and *ayb* are powerful tools for social control, and allow the community to exert pressure on a family through the way masculine gender identity is defined, in particular through the characteristic of control. Men are vulnerable to community pressure precisely because of this characteristic, which forces male heads of family to repress other members in order not to be seen as emasculated. It is also beneficial to younger women in the community that other young women conform, because this keeps the pressure off them. Once one young woman is seen to be rebelling against the norms their peers find their behaviour under closer scrutiny. This encourages young women also to cooperate in policing each other and to keep any aberrations well hidden behind their gender masks.

Such interference of the wider community in the lives of individuals and their families may seem exceptionally intrusive, but, as the Tebbutt (1995) study referred to above suggests, it is only quantitatively different from community control in the west. In fact, a certain amount of community control is vital everywhere since communities cannot exist as cohesive groups without a sense of underlying norms and shared understanding of how people should live and societies be structured (Singerman 1995: 50). So the survival of the community and society is actually dependent on the types of controls discussed here.

If everyone took as little notice as Tillo, if everyone were to defy the community secretly as Safarmo does, if young people were allowed to go their own way, taking no notice of their elders, this would threaten the glue that holds society together and chaos would doubtless ensue, a chaos that would be beneficial to no-one. This was the sort of chaos that occurred in actual fact during the civil war. People in Tajikistan perhaps rebel less against social controls today than they might otherwise do, given the relative weakness of the national government and the stresses of the post-Soviet period, precisely because they have seen the horrors that lack of control can cause and they want to minimise these.

The problem is, however, that it is difficult to draw the line between community pressures that serve to keep a community together and debilitating repression of individual members. Community pressures serve to ensure both that family hierarchies are supported in their control over subordinate members and that dominant members are held strictly to their function as intermediaries of community control.

In Tajikistan the threat posed by the constant attempts of the Soviet state to penetrate and influence the local culture, attempts that only ended with *perestroika*, has made the vigilance, strictness and repression of difference far more important than they might otherwise have been. This also legitimises parental repression of youth. When the community as a whole felt under attack, as happened during *hujum*, their reaction made it clear that in Tajikistan national honour was dependent on exactly the same attributes as masculine honour. Both men and the nation are disgraced if their womenfolk's gender identities are infringed upon but men's *nomus* remains untouched by actions such as rape, drug-taking or even murder.

The stories in this chapter make it clear that for both sexes the characteristics that comprise their gender ideals are those that men find important. The characteristics women prize in men – such as responsibility, kindness, caring and tenderness – are totally missing in the definition of masculine gender identity. Meanwhile, for men, the important feminine gender characteristics are not so much those associated with relationships between the sexes, as those connected with men's relationships with other men. In other words, the dominant sets of gender norms are essentially part of male struggles to attain, or at least preserve, their status vis-à-vis other males (see Gilmore 1987: 4).

In the course of these struggles anything that might conceivably be labelled *ayb*, and there are an extraordinary number of things that can be, may appear on the prohibited list and be used against a potential transgressor. The system is the more frightening in that, since the law is not written down, the boundaries can be moved in accordance with the whim of those who appoint themselves judges, which can make it very confusing. The vital thing is never to forget the importance of preserving one's good name, if necessary using gender masks to do so, since this provides protection lacking for those perceived as teetering on the brink of respectability. Someone from a prestigious background or who lives within visibly strict family controls will obviously, therefore, be less vulnerable than a person in the situation of a Tillo.

While the stories in the following chapters stress family and interpersonal relationships they also contain many further instances of the influence of gossip and how this can be used to coerce families into controlling their members. As Foucault suggests (1980a: 98), society is, in effect, a net, its threads connecting all its members. In Tajikistan these connections run, not from person to person, but from family to family, with the individual family members forming an internal circle of power relations at each node.

4   INTERGENERATIONAL FAMILY CONTROL

In Chapter 3, I explained how Tajiks use gossip and related tactics to force conformity to social norms, especially gender norms, and how control is most effective when applied to women through their menfolk, or directly to men via mockery or worse. It demonstrated that social pressure works on people not singly but as members of families, its force coming from the fact that each individual is enmeshed in a family, so that any hint of shame attaching to one member affects them all. The present chapter shows how powerful this is as a motivation for family members to control each other, so that potentially shaming behaviour will remain concealed within the family circle. It also shows how family members can manipulate internal power relations so as to take personal advantage of this social pressure.

PARENTAL POWER

Rustam is the eldest of four. He has two sisters, Khatiya and Sumangul, and a brother, Kurbon. Their family comes from Hissor but moved to Dushanbe some 20 years ago. When we first met, Rustam was in his late 20s and a handiwork teacher at one of the best Dushanbe high schools. His mother, Dilorom, was also a teacher and his father, Malik, a high-ranking Party official. Kurbon was studying to be a doctor, Khatiya a nurse, while Sumangul was still in high school.

Even today Malik is a strong believer in the Soviet socialist system and brought his children up to believe in its principles, including atheism. His code is that the world should be organised according to a strict hierarchy, in which everyone, especially the young, should know and keep to their place. As he was a Party official his children had to show an example and so they were not allowed to play with the neighbours' children and were scolded for the slightest rowdiness.

Rustam was an energetic boy who loved the outdoors, so he found the prohibitions very difficult to live with. He longed to join in the wild games of the neighbourhood boys but if either of his parents caught him he would be severely beaten, his mother often inflicting even more pain than his father. The strict control his parents exercised was the harder to bear because most other boys were allowed to run wild.

Whenever his parents permitted, Rustam would stay with his favourite uncle, whose wife was Russian, and who treated both her own sons and Rustam very kindly, allowing them to play outside as much as they liked.

As he grew older Rustam's parents took little notice of his progress at school. The only thing they demanded was obedience. Nevertheless, they wanted him to have a prestigious career and his father decided he should become a lawyer. This absolutely horrified Rustam, who could not imagine anything he would like less. Moreover, he was sure he would be totally unable to cope with the coursework.

Taking no notice of this Malik arranged for his son to enrol in Dushanbe University. Rustam set out on registration day feeling dreadful. On his reluctant way to the law school he passed by the Pedagogical Institute. Suddenly he decided to defy his father. He went in and signed up to study to become a handicrafts teacher.

When he told his father Malik became more furious than ever before. However, since Rustam was by this time bigger than he was, he could no longer beat him. Instead he had to content himself with calling him the worst names he could think of. Rustam's parents have never forgiven him this career change. Since then they not only have never praised him, they have repeatedly told him he is stupid and dull-witted.

Rustam was content at the Institute, especially as he managed to get a place in the student dormitory so he could live away from home. However, after graduating, completing his military service and starting his teaching career, he had no option but to return to live with his parents, since housing for single persons was virtually non-existent.

One day, soon after Rustam's return from the army, Khatiya brought a fellow medical student home with her. This was Zhenia, a divorced Russian woman, a few years older than Rustam. Rustam and Zhenia fell in love and became inseparable. Although both were living with their parents, Zhenia's travelled a great deal, and Rustam was often able to stay with her in their absence.

Over the next year their feelings for each other became deeper and deeper. The only things that marred their happiness were the fact that both sets of parents disapproved of their relationship and that Zhenia's fallopian tubes had been damaged when her former husband punched her in the stomach when she was pregnant, killing their child and causing Zhenia serious gynaecological complications. Rustam took her to every specialist in the country but they could find no way to remedy her condition.

The following year, Rustam reached the age of 23 and his parents decided to find him a wife. Although they had nothing against Zhenia personally they had no intention of accepting her as a daughter-in-law. She was Russian, older and, worst of all, she was infertile and had been married before, all major strikes against her, especially the last two. Healthy young men with a reasonable position in life should marry virgins. Anything else is unacceptable. Rustam was already being jeered at for being so obviously besotted by Zhenia. Were he actually to marry her he would become a laughing stock, which would humiliate his family.

Zhenia's parents were less strong in their opposition. As Russians they did not believe that their daughter had to obey them absolutely but they let her know that they believed nothing good could possibly come of a match with a Tajik. Although they could not stop her, they withheld their approval and made it clear that Rustam would never be welcome to live in their home.

Rustam and Zhenia continued to see each other, although by this time his parents had totally forbidden this. They even tried following him round town after work to see what he was up to, and he had to go to extreme lengths to get away from them to meet her.

Rustam was desperate. His love for Zhenia was one of most important things in his life. He tried as hard as he could to enlist the support of other family members. His mother was not in favour, as she thought Zhenia would be a most unsuitable kelin. Even Kurbon refused to support him. Unfortunately, his favourite uncle had emigrated to Russia, so his support was unavailable.

Rustam told his father over and over again that he could and would marry nobody except Zhenia. This made Malik furious. Finally, he gave his son an ultimatum: 'If you marry Zhenia you will bring shame on me and on the whole family. All our friends and relatives will laugh at me for allowing it. I absolutely forbid it. You will marry whomever I tell you to or I'll divorce your mother and abandon the family.'

This was too much for Zhenia, who could not face being responsible for breaking up Rustam's family. She told him she could no longer agree to marry him and that in any case she was doubtful whether she had a right to marry at all, infertile as she was. After vain attempts to get her to change her mind Rustam went to his father and agreed to marry whomever he selected.

With some input from Rustam, Malik and Dilorom chose a bride whom they could all agree on. However, on their way to make an offer for her, they were waylaid by the mother of a quite different girl, who tried to persuade them to offer for her daughter, Jumbul. After a short discussion Malik and Dilorom agreed to accept her. She was 19 years old at the time and also, like Rustam, a teacher. A few days later Rustam and Jumbul were introduced and permitted to go to the cinema together. After this, Rustam made no further attempt to see her. He did not like her but did not really care one way or the other. It just did not seem worth making a fuss about; he was already too emotionally exhausted. If he couldn't have Zhenia he didn't care whom he married. So he agreed. At this point Dilorom went to visit Zhenia, told her that her son's wedding had been fixed, and begged her to leave him alone now he was pledged to another woman.

Shortly thereafter Rustam and Jumbul were married and she came to live at his parents' place. Within three days of the wedding Zhenia and Rustam had resumed their relationship, now in the utmost secrecy, and their affair continued until she emigrated to Russia with her parents a few years later. Observing the tremendous grief both young people were clearly feeling at the prospect of separation, perhaps for ever, Zhenia's mother burst into tears and said 'We did very wrong to part the two of you.'

After Zhenia left, Rustam did not attempt to hide his grief and unhappiness from his parents. However, this changed neither their belief in the correctness of their actions, nor their certainty as to their right to choose the fate of the rest of their children.

Next it was Kurbon's turn to marry and Malik introduced him to Mukhayo, the daughter of a colleague. Kurbon decided he liked her well enough and agreed to marry her. However, after the wedding their relationship gradually deteriorated and he has come to realise he made a major mistake in allowing his father to choose for him, but since he has two children it is too late. He says if it were not for the children he would not live with Mukhayo for one more day.

When Kurbon married, Rustam moved his family into a flat of their own. However, he spends more of his waking time at his parents' than at his own home, visiting them *at least once a day. If he does not go over of his own accord his father sends Kurbon over to fetch him.*

Today Rustam has four children whom he adores, and on whom he spends as much time and energy as he can spare from his work and his emotional preoccupations. Even though he believes his father is right and one should treat children strictly, Rustam does not believe in severe corporal punishment. He spends less time with his children than Jumbul but gives them much more attention. Jumbul prefers them to keep out of her way and leave her in peace, and her relations with them are not very warm. While Rustam plays with his children and shows them affection Jumbul swears and shouts at them.

Malik realises that his sons are unhappy but, in front of them at least, refuses to accept any blame, insisting he did the right thing. He has not forgiven Rustam for choosing his own career and professes not to see anything special in his love for Zhenia. Although Malik does not much like Jumbul himself, he insists that the only reason his son is not happy with her is that he does not treat her with the appropriate authority and strictness. Malik claims the reason he and Dilorom do well together is because he controls her with an iron hand, never allowing her out of the house except with his explicit permission and making her wait on him hand and foot. Rustam is altogether too lenient. He helps with the housework, does not expect to be waited on and, worst of all, allows Jumbul complete freedom of mobility.

Part of Rustam's frustration with his parents comes from a feeling that they have never treated him as an individual with needs of his own. Their cruel behaviour does not derive, he believes, from lack of love but from failure to see him as anything but an appendage to themselves. It would not occur to them to put themselves in his place and consider his feelings. He is loveable only as long as he enacts the persona they want and only by doing this can he meet with their approbation. When he fails in this, especially if this threatens to shame them in any way, they appear to withdraw their love.

For Rustam this would be truly unbearable. In fact, the main reason he acceded to Malik's demands to abandon Zhenia was that he could not face losing his father's affection. After all, had he single-mindedly determined to do so he probably could have married Zhenia. They could have gone to Russia, for instance, to his uncle or one of her relatives. In fact, they did discuss this but decided against it because he could not bear permanent separation from his family.

A couple of years ago Rustam joined a private firm and now earns many times more than the rest of his family, so he finds himself obliged to support not just himself, his wife and children, but also his parents and siblings. Nevertheless, Malik still considers himself the head of the family and allows Rustam no greater say in family affairs than before. He has explicitly informed both Rustam and Kurbon that they, along of course with the rest of the family, will obey their father as long as he lives.

Rustam's father takes all the advantage he can of the authority accorded him as head of the family. Thus, even after Rustam moved out of his parents' home he was unable to separate psychologically from them. Rustam and his brother are forced to enact a subordinate style of masculinity in relation to their parents, especially their father, something they find very frustrating. The experiences of these young men, like those of Hamid (Chapter 3), bear out Butler's (1993: 95) contention that gender performance often tends to be enacted under constraints.

The material complications of trying to make his own way without family support make it doubly difficult for Rustam to escape his father's control. Finding somewhere to live was very difficult in Soviet Tajikistan. At the time Rustam was trying to persuade his parents to allow him to marry Zhenia they could not have got their own flat without years on a waiting list. Thus, without the support of at least one adult relative, they would have had nowhere to live after marriage.

Shahzoda is from the township of Khojamaston. When her boyfriend's parents offered for her in marriage her parents refused. She fought bitterly with them but to no avail. When they would not change their minds Shahzoda ran off to her aunt in Dushanbe, whom she managed to persuade to take her side. This aunt organised her wedding, since Shahzoda's parents declined to have anything to do with it. Afterwards Shahzoda and her husband returned to Khojamaston. For many years she had to sneak home to visit her mother when her father was out. Eventually her father started to speak to her husband. However, it took almost ten years before he again addressed a word to Shahzoda or acknowledged her as his daughter.[1]

Shahzoda was able to get a relative on her side and so she achieved her wish, even if this seriously damaged her relationship with her father and made things difficult for many years. But this was only possible because of her aunt's support, and because Shahzoda and her husband could live with his family. For Rustam and Zhenia things were considerably more difficult, since they had no support from either family.

For Tajiks the family has always been vital for material survival. During Soviet times the difficulties young people faced in earning a decent living wage often meant that parents made significant financial contributions to their children during much of their adult lives. Since independence, however, it is no longer necessarily the older people who make the most money. In fact at times the young make considerably more, as Rustam now does, since they are better equipped to take on the more commercial type of work. But even today the webs of connectivity that are used to procure jobs and other benefits still function via the family, which makes gaining or even holding on to a job almost impossible without their support. Thus, Malik was making use of a formidable tool when he threatened to break up the family if he failed to get his own way over the question of his son's marriage. Small wonder then that Rustam could not bring himself to risk losing his family.

Malik is determined to keep his son emotionally dependent and this is even more important now he is earning so well. It is not uncommon for patriarchs in extended families to do their best to stop their financially independent sons from psychologically separating themselves, fearing that any sign of independence will mean a significant drop in their own power. In Egypt, for instance, the patriarch of a peasant family has total decision-making powers over his sons and grandsons as long as he lives. However, sons who are more educated or who have worked abroad and can now afford to build their own separate homes may win some measure of emotional independence along with their economic self-sufficiency. Nevertheless, separation is viewed negatively, and fathers make the maximum use of this so as not to lose the prestige and power of controlling their sons, along with their daughters-in-law and grand-children (Weyland 1994: 163).

In Tajikistan much the same tends to be true. However, it is striking that Malik, a Party official and self-declared atheist, sticks even more strictly to tradition at home than many religious non-Party members. Perhaps this is because his contravening of tradition in regard to religious observance makes it all the more imperative for him to be seen to be following it in other respects. As he appears healthy and is little more than 20 years older than Rustam there seems little likelihood that the latter will be given a chance to lead his own life until he is too old for it to matter.

CONTROL OVER CHILDREN

Control over children is most important of all at the crucial moment of their marriage, when a family must be able publicly to demonstrate its mastery of the correct gender behaviour. At that time there is a great deal at stake, and the family's *nomus* can take a severe blow if things go wrong. Zhenia would have affected Rustam's and his family's *nomus* very negatively. This was much more important to Rustam's parents than the fact that she and Rustam had an enormous amount in common, were friends as well as passionate lovers and thus had all the ingredients for a truly happy relationship.

Malik clearly felt that had he permitted Rustam to marry Zhenia he would have failed in his own gender performance, as this would have demonstrated his lack of control over his son. He would also have lost the chance of an appropriately behaved daughter-in-law, since as a Russian Zhenia would have been unlikely to behave submissively to him and, of course, there would have been no grandchildren. All this would have seriously affected his standing in the community. On the other hand, once Rustam was married to Jumbul and had produced children Malik had proved himself a mature and successful man and his power position was enhanced by achieving control over this new family.

Now Malik expects Rustam to develop into a proper mature adult male by following his father's example in the way he exercises control over his family. But, to his consternation, his son does nothing of the kind, and is indifferent to his wife's behaviour. Perhaps it is because he feels Rustam does not fully live up to his masculine gender performance that Malik keeps him so strongly under control even now that he is reaching maturity, since his son could still do something that might damage his family's *nomus* and make his father a laughing stock. Malik has a potential rogue male on his hands, a Russianised son who has not completely accepted Tajik gender identities and can only be kept under control through the application of strong pressures. At least it is only within the family that they know that Rustam does not try to control Jumbul, so that his lack of correct performance in that respect has been kept private.

Rustam is strict with his children but he is also really concerned with their happiness and is very worried about their mother's poor treatment of them. Both Rustam and Kurbon are markedly closer to their children than their wives are. They are not alone in this. Mothers shout and swear at their children so much in Tajikistan that many swear words almost come to sound like the words of affection that are practically never spoken. Several women told me they realised they were taking out their frustrations with other things in their lives on their children but that they simply could not control themselves, that they feel at that moment as if all their problems are their children's fault, which thus justifies their behaviour. In return children get used to being screamed at and scolded, and appear to take little notice. In such a situation parents appear to feel that the only way to get their children to obey them is to hit them.

It is also noticeable that emotional relationships between parents and children tend to be at their strongest before the children reach their teens. By the time the children are over 12 the emphasis will be on control rather than love. Thus, the small amount of affection Rustam's parents ever showed him had vanished totally by the time he was 12, never to be expressed again. When Javhar (see below) was a teenager her mother, a nurse by profession, would knock her daughter's head against the wall if she did not immediately obey her. One of the few exceptions is Jahongul's mother, Nahdiya, who almost always speaks to her children in a kind and warm manner.

The women whom I know in Sayot tend to be too busy to pay much attention to their children most of the time, except when they annoy them. Until the civil war, most rural and many urban women had so many children they had a baby at their breast for practically the entire first 15–20 years of their married lives. After the first few, as each new baby was born the previous one would be turned over to an older sibling, thereafter receiving very little care from their mother. The youngest child of all seems to remain closer to her mother than her older siblings, who once weaned will rarely be touched lovingly by their mother again.

GENDER IDEALS FOR ADOLESCENTS

As long as they exhibit proper deference to their elders and behave in a quiet, orderly and obedient manner in front of them, most parents do not seem to bother about what their young sons get up to; it is preferred that they spend most of their time outside the home so they do not get in the way. Girls, on the other hand, are kept at home most of the time, helping their mothers and learning to wait on the male members of their families. Thus both sexes absorb the message early on that males are free, females tied to the home, and no male should ever be expected to carry out even the simplest of domestic chores.

At the end of eighth grade, if not earlier, many parents, especially in rural areas, remove their daughters from school. For her marital family a *kelin* is useful to provide household labour, not financial support, which should be left to the men, so what use will education be to her? This attitude has changed a little with the economic difficulties of the late 1990s but is still generally maintained in the Khatlon villages I have worked in and even to a certain extent in Dushanbe. Moreover, daughters are big responsibilities for their parents, as they need constant watching to ensure they never disgrace the family. This is one reason they are rarely averse to marrying them off young. Although married daughters can still shame their natal families, as long as they remain with their husbands it is the business of their marital families to control them.

Marifat was born in 1950 in Dushanbe, the eldest of several siblings. Both her parents were educated and worked outside the house. Nevertheless, they were convinced that the Soviet state was a corrupting influence, from which their children needed to be protected. They did not want Marifat and her sisters to have anything to do even with other Tajik girls and were totally opposed to their meeting boys under any circumstances.

For this reason Marifat was never allowed to attend school at all. She was kept at home all the time and allowed to play only with her siblings; she had no contact with the world outside their courtyard. When she was 13 she was informed that she was to be married. She had no idea what that meant. She was given pretty clothes and a lot of people came and there were dancing and other festivities. After all this she was taken to another house and put to bed. She begged to go home with her mother but she was told she must stay behind.

After her mother left she fell asleep. Later on in the night she woke up feeling a pain. She saw the young man she had been introduced to that day at the festivities lying in bed with her. Her ezor and his were pulled down and his penis was touching her. It was wet. She had seen her brothers' penises and knew they were for peeing, so she just assumed this man had been too lazy to go to the toilet and she scolded him for it. She did not know he was her husband, or indeed what a husband was. In the following days she hated it when her husband kept forcing sex on her but there was nothing she could do about it. He was 20 and much stronger than she was. Marifat was very unhappy living there with this man and his parents, and kept running home to her own parents, only to be scolded and sent back.

Somehow or other the KGB found out that she had been married under age and started to follow her parents and her husband's. This continued until she had her first child at the age of 14 years and 6 months, after which they were left alone. The KGB never tried to take her away from her husband. However, they succeeded in frightening her parents so much that they allowed her younger sister to attend school and did not marry her off until she was 18. Now in her mid-40s Marifat is a small, sad-looking woman, who does not feel she has ever completely recovered from the harm done by her premature marriage.

Marifat's story was doubtless not uncommon in earlier times, although I have not heard of any other such extreme case occurring at so late a date. I cannot help wondering why Marifat's parents clung to such a very strict and rigid, almost pre-revolutionary concept of what their daughter's gender performance should be, especially in view of the fact that both of them had been educated and were working in the Soviet system, and that it was already the 1960s when Marifat's marriage took place. Marifat also could not explain why her parents had been so much more reactionary than most other people's, especially considering they had been living in the capital. Neither she nor her neighbours could think of another family at that time where a daughter had been treated anything like so strictly.

CHOICE OF *KELIN*

In Tajikistan, by far the most important life decision for anyone is the choice of marriage partner. But this decision is rarely taken with the welfare of the couple themselves in mind. It is the young man's family who feel their needs to be paramount here. A *kelin* will spend her life with her marital family and thus affect all family members, so her selection is considered far too important to leave to an immature young man.

Jahongul's sister, Tahmina, was married at age 17 in 1993, when the civil war was at its height and rape an everyday occurrence; her widowed mother, Nahdiya, had decided it was better to marry her rather than risk anything happening to her. Tahmina was totally set against marriage. All she wanted to do was to go to university.

Nahdiya had contracted a debt with a man from Hissor and in exchange had promised her daughter would marry whichever young relative he chose, only stipulating that the young couple live in Dushanbe and Tahmina be permitted to study. The man chose his nephew, Rashid, and informed Nahdiya that the young man's parents had agreed to her conditions. At that point Nahdiya accepted the arrangement. Only after she had done so did she inform a horrified Tahmina, who did not know what to say. No matter how much she hated the idea she could not bring herself explicitly to refuse her mother or even to protest directly. 'We Tajiks have to obey our parents', she told me.

Tahmina was so depressed at being forced to marry that she was indifferent to the person she would be living with, possibly for the rest of her life, and refused an offer to meet him before the wedding. She just said, 'Whatever will be, will be and there is nothing meaningful I can do to influence my fate.'

After they were married Rashid's parents broke both their promises. Tahmina was forced to abandon all idea of studying and after a few months in Dushanbe ended up living with her in-laws in their village. She was extremely unhappy. It did not take long for Nahdiya to realise she had made a mistake but there was little she could do about it, for all she spent many a sleepless night lying awake worrying about her daughter's misery.

Tahmina wanted to leave her husband but was too afraid of the ensuing gossip – she thought she might thereafter be labelled as bad. She also thought she would never get another husband afterwards, or at least that he would most likely be worse than her present one. So she decided it was probably better to endure.

However, after the birth of her first child Tahmina decided that she had better start thinking about taking charge of her own life. Her health had seriously suffered from her pregnancy and her husband was not earning anything. When she became pregnant again she had an abortion and at the same time got herself fitted with an IUD. She categorically refused to consider having another child until Rashid proved himself more responsible and started to support his family.

Although she was never able to become a full-time student, in 1998 Tahmina started an external degree course at the University of Dushanbe. This is an independent study course, with only a couple of months of classes a year. She knows that this will be her only opportunity for an education and tries to do as well as she can, although it is hard to study in her parents-in-law's house and she has little access to books.

Meanwhile, after six years of marriage Tahmina has more or less come to terms with it and no longer considers divorce. She sees that other women have an even harder time than she does and that it makes sense to try to make the best of what she has.

Although Tahmina has neither father nor grandfather to boss the family, and on the surface her relationship with her mother appears relaxed, she still finds it impossible to speak out openly in opposition to her, even though she knows that Nahdiya really loves her daughters and very much wants them to be happy. Nevertheless, Nahdiya continues to hold the position that it is *her* responsibility to arrange her children's future and attributes the problems with Tahmina's marriage to the impossibility of finding decent young men in Tajikistan today, rather than to her actions in forcing Tahmina into the situation.

In the marital relation the formal power is on the side of husbands and their families, who can thus bend the situation to their advantage. As happened in Tahmina's case they often make promises to the families of future *kelins* which they break after the wedding when it is too late to back out. There are no written marriage contracts in Tajikistan and people can only hold others to their promises if they are in a position of power. Nahdiya is in a particularly weak position, as she is poor and has no mature man to support her. Moreover, she is far less educated than Tahmina's mother-in-law, which makes it even harder for her to confront her.

MARRIAGE FOR LOVE

When Javhar was in her last year at the Pedagogical Institute her mother decided it was time to think about getting her married. The first candidate she considered was the son of one of her brothers, whose family was both impoverished and sickly. Several of them had tuberculosis. Javhar was appalled at the idea of marrying into such a family. They had learned in their health classes at the Institute that tuberculosis was very dangerous and highly contagious and she had no intention of putting herself or her future children at risk from this. She was shocked that this did not seem to bother her mother, a nurse by profession. It took a hard fight but finally Javhar was able to convince her mother she would never accept her cousin.

Before anyone else had a chance to offer for her Javhar informed her parents that they would be receiving an offer from a fellow student. He was from a different mahalla, *which upset them and put them very much against the match. However, Javhar stood firm. She insisted he was the only man she would ever agree to marry and that if they forbade this she would not marry at all.*

Eventually she got her own way. Her parents, however, made absolutely certain that this insurrection would not be repeated by her sister, whom they forced into marriage with a man of their own choice.

Ten years later Javhar lives reasonably well with her husband, while her sister is married to an alcoholic, who not only does not support his family financially but also beats his wife almost daily. Her mother refuses to acknowledge that Javhar made a better choice for herself than her parents did for her sister. Instead of being thankful that at least one of her sons-in-law treats his wife decently, she continues to be upset by the match and says she will not be able to sleep peacefully in her grave because her daughter turned down her brother's son and instead married for love. Since the civil war, her dislike of her daughter's having married someone from another region has grown still stronger, because there is now a great deal more prejudice against 'intermarriage'.

In 1943, when Karomat was 17, the government started sending unmarried girls in their late teens to the war front as nurses. She decided that, as the eldest child and with her father already at the front, she couldn't possibly leave her mother and siblings. They held a family council and it was agreed she should get married to avoid being called up.

Karomat had a friend, Khudoydod, who had been kept out of the army by a minor health problem, and who had been quietly courting her for several years. Karomat and her mother discussed the situation and decided the best thing to do was for the young people to marry. On his return after the war her father was cross at the fact that his daughter had been married without his permission and said he would never have allowed her to choose her own husband had he been at home.

As an old woman Karomat told me she thought now that the only good way to marry is the 'clean Muslim way' – letting one's parents decide. It is best to marry without love because this will come with propinquity and children. It is not necessary for it to be there in the beginning. She said she would have preferred her parents to choose her husband for her. Then she would have been happy. I queried this and said that surely she had been happy most of her married life. She had married a man she had really loved and who had loved her, even if later on she had problems and ended up childless and divorced (Chapters 5 and 6) but she did not agree.

Looking back in old age Karomat sees her parents as the most important people in her life perhaps because she spent most of her life with them. She would doubtless have felt different had she had her own children and grandchildren. Moreover, Karomat said she believed she could have been just as happy with another man as with Khudoydod when she thought of him as connected to her bad luck in becoming a childless divorcee and speculated on the fact that her fate might perhaps have been more positive with someone else. However, reminiscing about her marriage usually appeared to make her feel happy. I wonder if, in fact, at age 17 she would as easily have accepted her father's decision to find her another husband as she later thought.

Javhar and Karomat both managed to take major decisions for themselves that influenced the course of their lives. Javhar used the strength and knowledge gained from her time living away from home as a student to insist on making her own choices. As the eldest child during World War II, Karomat was expected to take her father's place in helping her mother with decision-making, and this allowed her to have input into decisions concerning her own future, something that would never have occurred normally.

CRITERIA FOR CHOICE

How much parents in Tajikistan insist on making their children's choice of spouse themselves and how much leeway they are willing to allow their children will depend partly on the individual family, but even more on parents' perceptions of their own needs. A parent, especially a father, who considers either his own gender identity and/or his power base to be at risk, may feel it vital to compel his children to knuckle under to him and to be seen to be doing so, as did Malik.

No doubt it is the importance in patrilocal societies of finding a *kelin* to suit the family's needs that is responsible for the tradition that the boy's family should be the one to take the first step in arranging a marriage. It is also likely that the reason the main mover in any marriage tends to be the mother of the groom is because it is she who has the chance to meet young women and decide on their suitability, something that is very difficult for her husband to do (Tett 1995: 106). Even more important, it is she who will have most contact with the *kelin* after marriage, especially when the young couple will live with her.

The women in Sayot who participated in discussions on the subject of choice of *kelin* said they had all chosen their sons' wives. Generally speaking they seemed to have been motivated in their choice by practical considerations. These are especially important to rural women, whose *kelins* will be vital for carrying out chores both in the house and on the land, so they need willing girls capable of good hard work. Most of these families expect their sons, and thus their *kelins*, to live with them all their lives, which makes the choice doubly important to the family. All this most likely accounts for the fact that so few rural parents, at least in Khatlon, permit their children any say at all in the choice of their spouse. There are far more important considerations at stake than the personal relationship between the young couple. The welfare of the entire family will ultimately depend on its *kelins*.

In the village Tett studied, on the other hand, love marriages were common and young people very interested in the idea of romantic love. Moreover, the threat of *ayb* notwithstanding, many girls were allowed to study in Dushanbe (Tett 1995: 102–8). Clearly this village did not constrain its girls in the same way as the very religious villages in which the health project has worked in Khatlon, where girls have hardly ever been permitted to study outside the immediate neighbourhood and parents insist on choosing their children's spouses.

In Sayot women expect their daughters-in-law not only to be good hard workers but also to obey them unquestioningly, so as to avoid power struggles within the family.[2] Another important reason the Sayot women gave for taking a *kelin* was to supply their sons with a controlled outlet for their sexuality, but this still does not mean a woman will choose her *kelin* with her son's personal preferences in mind. In fact, they do not want him to be too well suited.

As the literal meaning of the word implies, a *kelin* (incomer) is someone grafted on to the family from outside, who can be removed quite easily without disturbing the essential structure. A man only has one father and mother but a wife can easily be replaced (see Patel 1994: 7). Therefore, unless they fall deeply in love, men will not put their wives before their parents. Women in particular want to come first with their sons, as their position in life will depend on them.[3] They believe family stability would be endangered if their sons fall in love. They are thus unlikely to welcome signs of this. Indeed, it is not unknown for mothers to try to force their sons to divorce if they think they are beginning to care too much for their wives.

The preference in many Tajik families has long been to marry off their children to their cousins (Kislyakov and Pisarchik 1970: 27; Shishov 1904: 360). A study carried out among pregnant women in Dushanbe at the beginning of the 1980s showed that 33 per cent of the women studied were in cousin marriages (Ergina and Rustamova 1983: 36). In many families, as in Javhar's, brothers and sisters put pressure on one another to marry their children to each other and insist they will be extremely offended if they do not do so. Very often parents agree to such marriages largely to avoid arousing a sibling's hostility and so causing rifts within the family.

In Tajikistan cousin marriages are not necessarily with agnates. Marriage in the maternal line is every bit as common, perhaps because marriage arrangements are often initiated by women. A number of women in cousin marriages complained to me bitterly about the frequency of birth defects in their children, which they attributed to generations of inbreeding. Nevertheless, in general Tajiks appear unaware of the dangers of this, as we found out when we brought up the subject with health project participants. Moreover, cousin marriages are no guarantee of good treatment on the part either of a husband or of his parents. If a woman in such a marriage is badly treated it may be harder rather than easier for her to have recourse to her parents' protection since family interests may intervene.

If there is no suitable cousin available or if the family prefers not to marry their son to a relative and does not immediately have another bride in mind for him, a potential candidate will be sought among their friends and acquaintances. The husband-to-be is not only unlikely to be consulted, he very probably will not even be taken into account. What his mother will consider is first how this girl would suit her and the family, and, second, how the two families would be likely to deal together, not the future relationship between the spouses. The girl's family will most probably focus on the material circumstances of the family and the ability of their daughter's future parents-in-law to provide a suitable amount of *kalym*. Although bride price is by no means universal in Tajikistan, those families that demand it often have very high expectations and even something as apparently trivial as offering poor quality dress material may be sufficient to put an end to wedding arrangements. It is noteworthy that insufficient *kalym* is an acceptable excuse for breaking off a match whereas a young person's dislike of a future spouse is not. However, most likely problems with *kalym* could be used as a face-saving excuse to allow families to withdraw from marriage arrangements.

Some urban families, and even a very few rural families, may allow a son to suggest his own candidate and, if she is found suitable, will make an offer for her. Daughters cannot have more than the right of refusal, since the girl's family plays a passive role here. However, in those rare cases that a girl has a boyfriend who wishes to marry her and who is able to persuade his parents to offer for her, she will try to see to it that this offer gets precedence, as Javhar did, although, like Shahzoda's, not all parents will necessarily agree.

When marrying a daughter parents are caught in the bind of the very narrow window of opportunity in looking for a marriage partner. They cannot simply go in search of a boy they like. They must wait for suitors to come to them. It is only in the case of cousin marriages that they can arrange things themselves. Moreover, there are only a couple of years between a girl's finishing high school and her arriving at an age where she will be considered on the shelf so they often grasp at the first opportunity that presents itself, irrespective of the young man's worth. Since parents consider the personal qualities of their son-in-law relatively unimportant this is an understandable position, especially as it would be a disaster if no other prospect for their daughter's hand turned up later.

RELATIONS WITH *KELINS*

Like Jumbul most *kelins* spend at least a few years living with their in-laws. Even where they have a separate home, custom demands that the young couple spend the first 40 days after their wedding with the groom's parents. In this way the mother-in-law gets to break in her new *kelin*, see what she is really like and mould her to her requirements.

At the same time the *kelin* finds herself in a new environment where she has no real ties. Isolated in her marital family, many a young woman feels bitter when her husband shows less strong feelings for her than for his own family and refuses to take her side. As well as endeavouring to keep this marriage bond weak, parents will have done their best to ensure their sons understand that it is to their own benefit to side with their parents. Thus, the life of a new *kelin* can be very hard:

Tahmina felt she was particularly badly treated by her in-laws. They made no pretence of feeling affection towards her. Tahmina could not understand how Rashid's family could treat her so, when she and her family were exactly the opposite with their own kelin. She loved her eldest brother Farhod's wife and the two had become close friends. Nahdiya also gets along well with her daughter-in-law.

Rashid's mother is quite different. She orders Tahmina around all the time. Except for the grandmother everyone else in the family goes out to work, including her mother-in-law, who works as chief bookkeeper to the kolkhoz, *so all the housework devolves on Tahmina.*

Tahmina is an excellent housewife. She had always kept her mother's home spotless. However, it is much more difficult to do this in a village. Just living there is rough after the central heating and indoor plumbing of their Dushanbe apartment. It is very hard work building wood fires, fetching water, washing clothes outside in cold water, milking the cow and cleaning the yard, especially in winter.

Tahmina has to get up early in the morning and start the fire going before the rest of the family gets out of bed. She is given a minimum of food, and scolded if she asks for more. If she wants to watch television or listen to music in the evenings she is told there is work to do and she is not there to sit around idle. She finds being treated like an unpaid servant almost intolerable. Village life is especially hard in cold weather and in the first few years adversely affected her delicate health. She was constantly in pain from her back, lost a great deal of weight and generally felt terrible.

Rashid was a student and earning only sporadically. Whenever he had money his sisters would inveigle it out of him. They would complain and give him a hard time if he gave any to Tahmina. Her sisters-in-law got presents from their parents as well as their brother but Tahmina got little from her husband and nothing from anyone else in the family. If she needed anything for herself it was usually her own mother who paid, despite her lack of resources.

When Tahmina finally became pregnant she was already quite anaemic and this worsened until she felt dizzy much of the time. However, her mother-in-law showed her no mercy and insisted on her doing the same amount of hard labour as before.

Tahmina felt so ill she went to town to consult her doctor. When the latter heard what Tahmina was made to do every day at home she insisted on hospitalising her in order to ensure she got some rest. Her in-laws were furious. They came to Dushanbe and tried to get her out of the hospital to go home with them.

For once Rashid stood up for his wife. He realised that if she did not rest the likelihood was that she would miscarry. They had spent a great deal of time, energy and money on getting her gynaecological problems treated so she could bear his children, and now his parents found it more important that she should do housework than that their son should have a healthy child. Rashid managed to persuade them to leave Tahmina alone for the time being. And they did so. Completely. While Nahdiya and Jahongul went every day to the hospital, taking Tahmina her meals and generally looking after her, none of her marital family other than her husband came to see her at all, not even her brothers-in-law, who lived five minutes away.

When Tahmina returned to the village her mother- and even her grandmother-in-law tried to make her carry heavy buckets of water, which her doctor had expressly forbidden her to do during her pregnancy. When she told them this they mocked her, saying they had both always worked up to the day they had given birth and started again immediately afterwards. They did not understand how this young girl could be so sickly. What was the point of having a kelin if they had to do the work themselves? Luckily, despite this treatment, Tahmina was able to carry her child to term and gave birth to a healthy daughter.

Young *kelins* are all too often harshly treated like Tahmina and few seem to be happy with their position in their parents-in-law's home. The attitude of Tahmina's sisters-in-law in treating their *kelin* almost like an enemy is very typical. It is as if they see their brother's wife as a rival for his affections. Young women have frequently told me they are treated like intruders in the family. Like Tahmina, an often-repeated complaint is that they are given less to eat than everyone else, even when they are pregnant and it should be in the family's own interest to see they bore healthy children.[4]

Once their sons are married women expect to do very little housework. They feel they deserve an easier time and prefer to sleep, or chat with friends or relatives, just keeping an eye out to check their daughters-in-law are carrying out their allotted tasks correctly. If a *kelin* fails to live up to her mother-in-law's requirements she is likely to find herself divorced and sent back to her natal family, so she is under a great deal of pressure, especially at first, to show herself obedient and hardworking in order to prove herself worthy.

Javhar might have married for love, she might be educated and have a job, but none of these absolved her from living with her in-laws or from fulfilling her domestic obligations. By the time of her marriage she already had a teaching job in a village near her husband's hometown. To get there by public transport was possible, but very time-consuming. Javhar insisted on keeping her job. Her parents-in-law insisted on her taking on a large share of the housework. This was especially important because her husband was the oldest of a family of boys so there was no other female to help her mother-in-law. Javhar's father-in-law was a high-level bureaucrat, entitled to a government car, which he made use of to have Javhar driven to school and back every day. In this way he was able to organise her life so that she had the maximum amount of time for domestic labour. This also enabled him to control her movements and ensure she never went anywhere without his permission.

Javhar felt totally trapped. She did not have one moment of freedom to do anything or go anywhere she wanted. She could not exploit her job or the necessity of travelling to and from it to make a window even to visit her parents, who lived a few minutes from her school, in the opposite direction from the town. The only way she was able to escape was to apply for a job near home. Her new post was in easy walking distance, which at least gave her the opportunity for a little bit of freedom, the car now being redundant. After a few years her eldest brother-in-law married, allowing Javhar and her husband to get a place of their own. Now she is her own boss Javhar is much happier.

It gives some indication of the relative equality women have with their husbands that it is not uncommon to hear them say with Javhar that once they left their in-laws' house and set up in their own place, they felt they were their own boss. This may not give them full autonomy but for most women it is a tremendous improvement since husbands are usually less difficult to handle and rarely interfere in the running of the home, even if they insist on compliance in other matters.

Lack of submission on the part of a *kelin* is often linked in the minds of their mothers-in-law with higher education, which is why a daughter with tertiary education commands considerably less *kalym* than one who left school after eighth grade or earlier. However, interestingly enough, it is Tahmina, who merely aspires to higher education, who stands up to her mother-in-law while Javhar, a graduate, shows herself more compliant. Perhaps, having forced her parents to accept her choice of spouse, she felt she had to get on with her in-laws whatever the cost.

Things get more complicated in families where two generations of mothers-in-law have to coexist. In this case the older woman may insist on choosing her grandsons' wives and in being the boss of her *kelin* as well as of her *kelin*'s *kelins*, effectively cutting the younger woman out of the power equation. The latter may well feel particularly badly done by, since part of the 'patriarchal bargain'[5] is that women eventually attain a position of power and that this should happen at the time they marry off their sons.

GRANDCHILDREN

Whatever women may state about their reasons for taking a daughter-in-law, a *kelin*'s most important function is, of course, to provide descendants for her husband's family. Therefore, she must prove her reproductive capacities by becoming pregnant as soon as possible after marriage. Failure to do so within the first year or so will give her husband and in-laws a good excuse to get rid of her. Many a young woman has been returned to her parents for this reason. Tahmina was very nervous that this might happen to her and for this reason happy to become pregnant.

However, her story also points up a strange dichotomy in Tajik life. Although the desire for children is very strong and a *kelin* must prove her fertility as soon as possible, parents-in-law and even husbands often do not seem very interested in the outcome of the pregnancy. Moreover, if a marital family decides to get rid of their *kelin* they do not seem to have any compunction about getting rid of the children also. It is rare to hear of a family whose father claimed custody of the children on divorce. In fact, I have not come across a divorce in those families where the man really cares for his children. Despite their dislike of their wives neither Rustam nor Kurbon wanted to risk losing their children through divorce. On the other hand I have come across only too many families who had abandoned their *kelins* together with their children with apparent ease.

When we discussed this with the women of Sayot, they all maintained that whoever else might behave so despicably they would not. They may have been reacting to the way we introduced the subject or they may, of course, have been genuinely against the practice but it seems to be increasingly frequent as life becomes more unstable and difficult. However, Tillo is testimony to the fact that disregard for grandchildren long predates the civil war. Her first marriage broke up in the early 1980s but her parents-in-law have never once bothered to have any contact with their grandchildren, nor does her second husband bother with the children he insisted Tillo have for him.

This attitude may owe something to the earlier high rates of infant and child mortality, which are likely to have meant that parents came to value the individual child less strongly. Such an attitude at least was expressed by Zora's mother, who herself had had nine children, when she felt that her daughter was expending an inordinate amount of time and energy caring for her sickly young son. 'Just let him die. You can easily have another who might be stronger', was her advice. Zora was shocked by this. She loved her son and did not feel he was so easily replaceable; besides she did not want to undergo another pregnancy.

However, the relatively easy abandonment of children upon divorce may be the result of the Soviet legal system. Although before the revolution it had been normal for men to keep their older children on divorce, as is the practice in other Muslim societies, Soviet divorce courts almost always awarded children to mothers (Pal'vanova 1982: 7). It would be interesting to study what this meant to families in early Soviet times. It is entirely likely that the strong reaction against women demanding divorce at that time was due as much to the fact that the family would lose their children/grandchildren along with their *kelin* as to the material high cost of divorce (Keller 2001: 75).

It could well be that the reason that fathers and paternal grandparents do not bother to stay in contact with their children by divorced wives is because once the children leave they have essentially abandoned the patrilineage. By definition, a patriarch is a man who controls the younger family members. Therefore, when their mother removes them from the control of their father's family, in essence they cease to be members of it, so that this family no longer feels any obligation towards them. The point of the insistence in most Muslim countries on children of divorced parents returning to their father's family before the onset of puberty may be largely to prevent such a situation arising.

RUSSIAN WIVES

Family relationships have become even more complicated in recent years since the economic situation worsened in Tajikistan, resulting in increasing labour migration to Russia, where the majority of male migrants form relationships with local women. Rustam is no longer in such a minority. Today there are thousands of Tajik men who have fallen in love with Russian-speaking women, with whom they have developed much more intimate relationships than those they have with their Tajik wives at home, to whom they were married by their parents but with whom they may have little emotional contact.

When they return for a visit, those who do not already have a wife are rarely able to escape their parents' insistence on marrying them to a Tajik woman, so as to provide a *kelin* for the family. In most cases young men will find it expedient to accede to these demands. One of the health-project staff said the wife of one of her relatives, who lives with them in the village, now has seven children, although during their eight years of marriage she has seen her husband only for a few months in total. He has several more children by his Russian wife, with whom he spends most of the year.

Young men who attend the health project's discussion groups occasionally ask for advice on successfully resisting parental imposition of a wife. Once, when this subject came up in Sayot, Mahmud, at 28 the oldest man present, related how he had managed to get his own way and still keep on good terms with his parents.

When I first went to work in Russia I got to know Olga and we fell in love. We got married and now have two children. A few years ago when I came back to Tajikistan for a visit I found that my parents had started to look for a wife for me here but I decided I did not want this. As far as I was concerned Olga was my wife and that was that. So I told my parents I would on no account allow them to find me a wife. When they asked why, I said I already had one in Russia whom I loved very much and that I was not going to take another. When they insisted I told them that unless they agreed to stop pressuring me I would return to Russia and neither visit them, nor support them financially any more. They have never again raised the subject.

Mahmud added that he did not intend to deprive his parents permanently of a chance to be with their grandchildren nor did he wish to spend the rest of his life in Russia. As soon as economic circumstances permit he will bring his family to Tajikistan and raise his children according to local traditions.[6]

What gave Mahmud the power to force his parents to accept his terms while Rustam was unable to do this? In the first place this is very probably because there does not appear to be any very great stigma attached to a

Tajik man's marrying a Russian woman in Russia. Rustam, on the other hand, wanted to marry a divorced, infertile, older Russian woman in Tajikistan itself – thus in full view of the community – something so outrageous in Tajik terms that it would inevitably have diminished his family's standing in the community. In view of Malik's high position in the Party, this would have been especially demeaning. In the second place, Mahmud lives in Russia and supports his parents financially. Rustam was still living with his parents at the time and had only a small income. Moreover, Mahmud does not seem to have greatly feared his parents' rejection but even now, when Rustam is in a much more favourable economic situation, he is unable to separate himself psychologically from his father, who still appears to believe he acted for the best and that his son's unhappiness is his own fault and has nothing directly to do with his parents' choice of wife.

CONCLUSION

The family relationships described here are not nearly as straightforward and clear-cut as one might assume from listening to Tajik discourse. The margin for variation of the norms is fairly small and very much dependent on a family's social position and the psychological strength of its members, particularly of the head of family. Although it may seem extraordinary that some families fear the slightest deviation while others seem to deviate unhesitatingly, closer examination usually reveals good reasons for this, just as with Mahmud and Rustam. In fact, the wearing of masks is often necessary to give the appearance of uniform compliance with the norms.

The stories narrated here have shown that it is possible for determined young people in some circumstances to find a way of making their own choices without alienating themselves from their families. They reveal that it is very often not those who choose conformity who are rewarded: those who, like Javhar and Karomat, made their own choices in life have also been the happiest, while many of the most unhappy – such as Jahongul, Tahmina, Javhar's sister and Rustam – are precisely those who have conformed.

I find it interesting how often young women, despite the constraints of their upbringing and the restrictive gender performances they are forced into, tend to be more decisive than their husbands, particularly after the birth of their first child. It is also notable that while young people are submissive to their own parents the level of submission of daughters-in-law to their mothers-in-law may be much less, despite the insecurity of living in a situation where they have little control and may be divorced at the whim of either mother-in-law or husband. This last is on the whole a new phenomenon, since, in addition to the general instability, the post-war situation, together with economic migration, has produced a huge dearth of young men, which allows families easily to replace an unsatisfactory *kelin*.

At the same time boys are every bit as strongly subjugated by their parents as girls in the matter of the one thing that *all* parents insist on from their offspring – obedience. The repetitive inculcation of this in children of both sexes results in submissive sons as well as daughters, as Rustam's story shows. As Jahongul claims (Chapter 5), young men frequently use the excuse of parental refusal to get out of marrying their girlfriends. This may be a ploy to get rid of them but mothers frequently do bring very strong pressures to bear on their sons and harass them with great determination if they go against their wishes. Few young men possess the degree of determination required to stand up against this day after day.

In the Tajik project of maintaining their own cultural identity, controlling sons is almost as important as controlling daughters. In many ways Rustam had accepted Russian cultural ideals, almost abandoning the most vital Tajik masculine gender norms, including control over women. If large numbers of young men were to behave as he does it would be virtually impossible to maintain their cultural separation. In essence what Malik was doing was preventing his son from opting out of Tajik culture. In fact, in one way this story could be read as a classic case of how the Tajiks have been able to preserve their traditions in the face of Soviet pressures to modernise.

Nevertheless, despite the harsh treatment that considerations of *nomus* and *ayb* cause parents to impose, most Tajik parents I met are loved by, and also claim to love, their children, even if the spiteful way parents often behave towards those children who manage to escape their control would suggest that on the parental side love is not always as strong as pride.

The stories in this chapter show just how important generational placing is to gender identity, as the way young men are made to submit, while older women find themselves in positions of dominance reverses the usual direction of gendered power relations.

These stories also reveal some of the main trends of the post-Soviet period, most especially frequent divorces, smaller family size and long-term migration, all of which will no doubt eventually result in fundamental changes in family structures and relationships.

5   THE INDIVIDUAL UNMASKED

One day I accompanied Jahongul to the office of an important personage in Dushanbe. The change that came over her in the presence of this woman was startling. The lively, chatty teenager, cheerfully giving me her opinions on everyone we passed in the street, turned into a bashful and timid young woman. Head hung, eyes fixed on the floor, hardly able to open her mouth, Jahongul almost whispered her answers. 'Look up, girl, and speak to me directly', she was told, but the more she was ordered to do this, the more intimidated she became. Afterwards, she was still constrained. I asked her what had come over her, why she had been so different. Jahongul replied that this was how a girl was supposed to behave in front of important people, even schoolteachers. In front of her mother too, Jahongul was different from the way she was with me, less free and much quieter.

Rustam too almost transforms himself in front of different people. Even his face changes, to the point where it is hard to recognise him as the same person. With his colleagues at work, with his parents, alone with me, Rustam presents extraordinarily different personas.

Of course, to a certain extent everyone makes these types of changes. However, in Tajikistan they assume a ritual quality, which I am convinced is linked to the spectrum of gender performances, accompanied as they are by specific physical attributes. The downcast eyes and hung head seem to be something that all girls have absorbed by the end of puberty. Boys do this much less. However, Rustam notably finds it difficult not to assume this stance when in the presence of anyone in authority. As I noted in my diary on the occasion of our first meeting, 'This young man seems pleasant but very shy. He was unable even once to lift his eyes to mine.'

To phrase it differently, the expressions accompanying the variant gender performances almost seem to reproduce in visible form the concept of the masks I introduced in Chapter 1. As I said there the masks serve to display stock characters, to make it easier for an audience to grasp what they are seeing. Jahongul comes on stage and there she is –

a submissive and obedient girl. Rustam does likewise. Such masks are useful to the actors because they stop people looking more closely at them and thus perhaps observing the irregularities and imperfections they are trying to conceal.

Although both Jahongul and Rustam (when he got to know me better) were able to chat in my presence with a freedom that I did not see them exhibit elsewhere, this does not, of course, mean that what I was seeing was not just another mask. However, with me there was no pre-set model. No-one had taught them how one behaved in front of a foreign researcher who clearly did not follow the same conventions they lived by, whose own gender performance was quite different from those they were accustomed to, who did not scold them, no matter what, and who seemed to be interested in listening to everything they had to say. It seemed to me that in fact they were relieved not to have to put on the same display as with other people and that they truly did let down their guard with me to a considerable extent, as the stories in this book demonstrate.

THE DREAMS OF YOUTH

Jahongul and her elder sister Tahmina were introduced in previous chapters. They are the elder daughters of a family of three girls and two boys living in the centre of Dushanbe. Their father was a factory inspector, murdered when they were very young, just as he was about to blow the whistle on fraud, leaving their mother, Nahdiya, to raise the children on her own. Nahdiya's own father had been killed when she was a child and her mother had few resources, so that the family is extremely poverty-stricken.

Before the civil war Nahdiya worked in a factory. She is only barely functionally literate. Despite years of living in Dushanbe and of inter-actions with her mostly Russian neighbours her knowledge of this language remains poor, but even her Tajik is highly ungrammatical. Nahdiya's husband, however, was educated and had wanted all his children to follow in his footsteps. She would very much like to be able to fulfil his wish, especially as she believes that only education will give her children a chance to raise their standards of living.

When I first met them in early 1995 the eldest brother, Farhod had been married for several years and was living near his wife's family. As was recounted in Chapter 4, Tahmina was living unhappily in her husband's village. The younger three children were still at home.

Sixteen-year-old Jahongul is in her last year at high school. She has many thoughts about life, thoughts that she cannot share with her family. She frequently comes over to see me and tells me at length about her wishes and dreams. She is so happy to have someone who listens to her that she pours out her words almost like a stream of consciousness. Often what she says on one occasion contradicts her previous statements but she does not seem to remember what she has said before, and just rattles on wherever her mind takes her at that moment. In the following passage I have put together extracts from conversations that took place over a period of several months in the first half of 1995:

Jahongul feels very sad for her sister. But she has taken what happened to her to heart and this has made her consider how her own life might turn out. Like Tahmina, Jahongul also wants to study but realises that very likely this will depend on her future husband and his family. Her sister's experience with marriage has not been good and Jahongul dreads things turning out equally badly for herself. In Tajikistan women have to do what their husbands tell them. If they insist on their staying home and not studying or working there is nothing women can do about it. Jahongul does not think this is fair but this is just how it is.

Like Tahmina before her, Jahongul will have nothing to do with boys. The last thing she wants, in fact, is to marry for love. She says she does not trust any man. She has seen enough to know how badly most men treat their wives, whether or not they have married for love. 'If I choose my own husband', she says, 'then he will be my responsibility. If he treats me badly I will have nowhere to turn. My family will say, "You chose him, you have to put up with him." But if my mother chooses him and something goes wrong I will say to her, "He is your son-in-law, you chose him, do something, protect me."'

Jahongul says that if a boy says he loves her she doesn't want to see him again. She thinks most boys are fools and doesn't want to have anything to do with them. Maybe someday she'll fall in love and then it will be okay. On the whole she wants a man to fall harder for her than she for him, so that she has power over him.

Jahongul says, 'We Tajik women are brought up to allow men to order us about; that is our tradition. There is nothing one can do to change tradition.' 'Why not?' I ask. Jahongul replies, 'How would it be possible?' 'Perhaps not for everyone but what about for you personally? Do you think you could change for yourself those customs you don't find good?' Jahongul didn't know, but she did think that the best marriage would be one where both parties had equal weight.

On another occasion Jahongul said she wished she'd been born into a Russian family so that she could go around with boys like Russians do, without incurring the sort of problems that Tajik girls have. However, she says one disadvantage for Russians is that they have to find their own marriage partners and sometimes a girl can date a boy for ages and he will never marry her.

Jahongul thinks that nowadays a husband is pointless, as few men can earn enough money to be worthwhile. Maybe it would be best not to marry at all. The most important thing in life is happiness and this comes from having everything. That is, one's own home, and a husband and children, and a job at which one doesn't have to work more than two hours a day. But it is important to find the right husband. Jahongul will have a competition. First she will study for four years and only after this start looking round to meet someone. Then she will spend a year observing him closely. If she doesn't find anyone she likes then she will live without a husband. I ask her whether it would really be possible to do this. She says it would. She could work and buy herself a flat near her mother's place and live there alone. She and her girlfriends would all meet once a week and she would have a good life. Of course, she would not be able to have children without a husband but that would not matter. If necessary she could adopt a child from an orphanage because after all it would not be much fun living entirely by herself. The best would be to live with a girlfriend who also didn't want to get married but she knows that, whatever they may say now, all her girlfriends will accept immediately someone asks for their hand and that will be that.

Jahongul says she will not be like that. She sees absolutely no reason whatever to marry. However, she knows she must. If only she could find a non-aggressive man, reasonably handsome, with a good income and a university degree, a good person, not the sort to shout at his wife, someone who would respect her. But such young men don't exist in Dushanbe today. On the contrary, they have all learned how to behave with women from watching foreign films and they call out to girls in the street and make it horrible to go out unaccompanied, and in general she thinks the best thing would be to shoot them all. In fact, Jahongul says she would like the war to start up again just so every young man in Tajikistan could be shot, so she wouldn't have to put up with all the stupid fools around the place.

Jahongul's idea of a good husband: first, he would be taller than she is. Second, he would be independent of his parents, earn a good living and have a flat of his own. A car would be nice too, but that could come later. He should be able to provide for her properly, although she doesn't want a rich man because then he would perhaps want more than one wife.[1]

Jahongul hopes her husband will have the guts to stick up for what he wants and not allow his parents to boss him around. She despises men who are too spineless to stick up for themselves. She thinks it is about time young people made their own decisions about how to live their lives and parents didn't interfere.

However, she fears her fate will be the same as Tahmina's, and she will end up living in a village and wearing a big headscarf.[2] She does not think Tahmina's husband is so very unsatisfactory because he does not treat her too badly; at least he doesn't beat her.

Jahongul wants everything – that is she wants to have money and for there to be goods in the shops and for her mother not to have to go to trade in the market at the weekend, and to have her own house and a car. She wants there to be proper lessons at school every day, to get into college and to be a student. She wants to be the best student in her class so that everyone will look at her and envy her. She doesn't know what might be the best career for a woman – journalism, business or something else. On the other hand she would quite like to be a secretary; she already has her typing diploma.[3] She might like to go to technical college to study to be a hairdresser, seamstress or book-keeper. She doesn't really know – just as long as she does something and doesn't just leave school at 17.

What she really wants is to be a lawyer and defend people, or perhaps to be a famous couturier and have everyone wear her designs, or a beautician or a hairdresser or maybe a midwife, which is only three years' study. Whatever happens, the most important thing is to study somewhere and have a student lifestyle. But in the end, most important of all, is to have a diploma and for people to say that Jahongul graduated from such and such an institute. But perhaps she doesn't really want to study and has only consented to think about it because her mother wants this so much. If she doesn't study she'll work somewhere, anywhere just as long as it is not in a factory.

Jahongul wants to know everything. By everything she means medicine and sewing and cooking. What she most likes to do is to cook and to clean so that everything in the house shines. But she would like to have her own office and secretary and order everyone around. She would like to marry a medical student so that she could have free medicine and medical care.

Her friends were discussing what would happen if their husbands were to marry a secondary or tertiary wife. One said, 'I'll be first and senior wife. I'll have all his keys, so I won't have any problems.' Another said, 'He can divorce me and I'll keep the house and will live happily and marry again for love if I choose.' Jahongul asked them, 'What if your husband keeps his keys or his house himself, then what will you do?'

In summer 1995 Jahongul left school. Soon afterwards, an offer of marriage was made for her. This time her mother, hoping not to make the same mistake as with Tahmina, insisted that her daughter decide for herself. The two families were not acquainted and Jahongul had never set eyes on the man whom she was being asked to marry but after thinking about it a little she agreed anyway. The deciding factor was that he lived in Dushanbe and had his own small flat, only a couple of miles from the centre of town, albeit in the same building as his parents, and was making a reasonable income from currency dealing.

By the time I returned to Dushanbe in December of that year Jahongul was married. Her mother had arranged for her to enter commercial school and she was studying to become a book-keeper. In early 1996 she became pregnant but, after many hours of labour, her child was stillborn. The experience left her so shaken she swore she would not soon, if ever, allow herself to become pregnant again. In spring 1997 there was a serious typhoid epidemic in Dushanbe, and Jahongul became sick after drinking water from a tap in the street. She remained in hospital for some weeks and for a long time afterwards was very weak. That summer, despite her vows, she became pregnant again and in March 1998 she gave birth to a boy after an even more difficult labour than the previous time. The baby has many health problems and will need long-term physiotherapy if he is ever going to walk.

Her husband was forced to stop working after laws against unlicensed currency dealing were passed and has become a watchman in the bank where his father holds a senior position. As a result they have a much reduced income. Furthermore, despite the separate flats, Jahongul and her husband do not really live apart from her parents-in-law and Jahongul spends much of her waking time in their flat, serving her mother-in-law. Jahongul's husband and marital family are very autocratic. Although she lives only a few miles away from her family she is rarely permitted to visit them and never allowed to stay overnight.

When I next saw Nahdiya in spring 1999 she told me she deeply regretted both her choices of son-in-law, saying that neither of them were any good and that she would not marry her third daughter to a Tajik. She will go to university first and only afterwards will they look for a husband for her. Nahdiya said that Tahmina's husband is incapable of earning any money, makes no financial contribution to the household, and is no help at all in looking after his child. Jahongul's husband brings home very little money, barely enough to pay for their son's therapy, and in addition beats her and keeps her from visiting her family. Certainly the one time I saw Jahongul after her marriage she looked terrible but we had no chance to speak privately, so I could not find out exactly what the matter was.

It seems that her mother's having chosen her husband for her has not protected Jahongul from violence, just as having her own flat has not protected her from having to serve her mother-in-law. There is no talk of her leaving her husband and returning home or of any attempt by her family to put a stop to her husband's violence. It is accepted as an unfortunate, but irremediable, fact of life.

Jahongul's constantly changing ideas about her future are typical of people who know they have no chance of being able to translate their dreams into action. In Jahongul's case this is not entirely due to Tajik traditions. True, her dreams relating to her choice of husband were un-realisable within that community but those to do with her choice of career were more a reflection of her personal situation. Her home environment is not conducive to intellectual development and the low standards at her school did not help. Moreover, despite the fact that tertiary education is supposedly free, only those capable of paying a large bribe are able to choose their field of study. The rest either go without or enrol in unpopular departments.

During the same period I was interviewing Jahongul in central Dushanbe I was also spending time on the outskirts of town with 16-year-old Sadbarg, one of Tillo's neighbours. The lives and aspirations of these two young women make an interesting contrast.

Sadbarg's family is from a lower social circle than that of Jahongul and they lead an almost peasant lifestyle, having a minuscule piece of land built into the hillside, where they manage to plant vegetables and keep cows, sheep, and goats in an unbelievably tiny space. In the summer one of the sons will take the cows to the mountains, just as they do in Sadbarg's father's home village. Sadbarg herself, having gone to school in central Dushanbe, has had more exposure to the town than her family's lifestyle would suggest and it is this perhaps that has allowed her to imbue the television programmes she watches with somewhat more immediacy and reality than most rural girls do.

When we first met Sadbarg was 16, the eldest daughter of a family of ten children, of whom three had died in childhood. Her father is illiterate. He was an alcoholic for many years and perhaps because of this all but two of the children, Sadbarg and her second brother, are somewhat mentally subnormal. Around 15 years ago their father lost the use of his legs and since then has stopped both drinking and beating his wife, which he used to do quite frequently.

Sadbarg is a conscientious, hard-working and lively youngster with lots of ideas of her own. She is not at all happy at home, where she feels very uncomfortable. Her mother is out much of the time, sitting for hours on a bench in front of the school across the street, where she has a job as a cleaner, although her second daughter, a pupil at the school, does most of the actual work. This leaves the housework in Sadbarg's hands. Despite all her labours the house is always filthy and smelly, since most of the children wet their beds every night and their mattresses are used as sitting mats in the daytime.

Sadbarg is doing an apprenticeship at a knitting factory while finishing her last year at secondary school. She is bored with working there and hates the unceasing noise of the machinery. Her only serious aspiration to further education is to study tailoring. However, her family does not have the money for this. Sadbarg would also like to study languages. She bewails the fact that she knows only Tajik and Russian; she doesn't even know Uzbek. Her dream, however, is to become a nurse.

Sadbarg thinks she is too fat and does not like her face or skin. Her brother tells her she is built like a tank and this makes her feel bad. In fact, she looks pleasant and quite bright but she longs to be gorgeous like the heroines of the soap operas and films she adores.

Sadbarg hates the fact that her parents are strict and she is never allowed to go anywhere except to work. There is so much of the world she would like to see and she is barely allowed to move round her hometown. However, in the last year she has managed to find ways to circumvent her parents' edicts. They believe the factory workday ends daily at four o'clock and so expect her home around five. In reality, problems acquiring raw materials have meant that she frequently finishes work much earlier, and that there are times when the factory remains closed all day. Sadbarg and her fellow apprentices never tell their parents of this. Every weekday they set off for work and return at the usual time. On those days – increasingly frequent – when they don't have to work the whole day they take advantage of this to have some fun. They may sneak into the cinema, go to the market, stroll around the centre looking in shop windows or sit in the park to eat their packed lunches.

However, they have to be careful. They cannot walk around freely but have to stick to areas they know their parents do not frequent. Should any of them find out what their daughters are up to there will be serious repercussions. Their parents believe that girls out on their own without strict control are always liable to gravitate towards boys. They would not believe these girls are not interested in boys. They just want a little freedom to chat, to exchange views, to learn about life, to feel like adults and not just children, obedient and silent.

Their parents, on the other hand, only care about one thing – their daughters' reputations. The remotest suspicion that they might have even the most innocent relations with a member of the opposite sex could be damaging. Gossips and spies abound. So the girls are always frightened they may be caught, and their adventures are fraught with risk. But it seems to be worth it, because they continue and, amazingly enough, remain free from discovery.

Sadbarg has no very clear idea what sort of future she would like but she does know that she doesn't want to lead the sort of life she is going to be forced into, that is to marry and have children and never see the world or do anything beyond domestic chores and perhaps some boring job. She would love to travel – especially to Moscow and to India. She has relatives in the former and thinks it would be interesting to see it. She has learned about India from Bollywood films, which she adores. She would like television programming to consist of nothing but Indian films, Latin American soap operas, and concerts of Tajik music and dancing. She doesn't see the point of most Russian programmes, especially things like the news, political commentary and so on. Best of all she loves the Mexican soap opera Wild Rosa. She has occasionally tried to watch the American series, Santa Barbara, but finds it too complicated and difficult to follow. If she had a choice about how to live her life she would like to live like Rosa did, once she discovered her rich mother.[4]

Sadbarg wishes she were a boy, so she could go anywhere she wanted and stay out all night and no-one would say anything, but a girl has to be home by five o'clock. Even before the war she had to. Parents are afraid that if girls go anywhere they will do bad things with boys, but that is not what Sadbarg cares about. She just wants to see new places. Her father has been to many Soviet cities but he never took her mother with her. Therefore, Sadbarg knows that married women don't get to go anywhere and that she will never be allowed to travel.[5] *If she were a boy and had the money she could go to Moscow, but as a girl she cannot. Her parents would never allow her. She doesn't want to get married before she sees Moscow but she believes her parents would throw her out if they heard her say that, or at least give her a lot of grief.*

Sadbarg doesn't know whether she wants to marry or not. She will just accept her fate. If no-one asks for her hand then she won't marry, if someone does she will, and that is that. She does not want to choose for herself, but wants her parents to do so in case her husband throws her out and she has nowhere to go. If she chooses for herself she believes that her parents won't take her back if anything happens. But if they choose for her and something goes wrong she will say, 'You see it's all your fault for choosing the wrong man.' However, she says, if he beats her she will just accept it and not do or say anything. That is the rule in Tajikistan. A wife must obey her husband no matter what. Husbands don't have to obey wives and it is bad that there is no equality in this. However, Sadbarg is not sure that there is any way this can be changed, as it is just how things are done here. But she says she doesn't have any choice about deciding not to marry because people here laugh at any girl who is not married by the age of 20 and say she is bad. Nevertheless, when her mother said that whether Sadbarg liked it or not she would marry her off, since if she didn't people would say 'That girl is no good.' Sadbarg retorted, 'Let them say it. Just see if I care!'

In fact, Sadbarg never got to study anything, but instead later that summer was married to a distant cousin, a schoolteacher. He is an orphan, living with his younger brother and sisters. Sadbarg is the oldest woman and so she has charge of the household. She likes this very much. She is able to take most decisions herself so she can order the house as she likes and it is cleaner and the family a great deal more pleasant than her own family. In autumn of the following year Sadbarg gave birth to a healthy baby girl. When I next saw her, a few months later, she looked happy. She was very proud of her beautiful daughter whom she had dressed in the prettiest clothes she could find. She had lost her puppy fat and was looking beautiful herself too. A few years later she had a second child.

The soap operas and films Sadbarg is so fond of have made it possible for her to dream of worlds beyond her own ken but not to imagine them having any realistic relation to her own life. She knows that breaking away from her parents' way of life will be beyond her capacities and even wishes. In any case, the lifestyles represented by the soaps are too far away from conceivable experience.

From her very unpromising beginnings Sadbarg seems to have had a lucky break with her marriage and to have improved her life by it. However, she is no nearer getting her wish to travel and see the world. I have not had a chance to ask her how she feels about this but in all likelihood she will now be more concerned about her children's future than about her own personal wishes.

Jahongul's fate has been very different. All her worst nightmares have been realised and more. She is married to a man who does not earn enough to support her properly. He mistreats her, but even so her family has not been able to help her. Living separately from her parents-in-law but in the same building allows her husband to beat her without interference from his parents while still placing her in a position of servant to her marital family. Into the bargain her son is an invalid who may never walk properly.

To both Sadbarg and Jahongul the lifestyles portrayed in the soap operas seem light years away. They are not from that segment of society that might be likely to travel abroad[6] and they can only marvel at, but not relate to, the characters depicted.

These two stories poignantly illustrate some of the principal issues that preoccupy young women in Tajikistan, and show how difficult it is to escape the narrow confines within which they are forced to live. For all their desires for a different fate from that of their sisters and friends both Jahongul and Sadbarg have ended up in very much the same circumstances. The strong similarity in the way the two girls talked about their reasons for not wanting to marry for love reflects a discourse on domestic violence that is quite prevalent, in Dushanbe at least. The suggestion is that since the civil war all the decent young men are either dead or have left Tajikistan, so that girls are forced to put up with the dregs. I have never heard it suggested that these same young men might have behaved very differently had they remained within the disciplined world of the Soviet Union, or even just not been subjected to the violence of war.

Jahongul sees that Russian girls have a great deal more freedom than she does, that they can have boyfriends, for instance. However, this freedom brings with it responsibilities. In the first place, responsibility for oneself. It is more difficult to run one's own life. It might be that one would not be able to find a husband at all. So perhaps it is preferable to allow parents to take responsibility. Neither Jahongul nor Sadbarg wants to accept responsibility for choosing her own husband. If their parents do this they believe it will absolve them should things go wrong. It is not their job to do anything about it. This is what things are like and it is not up to them to put them right. That is someone else's responsibility. Such attitudes largely derive from their relatively powerless positions since it is difficult to imagine how they could take responsibility in such a way as to change their situations in line with their dreams and yet remain within the boundaries acceptable to Tajik society.

Their only recourse in the case of a bad marriage would be to return to their parents. When Jahongul actually finds herself in this situation, however, she does not do this. She knows how hard her mother's life already is without landing her with not only herself but also her invalid son to support. Where on earth would she get the money? It is highly unlikely that Jahongul's husband's family would make any contribution should she leave him.

But Nahdiya is also in a very difficult position. She does not know what else she could have done to make her daughters' lives better. Despite her distress over the poor state of the traditionally contracted marriages of her eldest two daughters, she continues to uphold the customary way of life. Despite her wish to find a different sort of man for her youngest daughter she does not permit the latter to abandon any of the traditions.

On the other hand, she also has very few options. Living in Tajikistan, a different lifestyle is simply not open to her, nor can she imagine such a thing. None of the ways of making matches for her daughters that are sanctioned by local society would necessarily have had better results. Nahdiya could not possibly know if any of the other young men whose families offered for them would have turned out better, and divorce would probably only make things worse. In the absence of a mature male relative who could put pressure on her daughters' husbands or parents-in-law there is not much she can do. Her sons are too young to be taken seriously. Thus, despite her dominant position in the family, without a man behind her Nahdiya is relatively powerless.

It is clear from the stories of Sadbarg and Jahongul that the performances they give in front of their parents mask a great deal that they were willing to reveal to me. Sadbarg's parents had no idea she went out with her friends after school, nor were they aware of her longing to travel. Because she thinks even this last oversteps the boundaries of feminine gender norms in her social circle she feels she must conceal it. In her family girls are simply not supposed to express such desires. To show they even have them could be construed as a threat to parental authority. No wonder they prefer to keep quiet about them. But the same applies to Jahongul's family. Nahdiya certainly had no idea of all the thoughts going through her daughter's head. The outward show, the mask, she put on for her mother was to get on with the housework and keep quiet.

The narrow range of performances permitted to these women allows society to maintain the status quo. Unless they decide to vary their per-formances they will not be able to change things in their favour. However, as Butler suggests (1997b: 27–30), making variations significant enough to make a perceptible change in their lives would mean taking the risk of stepping outside the boundaries of acceptability. It is a risk that Sadbarg, Jahongul, Tahmina and Nahdiya, at any rate, do not consider worth taking.

THE WILL OF YOUTH

If young people were forced to choose between getting their own way and remaining within their families they would have little alternative but to choose the latter. There is nowhere for them to go if they leave home, nor any way of getting financial or other support. Today there are fewer options than ever open to most people, especially to young women. It is prohibitively expensive to enter an institute of tertiary education and students can no longer live on the minuscule government grants. Furthermore, a diploma is no longer necessarily a passport to a good job; indeed there are few jobs of any kind available and most do not pay well. It is very difficult to land one without family connections, and even to keep it once one has landed it. When it comes to layoffs the first to go are those not related to their bosses.

Moreover, it would be very hard to find a family who would accept an outcast from another family as a spouse for one of their children. Shahzoda, whose story was told in Chapter 4, could never have married her friend without her aunt's support. The increasing numbers of street children are a scary reminder of what can happen to young people without a family.

Friendship is not a practical alternative to family backing because what is needed first and foremost is not moral but material aid. Moral support is not much use when what one needs is a roof over one's head and food in one's stomach. Moreover, the personal sympathy of close friends does not have much weight when set against the (dis)approbation of the community at large.

In any case society is organised in such a way that close relationships are supposed to remain within the family. It is considered treachery to betray family secrets to an outsider. Since it is the family that suffers if secrets become public, trust is unlikely between mere friends, although it seems to be considerably stronger between women than men.

Sadbarg, for instance, could trust her girlfriends not to give her excursions round town away, since they would have been hard put to do this without giving themselves away too. The same goes for Safarmo and the friends she meets at night (Chapter 3). Perhaps trust between women works best when they are mutually dependent on each other's silence, since even women friends seem to be careful not to tell each other real family secrets. They seem to find it easier to tell an outsider such as myself, both because they think my Russified cultural background means I will not be shocked by their revelations and because I have nothing to gain by betraying them. Such trust is rare between friends.

On the other hand it is difficult to see much of it within the family either, since people seem wary of confiding in relatives. Like Jahongul and Tahmina, sisters may be good friends as children but very often they will see each other relatively little after marriage. Rustam never confided in Kurbon or his sisters that he continued his relationship with Zhenia after his marriage and had remained in touch with her after her departure from Tajikistan. When people have a real secret that could endanger their family's reputation, it is far too dangerous to confide in anyone. This is especially so for younger people whose chance of making a good marriage depends on their siblings' reputation (see Monogarova 1982: vol. I, 90) so that a potentially damaging secret told to one of them is unlikely to be safe (see Giovannini 1987: 68). Thus, discourse pits all siblings against each other, not just brothers against sisters.

It is hardly surprising then that close friendship seems rare in Tajikistan. The great majority of the men and women I interviewed claimed to have few, if any, real friends and only one or two people had anyone they could talk to about private or intimate matters. When Rustam was younger he had had three good men friends, all of whom had disappeared from his life long before I met him. One or two highly educated women I know in Dushanbe have close friends from their school days in whom they confide, but this is exceptional. Women often lose touch with their school friends on marriage.

Moreover, it can be difficult for women to spend time alone with their friends, as there are almost always intrusions and it is necessary to make great efforts to maintain privacy. Safarmo's group of women friends, described in Chapter 3, is quite unusual in this respect and I never heard of anyone else who laid such stress on friendship. Perhaps this is so important for Safarmo because she has no adult family members of either sex left.

Men and boys frequently go round in groups but it is unclear how close they really are to one another. From what I have seen they do not trust each other with secrets.

Thus, for most people there is no one to turn to outside the family. At least within it they receive some level of support, even if mostly material and contingent upon correct behaviour. The vast majority of Tajiks are largely dependent, both morally and materially, on their family structures so that those young people who are serious about making their own life decisions must try to negotiate with their families to find a solution acceptable to all parties. This is not easy for either sex.

It is made harder by the emphasis on unquestioning obedience that hinders the development of agency, something that tends to be even more difficult for men than for women, since so often they continue to live with their parents, remaining financially as well as emotionally dependent on them. Moreover, parents may accord their sons little more freedom of choice respecting their future lives than their daughters, so that they may be no better prepared for marriage than their brides.

Parents also retain responsibility for providing for their sons and their families. There is no suggestion that young people should wait to marry until they can afford to maintain themselves. In fact, young husbands who live with their parents are expected to put their earnings into the family pot and the household will be managed by their mothers.

Nor do men often develop a sense of responsibility for their children at birth. After all they have little to do with them in the early years when mothers do most of the caring. Rashid is a case in point. He remains dependent on his parents, especially his mother, for decision-making and for the rest leaves his daughter almost entirely to Tahmina, not bothering even to enquire about her welfare during the long periods they spend apart while he is in Russia or she with her family in Dushanbe.

The stories in this book illustrate the fact that underneath the surface uniformity the masks conceal many small aberrations, so that there is more room for difference in Tajik society than the formal discourse suggests. Just as in the west, youngsters give small experimental taps against the boundaries of parental authority, until they find themselves up against the limits. In Tajikistan, however, the boundaries are usually narrower and less flexible, and the option of escaping to a world outside the family upon adulthood considerably more limited.

The differing capacities young people have to stand up to their parents appear to a large extent to depend on the social status of the individual families, and especially on fathers' levels of self-assurance. Some, such as Rustam's, permit very little room for manoeuvre. Despite Tahmina's and Jahongul's lack of a father they also do not seem to have much space for this, perhaps because the absence of the usual male controlling figure compels them to prove they are as well-behaved as their contemporaries in order to preserve their family's reputation. Girls certainly have to be much more careful about going beyond the boundaries than boys, since they have more at stake in their gender performances. Nevertheless, they may be able to take advantage of their situation to step outside the conventional, as long as this is not publicly perceived as such and they do not go too far.

THE PERFORMANCE OF MASCULINITY

As Rustam's story shows, it is not just feminine gender that is problematic in performance. The correct performance of masculinity may also be complicated and onerous.

In the past few decades there has been a wave of studies of masculinity.[7] Victor Seidler recounts the difficulties of 'living up to masculinity' in Britain, and how he felt compelled to spend much of his adolescence doing all he could to avoid letting himself down and being labelled a 'sissy' or a 'weed'. 'I had to learn to please and ingratiate and to suppress my own feelings and responses, my own anger and frustration, so that I was liked by the others ... even if this meant sacrificing a sense of myself' (Seidler 1991: 17).

There is no reason to suppose that men in other cultures find it any easier to live up to the identities thrust upon them. In Tajikistan the contradiction between the image of the male as dominant and controlling and the subjugation of young men to their fathers, grandfathers and even mothers makes for its own special problems. The image of man as virile provider is also not unproblematic today with so few employment opportunities and the resulting necessity to keep one's family small. The apparent rise in domestic violence among younger couples is doubtless not unconnected with the struggles of young men to portray their masculine gender in the face of great odds. Not surprisingly, men's need to dominate their wives, not necessarily through physical violence, appears to increase in direct proportion with the decrease in other ways of displaying masculinity,[8] as in the case of Fayziddin (Chapter 1).

Decades of defending their ways of life against Russo-Soviet onslaughts have left Tajiks very aware that the performance of gender is culture-specific. They know, for instance, that *ayb* and *nomus* are not important to Russians in the same way they are to them. Both Tajiks and Russians are very ready with remarks about the difference in their respective female gender performances. Jahongul, for example, clearly has a good idea of the different gender performances open to Russian girls. However, there is much less comment on male gender performance, and what little there is tends to focus largely on the fact that Russian men do not insist on maintaining such strict control over their family members.

Nevertheless, as the following story shows, Tajik men are not only aware of the differences between the cultures, when circumstances demand it, they are also perfectly capable of moving between performances of Russian and Tajik masculinity.

Sayara's husband Eshmurod had been absent in Russia for a very long time and she was fed up, so she decided to go and fetch him back. After a long and tiring journey she arrived at the address he had given her and knocked on the door. A Russian woman opened it. 'Who are you?' she asked, 'And what do you want?' Sayara said she was looking for Eshmurod. 'Why do you want him?' was the response. 'I am his wife', said Sayara. The Russian woman looked at her and said, 'But I am his wife.' Just then Eshmurod came out to see what was going on. When he saw Sayara he invited her in and introduced her to the Russian woman, Tanya, as his other wife. Sayara was not pleased but she knew there was little she could do about it. She went in and agreed to stay with them for a few days. In turn Eshmurod agreed to return to Tajikistan with her for a visit.

Meanwhile, Tanya was preparing dinner. She called to Eshmurod to come and help her. Sayara watched in amazement as her husband, who in all their years of marriage had never lifted a hand in the house, worked alongside Tanya in the kitchen. When they sat down at table Sayara said to him in Tajik, which Tanya, of course, could not understand, 'So I see you can cook and do lots of other things I hadn't realised you were capable of. Next time you invite guests home in Tajikistan you can prepare the food and wait on them, I won't.' Eshmurod kept silent.

A few days later Eshmurod and Sayara were on the train travelling back to Tajikistan. When they arrived at the Tajik border Eshmurod turned to his wife and said: 'Those things I did for Tanya, they are how I behave in Russia. In Tajikistan I don't behave like that. You will not order me around like Tanya did, nor will you expect me to help in the house or make any other changes in the way I behave. It is one thing to do that in Russia, quite another here.'[9]

Eshmurod seems to have been trying to live up to Tanya's expectations of him, which were clearly very different from what Sayara's had been. The Tajik men in Russia who might see Eshmurod in this new persona are likely to be doing the same for *their* Russian wives, so they will not regard his behaviour as the aberration they would have at home.

Furthermore, the couple doubtless lives in Tanya's flat, and even Eshmurod's legal right to live in that town is likely to be dependent on her allowing him to register with the police at her address. Here it is the women who have the advantage. It is *their* town and their Tajik husbands are dependent on them, a situation very different from what the men will have experienced at home.

In the past Tajik men did marry Russians, meeting them, for instance, during their military service. Upon demobilisation they would bring their wives back with them to Tajikistan, hoping their families would accept them. In such cases the onus was on the women to learn to conform to Tajik feminine gender performances, especially if they lived in communities with a preponderance of Tajiks. I have seen such women wearing Tajik dress, speaking exclusively in Tajik with their children and following all the local customs, although those living in Russian-dominated Dushanbe were not expected to take on Tajik identity quite so strongly (Tett 1995: 168). For Tajik men to settle in Russia, even for part of the year, is very much a post-Soviet phenomenon resulting from economic necessity, and it has brought with it a new way of performing masculinity, which in the long run is bound to produce changes in Tajikistan itself.

ALTERNATE EXPRESSIONS OF MASCULINITY

In the previous chapter I examined the dynamics of Rustam's family relationships, describing how he spent much of his childhood being punished by his parents and is still repeatedly denigrated by them. Despite this, his public image is that of a relaxed, if somewhat subdued, masculinity, and he carries out the myriad small rituals of a male Tajik's life efficiently and with ease, including waiting on his elders and showing them respect at public functions. He is someone others turn to for help and support, appearing collected, decisive and resourceful. In other words, at work he appears highly masculine, something he is unable to do in front of his father. Nevertheless, behind his mask, Rustam is unsure of himself, timid and shy.

For all his need of his father's approbation Rustam is still able to view his behaviour critically. In the past Malik used on occasion to beat Dilorom, sometimes quite severely. Indeed, one of Rustam's earliest memories is watching his father beating his mother and vowing to be different when he grew up and especially never to hit a woman.

After Zhenia left Tajikistan Rustam had little to focus his emotions on other than his children, and he increasingly sank into melancholia and depression. He kept going only through instinct and routine. He was excellent at his work and adored by his pupils. In the absence of anything else to interest him he was putting in tremendously long hours in his school workshop and was always willing and ready to help anyone who asked for it.

Meanwhile, internally he was gradually subsiding into a twilight world from which external reality seemed more and more distant. The present was reduced to a primitive series of mechanical actions – getting out of bed in the morning, eating, going to work, coming home, eating again and then going to bed. The only milestones he could envision in his future would be the marriages of his children. His 'real' life was lived internally, with the 'ghost' of Zhenia ever walking by his side.

This 'half-life' was interrupted by a radical change of employment, when one of his uncles offered him a job as assistant buyer in his firm. Rustam had never thought about commerce before, and in any case such opportunities had not existed in Tajikistan when he was growing up. But he could no longer afford to maintain his family on his teacher's salary.

Once started in the world of business Rustam found himself fascinated by it. His job is to anticipate what people in Tajikistan will buy in these times of extreme economic hardship. When he goes on buying trips he has to judge which of the merchandise on offer will sell and which will not. Within a short time the wares Rustam was choosing were selling twice or three times better than those the other buyers brought back with them, and he was promoted to chief buyer. Nevertheless, his success at work does not compensate for the unhappiness of his private life and, however much his uncle praises him, his father does not show any more approbation than before. This all makes Rustam the more convinced that his outward competence is just a show and that in reality he is the failure his father proclaims him to be.

At the same time he was enjoying his job, which for the first time in his life brought him into an atmosphere where he was encouraged to think for himself and make his own decisions. During his career as a teacher this had been completely frowned upon. Both lesson plans and methodology had been fixed by the Ministry of Education, leaving him practically no leeway to develop anything himself. His parents had done their best to prevent him taking any initiative in his private life.

The new job forced Rustam into situations in which he had to make immediate decisions without the possibility of consulting his boss. He would be far away, without easy communication with Tajikistan and it would be entirely up to him to decide whether a line of goods would be likely to sell. After some initial trepidation Rustam found himself responding very positively to this challenge.

However, as soon as he returned home he would be confronted with his wife, or his father would start belittling him again and doing his best to ensure Rustam did not think his new job entitled him to think any better of himself.

Rustam's insecurities are clearly very different from those of the other men discussed in this chapter. He has grown up physically capable and coordinated, and is now able to support his entire family materially. He has proved his virility by fathering children and his relationship with Zhenia left him secure about his abilities to perform in bed. At work the other men look up to him and he is the object of envy rather than disdain. Indeed, the abyss of self-doubt that lurks underneath the surface is so well-concealed that it is unimaginable to those who have only seen his public face.

Karomat's husband, Khudoydod, was very different and apparently much more relaxed about himself. He was even able to put his love for his wife before his desire for children:

After her three children all died in infancy Karomat suffered a miscarriage at five months, brought on by manual labour while helping dig the ground for the fountain by the Dushanbe Opera House. The treatment she received damaged her womb and she became infertile. For some years afterwards she tried all the traditional treatments she could, including visiting mullahs and local shrines dedicated to fertility. When these didn't work she turned to modern medicine, but the doctors couldn't help either. Realising how very much Karomat wanted a child Khudoydod suggested they adopt. He even said they could pretend she was pregnant, stuffing a cushion under her clothes. They would arrange the adoption and then she could go away to 'give birth' and bring the child home with her. In this way nobody would know the child was not theirs. Karomat, however, would have none of it. If she could not have her own child she would not have one at all.

Karomat and Khudoydod lived in his paternal home. His older brother had a home of his own but it was not nearly so nice nor so big. After they had been married 18 years, Karomat's mother-in-law died. Immediately, her husband's relatives started to look enviously at Karomat and her husband living in their great place all by themselves and to put pressure on Khudoydod to take a second wife, or else to adopt one of their daughters. However, Khudoydod refused, saying he loved his wife and needed nobody else. But Karomat soon got tired of being on her own so much and doing all the housework. Khudoydod would bring his friends home or his relatives would come over, and she would have to cope single-handedly. And all the time her husband's relatives were offering him this young girl or that as a secondary wife. 'What is life without children?', they would hint. 'What is the point of having this big house and garden without children?'

While her mother-in-law had been alive Karomat had been fine, despite her childless state. She was happy with her husband, his relatives didn't bother her and her mother-in-law was even better to her than her own mother. But after her death, her in-laws' pressure started to get her down. Finally, she became fed up and decided to leave.

Once she had made up her mind there was no moving her. Her heart was cold. She wanted Khudoydod to divorce her so he could marry again and have children. But he wouldn't agree. He said he loved her and wanted only to be with her and that this was much more important to him than anything else, including children. He couldn't understand why she wanted a divorce and she never told him. He was sure it must be to marry someone else. He loved her so much and found her so beautiful he could not believe that other men would not be after her.

It took Karomat more than 18 months of working on him before he finally agreed to a divorce and at that point she returned to live with her parents. Khudoydod eventually remarried but Karomat never looked at another man.

Khudoydod chose for his second wife a woman who had been divorced after ten years of infertile marriage. With Khudoydod she did not become pregnant either, so she agreed to adopt a daughter. Later she insisted on blaming her lack of children on Khudoydod.

He became incensed and said that he had had children by Karomat but they simply had not lived. Furthermore, he told her he had additional proof that the problem was on her side. He introduced her to his son by a Russian woman with whom he had had a relationship after his divorce. Later, when this woman decided to emigrate to Russia Khudoydod took the child into his home and insisted his wife bring him up as their own.

In Karomat's old age her lack of children became a scourge to her because it meant that she had little left to live for and she would leave no trace of herself behind on earth after her death.[10]

I cannot help wondering about Khudoydod's second marriage. Was it that Karomat's problems had made him sympathetic to a woman for whom, perhaps, no-one else would have been likely to make an offer? Or could it have simply been that coincidentally he just happened to fall for an infertile woman?

CONCLUSION

The gender performances of these men and women are fluid and varying, employed in an attempt to maximise the few advantages they have, in situations basically stacked against them. Nevertheless, despite the fact that their personal identities were formed very much through subjugation and dependence, they have proved themselves capable of refusing to be mere victims. Their deliberate masking of their real personalities and the concealing of their agency in order to appear to conform to their parents' and society's demands, while secretly resisting, can be considered more than mere submission to necessity, their manipulation of situations yet another example of the use of the sorts of weapons at the disposal of the weak (see Scott 1985).

Because they do not conform to the outward performance of gender expected by Tajik society, the dreams and desires of young men and women usually remain as unexpressed fantasies, at the most secretly voiced to their best friends. The downcast eyes and silences of Jahongul, Rustam and the others conceal so many hopes and fears they can never articulate, especially those to do with deviant gender performances.

The insistence by the Soviet authorities that they had created a viable and wonderful new way of life in which difficulties and social problems were minimised has meant that all Soviet citizens were taught to regard problems as due to personal failings rather than those of the system (Humphrey 1983: 441). This makes people feel all the more helpless and inadequate when things go wrong. Given the lack of counselling and social support groups, most people have no way of obtaining meaningful help when they have problems. Essentially they have to go it alone. Families' fears of their weaknesses being exposed and exploited make it very difficult for anyone even to mention a problem outside the family circle. When, as so often happens, it is one's own family that has caused it, there is nothing for it but to keep the pain and confusion shut up inside and cope as best one can.

Rustam's abandonment of Zhenia has brought him little personal benefit in exchange for the sacrifice of his happiness. Although not exposed to the sort of physical maltreatment some of the women suffer nor forced to live with an autocratic mother-in-law, the psychological violence his own father inflicts on him is hardly less brutal nor in some ways less painful, and he also has to endure the agony of living with a woman he does not love. Jahongul finds herself in an even worse situation than any she had previously envisaged, unprotected from her husband's beatings, struggling to make ends meet on very inadequate means, serving her mother-in-law, and with an invalid child into the bargain.

This does not mean, however, that arranged marriages are necessarily unhappier than love matches, as I show in the next chapter, where I explore marital relations, in particular love and sex, and their significance in Tajikistan.

6 THE COUPLE RELATIONSHIP: LOVE, SEX AND MARRIAGE

MARITAL RELATIONS

'After marriage we Tajik women have to do what our husbands tell us. Without their permission we cannot leave the house, we cannot study and we cannot take a job', said Jahongul. 'It is our Tajik way to obey our husbands', said Tillo. Even Karomat agreed that this was unfortunately so.

Such reiterations of the 'magic formulas' of 'official' discourse produce the impression of strict adherence to gender norms. These women are announcing their acceptance of the traditions, their willingness to abide by them. This public acknowledgement of their duty to perform their feminine gender according to the rules makes it easier for them to get away with concealed deviations, advertises their husbands' successful performances of masculine gender and boosts family honour.

Outsiders listening to these women could be excused if they expected to find a nation of submissive, obedient wives, kow-towing to overbearing, dominant husbands, and indeed this is the image that many westerners have of Muslim life. But what actually goes on behind the closed doors of the marital relationship? How much power do husbands really have over their wives? What is more likely to be successful, marriage where the young couple have chosen their own partners or an arranged match? Is it reasonable for Tajiks to expect to achieve happiness through marriage and what role does love play?

Through the stories in this chapter I try to answer these questions by looking at aspects of marriage not usually on public display. They describe the most personal and intimate sides of human relations.

Life in an arranged marriage

Tahmina

It was Tahmina's wedding day and she set out with her family for Hissor for the ceremony. It was the first time that anyone apart from Nahdiya had met Tahmina's prospective husband and his family. Tahmina was very nervous. She wondered what this man, with whom she was perhaps to spend the rest of her life, would be like. The ceremony started. Tahmina looked at Rashid out of the corner of her eye so that no-one would notice. 'Is he good looking? How tall is he? Will he be kind or will he be harsh with me?' she asked herself.

Rashid was also nervous. He was so shy he could not answer when the mullah asked him whether he agreed to marry Tahmina. He just sat there blushing, his voice stuck in his throat.

Then the ceremony was over and Tahmina's family returned home, abandoning her with these unknown people. At first she thought it might not be too bad, after all Rashid had sisters with whom she would probably soon be friends, but to her dismay this didn't happen. They seemed to resent rather than to welcome her, as if she were an enemy come to take their brother away from them. Her mother-in-law was no better. This all made Tahmina feel extremely isolated. To be stuck in a village after living in Dushanbe all her life was an additional stress. The fact that Rashid, the person she was supposed to be close to, was away most of the time, and that when he was at home the two of them didn't get on particularly well, just made things worse.

Forty days after their marriage Rashid and Tahmina moved to his family's flat in Dushanbe. Tahmina was very beautiful and Rashid was extremely jealous of her. He would watch her everywhere they went, to see if she responded to any of the men who passed by, many of whom would look at her admiringly and even try to chat her up. This drove him absolutely wild.

Rashid would sometimes tell Tahmina he loved her but at other times he would say, 'I have no feelings for you. You are not my wife but my parents' wife. They chose you, not I.' He repeatedly asked her if she loved him and when she refused to say yes, Rashid decided this must be because she was in love with someone else. Irrespective of her denials she must have had a boyfriend before marriage.

They had been living in Dushanbe only a couple of months when Rashid decided he couldn't stand it any more. Since he couldn't watch over his wife 24 hours a day there was only one way to stop himself going mad with jealousy and allow him the freedom to do what he wanted without worrying about what Tahmina was up to and this was for her to live in the village with his parents. So, to her dismay, he insisted on her moving back there. She had been promised they would live in Dushanbe; she hated the village and living with his family.

This decision was not Rashid's alone. His mother had been pressuring him to bring his wife to live with them. She needed someone to do the domestic chores while she was at work and her daughters at school all day. Soon after Tahmina moved to the village her parents-in-law sold their Dushanbe flat, with the result that there was no longer anywhere to return to.

For several years after their marriage Tahmina did not manage to get pregnant, which deeply upset her. She would cry and cry. 'For Tajiks not getting pregnant is a tragedy', she told me. 'It is considered cause for divorce if a woman is not pregnant after three years of marriage.' And Tahmina had been married almost one and a half years.

'If I don't get pregnant what will I do? I will just go on getting older and older ... To a Tajik a 30-year-old woman without a child is just an old woman. She may be great at housework, she may have a good job but unless she can have a child she is useless.'

Rashid was very upset over Tahmina's failure to conceive and told her that she obviously did not love him because if she did she would give him a child. He was furious at the fact that one of his friends, who had married at the same time they did, was already a father, while Tahmina was not even pregnant yet.

Tahmina realised that Rashid's patience was wearing thin and that unless she became pregnant soon he would probably divorce her; she was not ready for this, even though she was not happy and did not believe she could ever love him. Their characters were too dissimilar, which made it hard for them to bond.

Tahmina often considered initiating divorce herself. However, she was too afraid of the gossip that might ensue. She did not want people to point at her and say, 'Tahmina failed, she was a bad wife.' Also, she did not know what would happen afterwards. 'Who knows if a second husband would be better than Rashid? In all likelihood he would be worse', she thought. She would no longer receive offers from young, unmarried men and an older man would probably be far more controlling than Rashid, so finally Tahmina decided it was better to remain with him.

She consulted a gynaecologist about her infertility and was given treatment, after which she at last became pregnant. Rashid was ecstatic. He immediately became less jealous and stopped watching over her so anxiously. He allowed her to spend more time with her mother and generally started treating her more kindly.

But after their daughter was born he returned to his old ways. The friction between them increased, but now, with her child's welfare to consider, Tahmina felt she was definitely no longer in a position to ask for a divorce. She had to put the child first.

In the last few years Tahmina and Rashid have worked out a reasonably amicable companionship based more on their mutual love for their daughter than on their feelings for each other. Tahmina has decided to try to be as happy as possible. She may not love Rashid but she could do a lot worse. At least he doesn't beat her. She feels she has a lot to be thankful for and has stopped blaming her mother for forcing her into marriage. Now their biggest worries are financial. Rashid has been to Russia several times but never managed to bring back much money. However, he has been able to find no source of income in Tajikistan and they are completely dependent on his parents.

For Rashid, his parents are still the controlling figures in his life, especially his dominating mother. He certainly does not appear to feel in control in his marital relationship. In some respects he appears to believe Tahmina is more in control than he is, especially with regard to her ability to conceive, interpreting her infertility as a deliberate refusal to bear him a child because she does not love him. He prefers to believe that this is an indication that her heart is not free rather than seeking in himself the reason for her lack of love. This would be scary, as it would place the responsibility for being lovable firmly on his shoulders.

The concept that a man is responsible for personally attracting and holding the affection of his wife is something I rarely heard mentioned in Tajikistan, where wives are chosen for men with little regard either to their own qualities or to the women's preferences (Chapter 4). Donish, for instance, appears to consider that whether a woman will become a loving wife depends on her character rather than on her husband's behaviour

(1960:180–202). Rustam is the only man in Tajikistan whom I heard voice a doubt about his lovability, but this was in the context of his capacity to attract a girlfriend, not in relation to his marriage. It is usually assumed that a husband who does not physically ill-treat his wife, gives her children and supports his family financially has fulfilled all the duties required of him. There is no discourse suggesting that men should behave nicely to their wives in order to gain their affection and love, other than by material gifts. Nevertheless, besides obeying their husbands, catering to their personal needs, bearing and caring for their children, keeping the house and yard in order, milking the cows and working on the private plot in the village, or holding down a job in the town, it appears that women are also expected to love their husbands. At least this is what Rashid demanded. Even Rustam seemed to be hurt that Jumbul did not care for him, despite the fact he made no pretence of loving her.

Rustam

The first time they were alone after their wedding Rustam told his wife he had no feelings for her. He was passionately in love with another woman and had only agreed to marry Jumbul because of the tremendous pressures his parents had applied. Jumbul told him she knew about his relationship with Zhenia. When Rustam asked why then she had agreed to marry him, she replied her that mother had told her to.

Rustam felt very weird with this woman, this stranger, expected to sleep in one room with her, have sex with her and spend his life with her, when they had not the slightest psychological contact. He could not bring himself to believe that she was actually his wife. It felt so unreal that he was supposed to live with her when all he could think of was Zhenia.

After his marriage Rustam spent even less time at home than before, ignoring Jumbul as much as possible and using all his ingenuity to figure out ways of spending time with Zhenia without being discovered. He started an evening course at the university to give him a legitimate reason for being absent most evenings and on weekends.

Even after marriage Rustam still hoped that something would happen to save him from a lifetime of living with Jumbul and allow him to marry Zhenia instead. He deliberately chose to have sex with his wife only during her safe periods so that at first she didn't get pregnant. However, when nothing intervened to free him from her, deciding that life would be better with children around, he decided to impregnate her. After this he felt as though he had closed off all possibility of escape and was serving a life sentence.

After Zhenia's departure Rustam concentrated his mind on the thought that he would soon be able to visit her in Russia but, on realising it might be years before he could afford to do so, he fell into despair.

Shortly afterwards one of Rustam's colleagues became interested in him. She was really sweet and attractive and he tried his best to reciprocate, but in vain. Eventually he had to tell her that there was no point; he could not have a relationship with her while Zhenia had such a strong hold on his heart. She was very disappointed and told him he was probably one of those people who loved only once in a lifetime. Nevertheless, a few years later Rustam was ready to start looking at other women once more and had a series of affairs, none of which lasted long because each time, after a few weeks, the woman concerned made it clear that what she wanted from him was financial support, not love.

Finally he gave up and decided he would just have to try to get emotional support from his wife. So he started trying to get closer to her. He would put his arm round her when they sat together in the evenings, and even tried to hold her hand when they went out together, as he used to do with Zhenia. But Jumbul pulled back from every gesture, using the convenient ayb as justification for keeping all physical and emotional contact with her husband to a minimum.

Finally, Rustam decided it was useless to attempt to fall in love with her. It just wouldn't work. He did feel some affection for her, but as the mother of his children rather than for herself. Recently he asked her what he meant to her. She replied, 'Personally very little. I only want two things from you – money and for you to be a good father to our children.' Rustam found this cool statement very painful, even though he does not love her either. He feels scarcely more contact with her than when they first married and believes their relationship will never improve. If he thought he would be awarded custody of his children he would sue for divorce, but he knows this would be highly unlikely.

Jumbul would like Rustam to give her much more money for her personal expenditure. She spends her own meagre wages and as much of Rustam's as she can on buying clothes and entertaining her colleagues. Rustam spends very little on himself. The bulk of his wages goes on household needs, the children and his parents.

Rustam could not help contrasting Jumbul's attitude with Zhenia's. From the beginning they had shared everything, down to the last crumb. Money meant so little to her. When the problems with Rustam's parents started and it became clear that he and Zhenia would not be able to live with either family if they married, some of Rustam's colleagues jokingly offered them a windowless storeroom as a home. Zhenia immediately said, 'I would be happy to live anywhere as long as it is with Rustam. I do not care about anything else as long as we are together.'

After Zhenia left Tajikistan Rustam had no real friend. There was not one person in whom he could confide, with whom he dared discuss his feelings, his desperate need for her. His colleagues and acquaintances only mocked him for being so emotional and for what they saw as his stupidity in falling so crazily in love, especially with someone as unprestigious as Zhenia. So he shut himself off psychologically from the outside world and lived off Zhenia's image, which he kept close to his heart.

The years passed with the only contact between them letters and the very occasional telephone call. Zhenia had no phone and the connections were very difficult. Then Rustam got his new job and started to save. He had soon put enough aside for a visit, and wrote in great excitement to tell her so. He had it all worked out. He would tell them at home he was going on a buying trip so no-one would know what he was up to. But then the shock came. Zhenia sent him a telegram, which read, 'Do not come to me.' This, Rustam took to mean that she considered their relationship over. He was utterly devastated and spent several nights staring sleeplessly at the ceiling while the place she had occupied in his heart slowly emptied out, leaving an unbearable vacuum.

Rustam could not understand how Zhenia could just finish their eleven-year-old relationship in this curt manner. He wrote to ask what she meant by her message but never *received a reply. Rustam now wishes with all his heart he had had the strength to defy his father and refuse to marry Jumbul.*

Since Zhenia's telegram Rustam has become very depressed. For years he had refused to admit to himself he had lost her, thus postponing the suffering of accepting this. By keeping himself in a dreamlike state he had been able to make believe Zhenia was really with him. In this way he had also refused to face up to the consequences of his own actions in letting her go. But now he was suddenly confronted with the finality of his loss, something that has been only slightly less unbearable for him to accept because it is so long since he last saw Zhenia that she is no longer completely real to him.

Now he feels totally alone. He only manages to stand his life with Jumbul by cutting their contact to a minimum. He leaves home early in the morning and rarely returns until late. He even spends much of his weekends and holidays in the office. It is much more bearable there than at home, even though his dreams have deserted him along with Zhenia. He feels more desolate, more lost, than ever before and believes himself destined to spend his life emotionally alone.

Rustam had been taught by his father that women's function was to serve men and he had been conditioned not to take their feelings into account. Moreover, he was so wrapped up first in Zhenia and subsequently in the pain of losing her, that he seems to have scarcely noticed anything, or anyone else for years. As a result, he paid virtually no attention to his wife. It does not seem once to have occurred to him to consider Jumbul's feelings, to think about the fact that she might also be suffering, or wonder what the effect on her might be of finding out as a new bride living in unfamiliar surroundings, when it was already too late to back out, that her husband was in love with another woman.

Rustam also still resents the fact that she rejected his attempts at bringing them emotionally closer together at the time when *he* wanted this, after nearly four years of virtually ignoring her. He feels extremely hurt that she does not appear to have developed any feelings for him. In other words, he believes with Rashid that his wife should love him irrespective of his behaviour towards her. If she does not it is *her* fault, not his. Interestingly enough, while Rustam thinks he is too ugly to attract another woman like Zhenia, he does not seem to think he is to blame for Jumbul's inability to care for him. He believes this is because her values are all wrong, because she cares only about money and possessions, rather than about human relationships and emotions.

The theme of alienation looms large in the stories both of Tahmina and Rustam. For Tahmina it is a double alienation since she is in a new and unwelcoming, if not downright hostile, environment. However many problems she might have with her husband she expected to have a good relationship with the women around her, so their rejection has in some ways been harder to bear than the problems of her relationship with Rashid.

Tahmina would not call herself happy, but since she decided to try to make the best of her situation she has at least found a measure of contentment. She no longer lies awake wondering whether to leave Rashid but rather how to solve their financial problems. The only way she can get free of her mother-in-law is if she and Rashid can afford to move into their own home. As Rashid is the oldest son they should be able to live separately when his brother marries but their financial situation will not allow it.

Rustam does not have to live with his in-laws but it is perhaps no less difficult for him to put up with the hostility of his own parents. This is very confusing for him. On the one hand he loves them, wants to please them and dreads them saying nasty things to him. On the other, he risked arousing their ire if they found out about the continuation of his relationship with Zhenia.

While Rustam is indifferent to the personal charms of his bride, Rashid, with no prior emotional commitment, found himself attracted to Tahmina at first sight. But a great deal more than mere physical attributes are necessary for Tahmina to develop positive feelings towards him. It is how he treats her that counts. Had their sexual relations been good, things would no doubt have been very different (see below). As it is, the realisation that while a few women are happy in their marriages, more suffer at the hands of violent and unpleasant husbands, brings Tahmina to count her blessings rather than long for a happiness she feels no hope of attaining.

At the age of 22 it seems that her life is already set in the pattern it will follow until she is old and she does not see the point of being unhappy all that time. She has also rebuilt her relationship with her mother since Jahongul's marriage turned out so badly, especially since 1998 when Nahdiya had a stroke and almost died.

Robiya

Robiya is 29 and comes from a village in Kofernihon. When she was in high school she fell in love with a student from the Dushanbe Pedagogical Institute, who had come to the village for teaching practice, but he left at the end of term and never contacted her again. Robiya didn't know where he lived so all she could do was to wait for him to get in touch.

Meanwhile, she finished high school and wanted to go to Dushanbe to study, but her mother would not allow this. Robiya wanted to be a poet. Although her mother refused to allow her to study Robiya worked on her poetry by herself in her spare time, putting all her feelings for her friend into this.

Several years went by. One day a lad from her village who had also studied at the Pedagogical Institute told Robiya her friend had graduated and gone home and that it was pointless her waiting for him any longer. She was upset but it had been a long time since she had seen him and her feelings for him were no longer very strong.

When Robiya was 22 her mother decided to marry her off and found her a husband from the central township of Kofernihon. They were married in April 1988. Although they had not known each other before the wedding they liked each other immediately and quickly fell very much in love. They were extremely happy together, except for the fact that she didn't seem to be able to conceive, but she went for treatment and had just succeeded in becoming pregnant when the civil war started.

Robiya's husband was unjustly suspected of favouring the Opposition. One night a group of masked men came and asked him for money. He gave them everything he had. After this Robiya begged him to leave the house. She wanted them to go to her mother in the village, or anywhere else where it was unlikely he would be found, but he refused. A few nights later the men came back. As soon as Robiya opened the door they put a gun to her head and demanded her husband. When he came out they ordered him to accompany them. Her husband turned to Robiya and told her not to be afraid. Then he went off. She never saw or heard from him again. That was in 1993. His family searched far and wide but found no trace of him. They looked in Afghanistan, Pakistan and all over Tajikistan. They even showed his photo on television, to no avail. They have now given up all hope of his still being alive.

Robiya refuses to believe this. She has decided to wait for him as long as it takes, if necessary for the rest of her life. Meanwhile, shortly after his disappearance she gave birth to his son, so at least she has something of him left. After they decided her husband was dead, her parents-in-law asked Robiya to leave their house. Her son is now living with her mother in their village while Robiya is working in Dushanbe. Her mother has been trying to get her to marry again but she refuses. In Dushanbe there are several men after her but she will not pay attention to anyone.

Robiya is one of the success stories of arranged marriages. Perhaps she and her husband were especially compatible or perhaps it was that she had already been in love once that made her emotionally open to her husband, or both. In this she was unlike Tahmina, who had never allowed herself to become emotionally involved with anyone before her marriage.

Marriage for love

Tillo

Chahonbek started to court Tillo at the end of 1994 when he was 30 years old and she was nearly 35 and had five children from her first two husbands. Chahonbek was still married to his first and primary wife by whom he had three children. At the beginning of 1995 Chahonbek decided he wanted to marry Tillo. It took a long time for him to get her to agree but eventually she did so. Tillo told me that this was because she had fallen in love with him. However, she told her neighbours she had married him so that he would provide well for her and her children, even though she was doing pretty well financially.

Soon after the wedding one of Chahonbek's friends told him that Tillo looked like a television star and recommended him not to let her go to work because she was much too good looking. Chahonbek came home and told Tillo. He said that he would never,

ever allow her to work outside the house again. He threatened to take a knife or gun to her if he caught her even saying hello to a man and forbade her to leave the house or even to stand at her front gate. 'If I ever catch you talking to a man I will kill you and then myself', he said.

Chahonbek says he is aware that such jealousy is a sickness but he cannot help himself. The thought of Tillo having the slightest thing to do with another man makes him ill. If he sees a man so much as looking at her in the street he immediately says, 'That's your lover saying hello to you.' He refuses to believe she didn't have a lover while she was single, even though she swears it on God's name. He says he doesn't trust any woman.

At that time Chahonbek had a good job as deputy director of a factory so there was no immediate need for Tillo to work. This did not stop her hating being forced to stay at home all the time. When Chahonbek was at work she would often visit her immediate neighbours, although she didn't dare go any further. The rest of the time she was bored stiff. She is not interested in reading and expects her daughters to do most of the housework. She finds her main interests in chatting with her friends and in being active outside the house. When deprived of these she would generally end up sleeping the day away.

Although she chafed against the restrictions Tillo did not refuse to obey Chahonbek. She felt she had no option but to do so, since Tajik women were expected to do what their husbands told them. She was the more inclined to comply, since she was in love for the first time in her life. She would spend all day waiting for him to come home. She said the two of them were so much in love that all they did when apart was to think of one another and long for the moment they could be together again.

Nevertheless, she was glad to share Chahonbek with his primary wife because this gave her some respite. When he slept at her place he insisted on making love all night and then wanted her to get up very early, fetch him water to wash in and make his breakfast before he went to work. She found this absolutely exhausting. It was good that he spent alternate nights with his primary wife.

Nevertheless, Chahonbek much preferred his time with Tillo because they really loved each other. In theory, on the days he spent with his primary wife he and Tillo should not have seen each other. However, he usually dropped in to see her after work, since he missed her so much. Tillo did not know life could be this wonderful. 'Living without a man is boring. A woman needs a husband to make life interesting', she said.

But her marriage was not all gain. In the evenings Chahonbek would return from work around 7.00 p.m. and Tillo had to give him his meal immediately and also be ready to sit with him and talk, and not allow her children to annoy him. Chahonbek smoked a great deal, which Tillo didn't like. He also drank alcohol and tried to get her to drink with him but she wouldn't, not even when he taunted her with the fact that his primary wife did so. Tillo did not like the idea of drinking alcohol. She thought it was a sin. Muslims should not drink.

Everyone laughed at Tillo for agreeing to become a secondary wife, which is considered demeaning. But Tillo thought it was a good solution for her. When she first married Chahonbek she thought that, as a secondary wife, she would have all the perks of being a wife without any of the problems. A secondary wife, according to her reckoning, would have a nice warm emotional relationship with her husband without the need to take care of such material requirements as washing his clothes and, above *all, without having to bear his children. As long as he had children by his primary wife with whom he was still living, he would not need to have a child with her. She would be able to get on with her life just as before, but with the added emotional support of a husband. However, it did not quite work out like that.*

A few months after Tillo's marriage Chahonbek's primary wife came over one evening, carrying a large knife. She started screaming at Chahonbek about his bad treatment of her and trying to run him through. He managed to get the knife away from her without any damage but became so incensed he said three taloqs *and that was that. The following day he brought all his belongings over to Tillo's place. Not long afterwards one of his children died and Chahonbek blamed his former wife's indifference. A few days later he took his remaining children from her home to be brought up by his brother in their native village, saying he considered her an unfit mother.*

The shock of all this calmed his former wife down. She now deeply regretted provoking Chahonbek to lose his temper and renounce her. She felt so bad about it that she came and told Tillo she wanted Chahonbek back, on any terms at all, even if only for one night a week. Tillo was in favour but he categorically refused. This made Tillo feel really bad. She had never meant it to turn out that way. She had not intended to hurt his former wife, to steal her husband from her. 'She is also a woman like me', she said. This was the first time I heard Tillo express any fellow feeling for her. Before this she had only had bad things to say about her: how unattractive and what a bad housekeeper she was, and a nag and so on.

Now that Tillo had become his primary wife Chahonbek began putting tremendous pressure on her to become pregnant. But she absolutely loathed the idea. For years she had been grumbling about the five children she already had. If she had had any sense at all, she would say, she would have left it at two. She finds her children intensely irritating and would much prefer to be without them. She certainly didn't want a sixth.

Chahonbek took no notice of this. He said he wanted her to give him the pleasure of having a child for him. She gave her other two husbands children and if she really loved him more than them then surely she would give him one. She told him over and over that she didn't want another child but he wouldn't take no for an answer.

After he divorced his first wife Chahonbek started to press Tillo to have her IUD removed. She would agree to this, but then would always manage to put it off until the following month. In this way she managed for a long time to postpone getting pregnant. She said she would tell Chahonbek she had had it removed without actually doing so, in order to stop him badgering her. Then she would pretend to be trying to get pregnant. However, Chahonbek did not fall for this. He insisted on taking her to a doctor friend. Finally, Tillo decided perhaps it would be better to have another child than to suffer so much pain from the IUD, as well as put up with Chahonbek's constant nagging.

In summer 1995 Tillo removed her IUD and immediately became pregnant. However, this pregnancy was very difficult and she miscarried at four months. She started bleeding and rushed to the toilet, with blood pouring out of her. She continued haemorrhaging severely for two days. Chahonbek wanted to take her to the hospital but she said, 'Why bother? I've just had a miscarriage, that's all. It's over and done with.'

But then she collapsed. Chahonbek rushed her to the hospital. When the doctors told him she was as good as dead he pleaded with them desperately to save her. So they stopped the bleeding and gave her intravenous liquids, glucose and so on. Eventually she returned to consciousness. Her blood pressure had been practically zero and the doctors told her afterwards that in another 15 minutes she would have died. Chahonbek paid US $300 for her stay in the hospital. After she was discharged he made sure she ate well and she soon began to feel healthy again.

The doctors told Tillo that she should on no account get pregnant again within the following three months. They did not take any precautions to prevent this; however, she was lucky and it did not happen. Immediately the three months were up Chahonbek started badgering her again, 'Just have one child for me. What kind of a life is this without a child?' Tillo believed if she didn't have his child soon he would leave her. She got pregnant again, but by the time the baby was born their relationship had become very fraught and Tillo was relieved when it was stillborn, especially because it was a girl. She was sure that even had the child lived Chahonbek would not have stopped pressuring her to have another until she gave him a son.

Soon after Chahonbek had come to live full-time with Tillo he started to buy electronic goods. First he brought home a colour television and later a VCR. However, not long after he had bought this last, the factory where he worked was forced to halt production and his pay-cheque was significantly reduced. Nevertheless, he continued to spend all day out of the house and to buy things as before.

Later it turned out that he had borrowed an enormous sum of money from some mafia acquaintances in order to buy heroin, which he had been intending to sell at a large profit. Unfortunately, instead of doing this he had started to use it himself, thus squandering almost the entire loan.

He stopped buying any but the bare essentials, even reducing their food to a minimum. He began to resent having to support his stepchildren and to bring home just enough meat, butter and other more expensive foodstuffs to feed himself and Tillo. The two of them would eat together in an inner room while the children remained outside. When I saw what was going on I asked Tillo how Chahonbek got on with her children and whether he treated them well. She replied that he was fine with them, that they had no problems, although it seemed clear to me that he tried to have as little as possible to do with them. He even refused to pay for Tillo's younger son to be circumcised, which caused a big scandal in the neighbourhood. The children were often so hungry they would go round scrounging food, thus making their mother's neglect of them public and arousing the disdain of the neighbours even more (Chapter 3).

Then one day Chahonbek vanished. Tillo did not know what had happened to him. She thought he had perhaps been arrested but the following night several armed men came to her house demanding money or they would kill her and her children. She said she had no idea what they were talking about and had no money to give them. This was the first Tillo had heard of Chahonbek's loan and she was horrified. It turned out they had kidnapped Chahonbek and were now warning Tillo of the seriousness of the situation.

A couple of days later Chahonbek was released. He returned to Tillo and told her they must go away and work as traders until they could amass enough money to pay his debts. His family would help them obtain wares. Tillo felt she had no option but to agree. So, leaving the children in charge of her second daughter, at that time about 16 years old, she and Chahonbek left. They were away for over six months during which time the children were left completely on their own, except for the occasional sack of flour or a few roubles that Tillo managed to send them. This was far from adequate to support them, however, and had it not been for the neighbours the children would have been hard pressed to survive.

Eventually Chahonbek was able to pay off most of his creditors and he and Tillo returned home. But they still had debts to his family and to her neighbours, who had kept her children going all this time. They were even living on borrowed money, as neither of them had a job.

At this point, Tillo's elder son, then 15, decided to go to Moscow to look for work. Sadbarg's (Chapter 5) second brother and he were best friends and planned to go together. Tillo was not happy about this and refused to give him any money. So he sold their television set, and used the proceeds to buy himself a train ticket. When they found out, Tillo and Chahonbek beat the boy so badly he had to remain in bed for several days. This upset him so much he swore he would have nothing further to do with his mother and as soon as he was well enough he and his friend set off for Moscow.

Tillo is generally very hard on her children, routinely calling them the most appalling names. Perhaps her resentment of them derives from their symbolising her lack of control over her life. She openly admits finding it difficult to have any positive feelings for them, thinking of them as a cross she must bear because she was stupid enough to give birth to them. And she does not try to conceal her feelings from them, often bemoaning the fact that she did not take control over her life until after her second husband had left her. Before that she had never thought it possible to make any decisions for herself. She had passively accepted whatever happened to her. She now bitterly and vocally regrets this.

With neither herself nor Chahonbek earning, Tillo was concerned about how they were all going to live. She tried to discuss this with Chahonbek but he refused to listen. Something would turn up, he just knew it. Tillo proposed that the two of them jointly start a trading venture similar to the one she had been involved in before their marriage, travelling to Russia, the Emirates, Iran and other places to buy goods, and bringing them back to Tajikistan to sell. But Chahonbek neither wanted to go on his own nor to take her with him.

When they made no attempt to pay back their current debts their creditors started threatening them once more. This time Chahonbek fled Tajikistan, leaving Tillo to face them alone. She made an agreement with them to give her time to pay, and then immediately restarted her business. She was so successful that within six months she had managed to pay off all their debts. Meanwhile, her son in Moscow had ended up in prison and Tillo was forced to find the money to buy him out. Four and a half years after marrying Chahonbek, Tillo's life is slowly coming back together again. However, those years have wrought considerable havoc. Her relations with her family are practically non-existent. Her health has suffered severely. Her elder son has never really forgiven her and her younger children feel quite hostile towards her.

She is still not sure whether Chahonbek will ever return to her, nor what will happen if he does. She would like to divorce him but doesn't know how. Only a man has the right to say taloq. *Tillo very much regrets ever marrying him and says if he will only divorce her and leave her in peace she will never marry again. She does not have much hope of this, however, as Chahonbek has no money and only a small flat of his own in Dushanbe. She knows that it will be only too easy for him to return to her house if he decides to come back. She fears his return partly because she knows she still has a soft spot for him and that this would make it more difficult to throw him out definitively, besides she is not sure she physically could get rid of him if he were determined to stay.*

The story of Tillo's third marriage shows the complex power struggles between these spouses. Chahonbek manages to force his wife apparently to obey him but can neither conquer her spirit nor stop her from rebelling in his absence. At the same time she cannot impose her wishes on him, even when he is in a desperate position and needs her help to pay his debts.

It is not clear what Tillo thought she would get out of marriage with Chahonbek in the first place. The discrepancy between her telling her neighbours she married for financial reasons and saying to me that she did it for love was striking. Was she telling each of us what she thought would be the most acceptable? Or did Tillo express her real feelings to me, but find this inappropriate to say to Tajik women who would doubtless have thought her insane? As an honorary Russian I would be expected to believe in love rather than material gain as a valid reason for marriage. Tillo's behaviour would seem to suggest that this last might have been the real reason. However, it is entirely possible that *both* factors were important and that she was merely saying what she felt most appropriate to each of us. And there may have been a third reason also – Chahonbek was really pressuring her hard and she may have felt she had little recourse but to marry him, especially in the light of her brothers' treatment (Chapter 3).

Tillo's experience shows that marriage for love does not necessarily work out any better than an arranged marriage. However, both love matches and arranged marriages *can* be happy. For instance, as opposed to Tahmina's and Jahongul's unhappy fate, their mother Nahdiya, like Robiya, was extremely happy in her own arranged marriage. Karomat was also happy until her in-laws started interfering (Chapter 5).

Karomat

Karomat was very happy as a young bride living with her mother-in-law and her husband. He was quite different from her father. When Karomat was a child her father had treated his house like a hotel. He had five daughters and would expect all of them to wait on him, as well as his wife. He would come in the door and shout, 'Boots!' and one daughter would rush to take them off, another to clean them, while a third would lay the dastarkhon, *as their mother prepared food. After eating he would lie down, and the whole family would tiptoe around so as not to disturb him.*

Khudoydod was not nearly so demanding. He was a long-distance lorry driver on the Dushanbe–Khorog run, which would take five or more days at a time. Then he would have a few days off, during which he would do a lot of work around the house although, of course, not women's work. He loved to have Karomat helping him while he fixed things. He liked her to be near him always when he was at home. He would dig the vegetable plot while she planted. However, Karomat did not have much time for this because she had her own work to do.

After World War II was over her still unmarried sisters returned to school. Karomat wanted to study also. However, Khudoydod would not let her. He said that if she did this she would be no use to him afterwards. Girls who studied were ruined. They either slept around or married 'foreigners' – Uzbeks, Tatars or even Russians. He did not want an educated wife. In the end Karomat agreed not to study even though she wanted to very much. She was always a quick learner and loved knowing things. Her sisters all went on to tertiary education and married fellow students – Tajiks. None of them lost their reputations.

Khudoydod's worst failing was his jealousy. Karomat was not allowed to leave the house unless he or his mother accompanied her. The only place she was permitted to go on her own was to work. But there were times when Khudoydod did not even allow her to have a job at all. After her third child was stillborn he ordered her to stop working.

Karomat got very bored without children to keep her occupied, especially as Khudoydod was away so much. So after some time staying home she asked for permission to work again. He told her he had made her stay at home because the neighbours had been mocking him for being unable to support even one wife and explained that was why he didn't want her to go out to work again. She said, 'But the wife of this friend of yours works and the wife of that relative. Are they worse than me or am I worse than them? Why shouldn't I work?' Finally, he said, 'Okay, go out to work then. I don't want you to be bored. Probably the people who said those things to me are our enemies. Go back to work.' So she did.

Karomat was very happy with Khudoydod. Their personal relationship was great at every level. 'There's nothing better in the world than a husband and wife together', she said. 'They look after each other when they are sick, give each other massages, bring each other things to eat and drink, and do lots of other nice things for each other. They respect each other; the wife obeys her husband and they are happy together.'

Unfortunately, Karomat and Khudoydod did not remain together for life, since she insisted on divorcing him so he could have children (Chapter 5). However, despite the divorce and all the years since, Karomat never stopped loving him. She almost always spoke of him with great affection and continued to call him 'my husband'. When he came to her father's funeral she was very excited and pleased. Had she been less proud she might never have divorced him, but she could not bear the daily reminders of her failure to provide a living child expressed by Khudoydod's relatives. She often voiced her regret at the circumstances that had made her feel compelled to divorce him and, especially after her parents died, felt lonely without him. Although she had a number of offers of marriage after her divorce, she would never contemplate accepting any of them. She said she could not understand how, having been to bed with one man, a woman could ever bring herself to touch another.

The best thing about being divorced was being her own boss. For all their good rela-tionship Khudoydod took it for granted that Karomat should obey him and she had never been completely comfortable with that, being generally very outspoken and not liking to rein in her tongue. So it was difficult for her to keep quiet in front of Khudoydod, just because he was a man.

Once again the norms that allow men to boss their wives made things difficult for the woman. Even such a loving spouse as Khudoydod could not accept equality with his wife, despite her strength of character. But at least Karomat received real joy from their relationship, and had a good life afterwards with her beloved parents. Hard as it was for her to end up on her own as she did, Karomat still seemed to me to have lived far more happily than most other Tajik women. She also really enjoyed her 25 years working at the textile factory and missed this in retirement.

Karomat and Robiya had as happy marriages as any among the women I met in Tajikistan. Their stories demonstrate that love is possible in either arranged or love marriages, providing the circumstances are propitious and the partners willing. One thing they both had in common was that they had stepped outside the convention that refuses girls permission to have pre-marital emotional contact with someone of the opposite sex, experiences that had awakened them emotionally and thus prepared them for marriage. They were also very lucky in having husbands who really loved them and treated them well, a rare occurrence in Tajikistan, irrespective of how the marriage is contracted.

Gender relations in marriage

The important thing for many men is not so much that their wives actually submit to them, as that they *demonstrate* public submission. Therefore, in front of others Tajik women have to be careful to keep their gender masks in place, in order not to shame their husbands.

Many Tajik men now migrate to Russia where, like Eshmurod (Chapter 5) they have married again. Despite the fact that they have learned to enjoy more open relationships in Russia, which makes them complain of boredom with their Tajik marriages, these men refuse to allow either their wives or their daughters greater mobility or exposure to the outside world. For all their grumbling, the last thing they actually seem to want is for their Tajik wives to become Russified. Eshmurod makes his attitude clear in his insistence on changing his gender performance on his return to Tajikistan. There is no way he would allow his wife to change hers instead. The same appears to be true for most men in Sayot.

It is impossible to know how much this is due to social pressures that would call their masculinity into question if their wives do not conform, and how much to their wish to continue their relatively comfortable domestic situations. It is likely that both are important factors. They certainly weigh heavily against any perceived benefits these men might gain from their wives making changes in their gender performances that would make them more interesting to live with.

SEXUAL RELATIONS

The marriage bed is the place where gender performance is at its most critical, where the whole façade of a person's performance will be shown to have a sound basis or revealed to be false. The successful start of marriage is dependent on the woman demonstrating her femininity through bestowing her virginity on her husband, a symbol of her willingness to belong submissively to him only. The man must prove his masculinity by a demonstration of his virility, a symbol of his ability to control. Together they confirm their parents' success in producing children capable of the correct gender performances, thus preserving family honour. Conversely, the masculine-seeming man who cannot achieve an erection or the most apparently compliant woman who cannot prove her virginity at the appropriate time is shown up as a failure.

Most married couples know each other very little, if at all, before their wedding night and any emotional relationship will have to be built up after this. Since almost the only time when most couples will be alone together will be at night in the bedroom, this puts even more onus on the quality of their sexual relationship, as it is practically the only personal contact they will have, unless or until they get a separate place of their own.

This is one of the moments, however, when the rigidity of Tajik gender norms and the puritanical nature of the Soviet state combine to make it extremely difficult to develop mutual sexual enjoyment. The latter is responsible for young people's almost total lack of knowledge about sexual matters, while the former makes it practically impossible for most girls to have a chance to explore their own sexuality before having to have intercourse on the first night of marriage. The result tends to be inevitably that few men are either knowledgeable enough to make their brides enjoy sex or sensitive enough to care when instead it becomes an agonisingly unpleasant and even abusive experience, if not (virtual) rape. For women sex is made even more problematic because up until the moment of marriage this has usually been a mere chimera, something that they may in fact not even have been fully aware existed.

Marital sex

In Tajikistan and culturally related societies, the wedding night is the occasion for the young couples' symbolic transformation into adults. The perforation of the hymen makes the bride a woman, ready to bear children. The 'public' act of perforating it on his wedding night brings a man to full adult sexuality (see Lindisfarne 1994: 92). This was so important that before the revolution, when marriage was very expensive for the groom and many families were poverty-stricken, the poorest men might spend years saving up to marry a virgin even though marrying a divorcée or widow would have cost very much less (Shishov 1904: 364).

This sheds further light on Malik's refusal to allow Rustam to marry a non-virgin and on that of those young Tajik men who refuse to marry their non-virgin girlfriends, even when they were responsible for the loss of their hymen. This would deprive them of that supreme moment of transition. However many times a man might previously have had sex, however many virgins he may have deflowered, it is the wedding night that counts because here he is publicly demonstrating his virility. This may also partly account for the fact that so many men deprived of this vital rite of passage by being forced to marry the girlfriends they had previously deflowered, subsequently show them considerable violence.

Looked at from this angle, one could say that the bleeding of the bride on her wedding night is in reality more important as a demonstration of her husband's virility than of any attribute of hers. Her virginity is a requirement for her husband to be able to complete his passage into adulthood. This is perhaps the answer to why it is so vital for girls to preserve their virginity for the marriage night. Naamane-Guessous tells of one mother who never fully accepted the fact that her son had chosen to marry a divorced woman. Sixteen years later she managed to force him to divorce his first wife and marry a virgin so he could have the pleasure of defloration (1991: 124). Finally, her son had become a 'true man'!

But the first night is of course only the start of sexual relations. For those few couples that click it will be great, but for most it can be highly problematic, especially where the woman really suffered on the first occasion and now dreads sex. Under Muslim law a woman does not have the right to refuse her husband (Bouhdiba 1975: 111). Tajik women may not know this but they rarely dare rebuff them. It is impossible to assess the incidence of marital rape in Tajikistan. Although rape within marriage has been a crime since Soviet times, as far as I know nobody has ever made a formal accusation of this, even if the sexual practices many of the health-project participants described could certainly be classified as such.

Davlatpochcha

When Davlatpochcha married for the first time she knew vaguely that a man sticks something into a woman somewhere but not how, what or where. This she only found out on her wedding night, when her husband behaved so repulsively towards her that afterwards the very idea of having sex with him was revolting. Being with him was like having a dog in bed. He was ugly and she couldn't stand him to touch her.

Immediately after marriage Davlatpochcha became pregnant. Her grandmother told her she should have lots of children – preferably ten. Davlatpochcha was totally ignorant and just went along with what people said. Her husband made her pregnant and she produced the children. In any case what else could she do? It is a sin to have an abortion; it is like taking a life. So she had four children, at 18-month intervals, after which her husband divorced her, leaving her alone with the children.

With Saydali, Davlatpochcha's second husband, she started to enjoy sex for the first time, at least when he was not too forceful. Her first husband, a big brawny man, had a small penis. Saydali is not big but he has a very large penis and sometimes thrusts so hard he hurts her. When she complains he just says, 'Nonsense, you have four children. This can't possibly hurt', and continues as before.

It is also painful if they have too much sex. Saydali wants sex virtually every night, sometimes several times, and cannot bear to wait the few days for her period to end, although he knows it is a sin to have sex at that time. Her IUD makes it still more painful. The doctor told her to wait twelve days after insertion before having sex. However, as soon as they were married Saydali insisted on having sex right away. This started her haemorrhaging and she also began to experience abdominal pain but she could not be bothered to go back to the doctor. She thought that if she just ignored it the pain would go away on its own.

Despite his encouragement Davlatpochcha is too embarrassed to tell Saydali what she would like him to do to make sex more enjoyable for her. However, when it does not hurt she quite often has an orgasm. She finds this both incredible and wonderful. Before her second marriage she had not realised such a sensation could exist. Davlatpochcha is also happy when Saydali tells her how much pleasure she gives him. He loves her body. It is just the shape Tajik men admire – a big bottom, and a small waist and breasts, which Saydali especially likes to stroke.

It is only recently that Davlatpochcha has begun to feel desire and she thinks this is partly due to the love she feels for Saydali and partly to her age. She thinks that this last has helped her experience arousal but also that sex should be associated with love, otherwise it is not pleasant. She and Saydali have a good time in bed because they love each other and he enjoys this as much as she does. For both of them it is the first time they have fallen in love.

Saydali was not really in love with his first wife, who hated sex, and so he did not like sleeping with her. She was not attractive, especially after having seven children. During sex she would just lie there like a lump and cry because she disliked it so much. For this reason, Saydali had lots of girlfriends and was hardly ever home. But after his marriage to Davlatpochcha he said he did not need to stray because she fulfilled all his needs.

Nevertheless, their happiness did not last. A couple of years after they got married Saydali lost his job and when he couldn't find another one he started to drink heavily and to take drugs. Then he would come home very late and insist on having sex virtually non-stop, all night long, so that she would be in a dreadful state by morning, all swollen. Eventually he made her life so unbearable she threw him out.

Tahmina

On the third day after Tahmina's wedding one of her sisters-in-law said something about sex. Tahmina asked, 'What's that?' Her sister-in-law said, 'Don't you know? Your husband sleeps with you and then you bleed a lot.'

Tahmina had never heard anything about this. She thought babies were just given by God. 'After all, we Tajiks always say we will have as many children as God gives.' She thought the wife and husband lay side by side in bed and the wife got pregnant through her menstruation. This was what she had understood people were referring to when they talked of women bleeding at marriage time. She did know that she had to be careful not to jump too much or do anything that would make her a woman and not a girl[1] but she had never known why. She had had no idea of the existence of sex.

Her sister-in-law's mention of it told Tahmina very little. It was just enough to get her frightened. For a week she managed to go to bed so late that Rashid was already asleep. Then finally she was persuaded to go to bed at the same time as he did and agree to having sex. Rashid was quite gentle and used persuasion rather than force. However, it took him 3–4 hours to be able to get an erection and then the sex hurt so much it was awful. Her head hurt and she had a bad pain between her legs. Afterwards her stomach and back hurt also. The next day she felt so ghastly she could hardly move. Nevertheless, Tahmina thinks she was lucky to have been able to wait until she was at least somewhat psychologically prepared and also that Rashid was relatively gentle. She has heard from other women that most husbands insist on sex on the very first night and that some just remove their wife's clothes, by force if necessary, and rape them.

A week after they first had sex Rashid wanted it again but Tahmina absolutely refused. She was even more afraid than before, since now she knew how much it hurt. Eventually he persuaded her and they did it again but it still hurt a great deal. By now she so much hated his touching her that even an accidental brush of his hand was torture. At night she would wait until he was asleep and then roll as far away from him as possible, to prevent any chance contact. She particularly hated it when Rashid wanted to French kiss. Before her marriage she didn't know such kisses existed and she found them disgusting.

It definitely hurt less if they had sex every week, especially if they had it several times. Despite this Tahmina tried to avoid it as much as possible. Most of the time when Rashid wanted sex she would say, 'Just a minute', or make some excuse and then wait in the next room until he went to sleep. Then he wouldn't wake up until morning. Usually after that it would be a week before he'd ask again. In the village Tahmina mostly refused because they don't have a bathroom inside the house and she hated not being able to wash properly.

While they were living in Dushanbe they settled down to having sex once every 2–3 weeks. But they started to lose a lot of weight and thought it was because they were having too much, so they cut down. Neither of them was really enjoying it. Then Rashid discovered he had inflammation of the penis. After he was cured he wanted sex more often. However, gradually they settled down to once a month.

Tahmina couldn't understand how Rashid could possibly get pleasure from this unpleasant act, but he told her he did and however extraordinary she found it, she had to believe him, otherwise why would he want to continue?

Before Tahmina married lots of boys in her class told her they loved her or that she was attractive to them. But as soon as one of them said such a thing to her she never wanted to speak to him again. The very idea he might want to touch her was completely repulsive. After several years of marriage she had still never experienced sexual arousal. Indeed, she couldn't begin to imagine what this could possibly feel like. Hoping to learn more about it, she confessed her problem to a group of young women in Rashid's village,[2] *who appeared to know more about sex than her friends in Dushanbe, and to enjoy it more. One of them lent her a book on sexual positions her husband had brought back from Russia. Tahmina leafed through it but found the pictures repulsive. The book made no mention of women's erogenous zones and Tahmina knew nothing about these.*

After Tahmina got pregnant Rashid agreed not to have sex until after the baby was born. He told her he didn't want to risk harming the baby merely for a few moments of pleasure. Some of the women in the hospital ward she stayed in during her pregnancy said that after their first child was born they began to love their husband and want sex for the first time. Tahmina began to hope this might happen to her, as she was convinced it would improve her marriage. She realised that it was Tajik women's embarrassment about sex and lack of enjoyment that caused so many of their husbands to seek Russian girlfriends.

However, the baby's birth has not made much difference. Sex is less painful but still not arousing. At least being used to it she does not mind it as much. She knows that she must not refuse Rashid all the time or he will find a Russian woman and maybe bring her back a disease.

Rustam

Rustam had been interested in sex and had started discussing it with his Russian school-friends in his mid-teens. From them he had learned how to arouse a girl and about the existence of the clitoris. He believes that it is the man's duty to make sex enjoyable for the woman.

He was initiated into sex at age 17 by a Russian girl. Afterwards the first thing he did was ask, 'Are you pregnant now?' The girl explained to him about the safe period and subsequently he used this method of contraception with his other girlfriends.

Before Rustam married nobody in his family told him anything about sex, although they did not know he was experienced. The only person to say anything beforehand was his grandmother. 'You will have to prove you are a man now', she admonished him, before he was dispatched to have almost public sex with his bride.

This consummation was one of the most painful experiences of Rustam's life. He was sent into a room in his parents' house with both his family and that of his wife next door, able to hear almost everything that transpired. In this room Jumbul was waiting for him. He found it degrading and humiliating to be forced to perform such an intimate act with a stranger. Having to do it virtually in public made it much worse.

It was not made any the easier by Jumbul's insistence on the utmost modesty. She made him turn out the light. She would not remove any garments beyond her ezor. He tried to stroke her to get her aroused before penetration, but she did not welcome his caresses, telling him it was shameful to do such things. It took the most tremendous will power and strength of mind to force himself to concentrate enough to get, and maintain, an erection.

While Zhenia was still in Tajikistan, Rustam performed his 'marital duties' as rarely as possible. Jumbul never allowed him any more freedom than before. Every attempt to make sex more pleasurable for her, or more interesting for him was met with a protesting 'ayb'. What a contrast to Zhenia, with whom he made love whenever her parents were away from home, which fortunately was frequently. Being in bed with her was absolute heaven. She was experienced, uninhibited and loving.

It took the birth of four children before Jumbul began to feel any sort of sexual awakening. At that point she began to undress totally before sex to give Rustam access to parts of her body he had never before touched. And for the first time she began to reach orgasm. However, she remained adamant that only one position was respectable, that the light had to be out, and that she was going to take no active part whatsoever. She also made it clear that her new-found sexuality did not come in any way from increased feelings for Rustam. It was purely a matter of horniness, not a sign of desire or affection for him, still less of love. Indeed, if he tries to show affection rather than merely satisfying her sexually she shies away and tells him not to mess about but to get on with it. This he finds very frustrating since for him sex is about the expression of caring.

Sitora

When Sitora and Haydar got married, her in-laws' house had only one room so she and her husband had to share it with his parents and other family members, separated from them only by a curtain. When her husband wanted sex he would give her a special sign so she could prepare herself. The young couple would then go to bed first and the others would wait up to allow them time by themselves. They would make love and then lie in bed until the others had come in and fallen asleep. Afterwards they would tiptoe quietly outside and wash. Later they built on another room so they could have privacy. Of course, it is not pleasant to make love when other people are around.

During the first three years of their marriage Sitora got no enjoyment from sex but she liked being with Haydar, even though he did not know how to arouse her and she didn't understand the point of it all, aside from conceiving children. When she was first married her mother-in-law told her that she should just give in to her husband's desire for sex whenever he wanted, to prevent his going to another woman. So she did.

Haydar's job sometimes allowed him time off in the afternoons and then he would come home at midday for sex and food. Sitora found this a great bore.

Then one day, Haydar's workmates started to discuss how to turn a woman on. One of the Russians explained what a man should do for his wife to enjoy sex. He said that the woman had to climax first and only then should the man let himself go. Haydar confessed he had never given any thought to his wife's pleasure. The Russian was amazed that she had allowed him to get away with it and neither taken a lover nor been annoyed with him. Haydar said that neither of them had known that a woman could enjoy sex so it hadn't occurred to his wife she had been hard done by.

That afternoon Haydar went home and wanted to try out what he had learned. Sitora became absolutely furious, accusing him of having taken a lover and of practising on his wife the tricks he had learned with his mistress. 'Don't treat me like your whore!', she told him. Haydar protested his innocence but Sitora wouldn't believe him. Every night he tried to give her pleasure in bed and every night she would be angry with him. Eventually he couldn't stand it any more and told her where he had learned it, but she didn't believe him.

Then, a few days later she was talking with a Russian friend who explained that men discussed sex among themselves and that Russian men were much better informed than Tajiks. Sitora realised that what Haydar had told her had probably been true and she went home and apologised for having misjudged him.

Only then did she allow him to try out what he had learned and it was really great. Haydar was very tender with her and showed her so much love. After that they never again had sex without his making sure she enjoyed it and they began to have a wonderful time in bed together so that their relationship became even better than before.

The contrast between these men's attitudes to their own sexuality is striking. Saydali is clearly highly insecure in his masculinity, needing to prove it over and over, while the other men are much more relaxed. Rashid seems to come from a different world from Saydali and to know little of other men's sex lives if he thinks sex a few times a month excessive. It would be good if someone like Haydar's workmate could give him some tips, but it is unlikely Tahmina would respond. She was horrified at the idea of so much physical contact when I discussed with her ways to help her learn to enjoy sex. Although Rustam has no special interest in Jumbul he nevertheless does his best to give her pleasure, if only because it is more satisfying for him to have a responsive woman in bed. Despite the emptiness of sex with someone for whom he feels nothing, Rustam says that as long as he has a wife, even one with whom he has no rapport, he would rather have sex with her than masturbate.

Most Tajik men do not appear to consider their wives' needs, perhaps because they have never known what it is to have sex with a responsive woman. As girls are usually too frightened to dare go in for petting before marriage they rarely have any understanding of sexual feelings and the obligation to preserve their virginity, dinned into them from childhood, often continues to inhibit their sexual feelings even after marriage. This may account for the fact that young Tajik women so rarely seem to experience sexual arousal.

It is impossible to know how many of them would have experienced this from the start of their marriage had their husbands been able and willing to arouse them. Unfortunately, although there is no discourse favouring female frigidity, many men are made nervous by a sexually responsive wife as they feel she may become unfaithful. Men who spend long periods away from home are particularly anxious on this score. There is thus a fine line between women enjoying themselves in bed and being considered (potentially) loose women.

Davlatpochcha and Jumbul seem to have grown into their sexual feelings as they got older. It is impossible to judge how much the former's enjoyment with Saydali came from the general horniness she had begun to feel, how much from her love for him and how much from his greater skill in bed than her previous husband. Most probably it was from a combination of the three. It is much too early to have any indication of how Tahmina's sexuality will change as she gets older but perhaps she too will start to want sex. Maybe then she will come to care more for Rashid, especially if he learns to satisfy her in bed.

Compatibility is not considered important in a society that prizes sex largely for producing children. But things are changing with greater exposure to the outside world. Younger couples, at any rate, are starting to expect something more out of their sex lives and if they do not get this there will eventually be problems. Even in Sayot, before the health project had got round to broaching the subject of sex, several of the younger women complained that they did not feel pleasure with their husbands.

The fact that so many previously unresponsive women develop sexual feelings around the age of 30 concurs with western sexological research that shows women becoming increasingly sexual with age (Hite 1976: 349ff). However, sex is not a purely physiological phenomenon and it is likely that the lack of sexual arousal in young women is in some measure connected to a lack of emotional response. Tahmina was not just sexually, but also emotionally, repressed. Before marriage she had feared the possible consequences far too much to allow herself any response to boys' attraction to her. Such emotional repression cannot help but have repercussions. Since sexual response is very much dependent on emotions this may be why it was that women who allowed themselves to feel emotionally connected to men before marriage were relatively quickly able to develop sexual feelings once their husbands learned how to arouse them.

Desire and passion

What place do desire and passion have in the sexual relations described above and what do these signify (see Lindisfarne 1994: 91)? Psychological research has shown important distinctions between sexual arousal, horniness and sexual desire. The first is a physical state marked by penile erection or vaginal lubrication. The second is a mental state of undirected sexual tension, while the third is sexual tension focused on a specific object (Shaffer 1997).

The difference among these can be illustrated by a comparison of Rustam's relations with Zhenia and Jumbul. For Zhenia Rustam felt *desire*, which he delighted in giving sexual expression to as often as possible. For Jumbul he feels little or nothing, so that he has sex with her only when he feels generally *horny*. He does not get *aroused* by thoughts of her but on the contrary uses thoughts of another in order to be able to become sufficiently *aroused* to be able to perform with her.

Similarly, Zhenia felt *desire* for Rustam, while even now that Jumbul experiences *sexual arousal* and orgasm Rustam does not believe this to be the result of specific emotions towards him but rather of an *undirected need for sexual release*. She never initiates sex, not even by doing things like dressing nicely or wearing scent to put him in the mood, nor does she behave other than passively either before or during it.

For many Tajik men their sexual feelings do not appear to be focused on a specific object of desire. In view of the fact that a man may not necessarily be especially turned on by his wife, particularly if she exhibits no significant sexual or emotional interest in him, this is not surprising. In the circumstances it is more surprising that there are couples like Sitora and Haydar.

In the second volume of his *History of Sexuality* (1992) Foucault asks how a person comes to see himself as a subject that can desire. Butler takes this further and asks, '[W]ho is it who is able to recognize him/herself as a subject of sexuality and how are the means of recognition controlled, dispersed, and regulated such that only a certain kind of subject is recognizable through them?' She further suggests that the development of agency is intimately linked to the development of sexual desire (Butler 1999: 19).

Butler is insinuating here that it is particularly women who are unable to recognise themselves as subjects of sexuality and thus to experience sexual desire. For Tajikistan it can further be said that most women have also been unable to conceptualise themselves as subjects of passionate love. Despite Tahmina's hope that she will one day feel such love this remains an alien emotion for her.

Segal points out that young women need narratives of desire in order to explore their sexuality. Physical experience alone may be insufficient (1994: 264). Both Butler and Segal are saying that in societies where there is no discourse on females as subjects of sexuality it will be difficult for them to experience sexual desire, that is, to allow themselves the freedom to focus sexually on a chosen person, rather than merely experiencing their sexuality within a socially sanctioned relationship with someone they may not be especially attracted to, and with whom they may not experience even arousal, let alone orgasm.

The taboos on public discussion of sex in the Soviet Union, together with their sheltered upbringing, mean that, like Tahmina, many girls in Tajikistan are unaware that there is anything to be a subject of. They are raised as non-sexual beings and many remain non-sexual all their lives.

In Sayot, when we held a group discussion on the function of the clitoris in female sexual arousal most of the women present were fascinated. A few of the younger ones wanted us to explain this to their husbands, who understood little beyond 'moving their penises in and out'. However, one of the older women said, 'I have felt nothing except distaste for sex throughout 20 years of married life and the birth of seven children. I don't think anything is likely to change my feelings now. I am only too glad to be left in peace.'

For this woman marriage removed her ignorance of the physical existence of sex only as far as she learned of penile penetration and understood this could cause pregnancy. She did not even have much idea how this last happened and associates sex solely with pain and discomfort.

Foreplay is virtually non-existent in the practice of most Tajik couples. If it takes place at all it tends to be a perfunctory caress of the breasts, mainly for the man's own pleasure. There are no books to help them learn anything else. There are many men like Haydar, who are unaware that women are capable of enjoying sex. Rustam, indeed, was something of an exception. He was very lucky to have been able to learn about female sexuality from his Russian classmates and to have had experienced girlfriends to teach him more. The one woman in Sayot who said she really enjoyed bed with her husband, and who clearly had good communication with him, was a woman in her late 20s, who had spent many years in Russia.

It would seem then that the majority of Tajik women are denied the remotest possibility of becoming subjects of desire, by being locked into marriage with men who do not arouse them in bed and for whom they feel little positive emotion. The prospect of their desire focusing on a homosexual object instead is remote in the extreme. This is so far outside the comprehension of most women that hardly anyone would admit to ever even hearing of there being lesbians in Tajikistan. The very thought appeared to terrify the members of the women's organisations whom I asked about this. How much this is a reaction to the gross violation of Tajik gender performance lesbian practice would represent and how much a reflection of the anti-homosexual discourse of Soviet times is difficult to say. Nevertheless, a very few apparently lesbian couples, where at least one of the persons involved appeared to be intersexed (Chapter 1), were known in the small towns around Sayot, where they seemed to be accepted perhaps because it was realised that they were not true women.

Male homosexuality, although not encouraged, is openly discussed and some men are known to be gay, although I have so far found little evidence of premarital homosexual relations among adolescent boys.

Are Tajik men better able to recognise themselves as subjects of desire than women? Men are certainly strongly encouraged to be sexual. Islamic discourse prioritises sex as an important path to spiritual union with God (Bouhdiba 1975: 16, 21, 106). Although the Qur'an suggests it is preferable to have only one spouse (Omran 1992: 18–22) the permission for polygyny and divorce suggests to many Muslim men that having multiple sex partners is perfectly acceptable and even preferable to too strong an emotional bond with one spouse that might distract one from one's duties to God. Moreover, the Prophet is reported to have explicitly stated that having sex with one woman is exactly the same as with any other (Mernissi 1987: 8ff).

The Muslim heaven is conceptualised as a place where the main pastime will be sex and where, besides their wives, men will be supplied with multiple partners in the shape of *houris* – living sex dolls who are always virgins and who return to their virgin state immediately after each sex act (Bouhdiba 1975: 95–6). This further situates discourse on male sexuality firmly in the camp of undirected sexual tension and away from a specific object of desire.

Thus there is a very fundamental Muslim discourse that depersonalises sex for men, while privileging relations with a virgin above all other sexual experiences. As stated above, defloration is the ultimate proof of virility and something that each man should experience at a minimum once, on his wedding night (see Lindisfarne 1994: 89).

A man's ability to impregnate his wife is also important in Tajik discourse on sexuality, which is doubtless why Rashid felt so much humiliation at Tahmina's failure to conceive. Men are also anxious to have their first child as soon as possible in order to tie their wives more firmly to them. They know it will be much harder for them to leave the relationship once they have a child. This is probably another reason why Rashid was so anxious for Tahmina to become pregnant.

If men experience their sexuality as undirected horniness then it will not much matter which woman they mate with. This is probably in part why so few men refuse to accept their parents' choice of a wife. In fact, the moment of spousal selection is the time – more than any other – when both men and women are treated not as individuals but as virtually interchangeable members of an object class (Shaffer 1997: 10) by parents who generally choose their sons' spouses in the hope that they will not come to feel passionately for them. The resulting lack of real sexual and emotional involvement after marriage restrains any tendency for either spouse to focus strongly on the other, and encourages husbands to stray.

Malik's inability to grasp why Rustam is so upset at having his desired object replaced by another woman may well derive from his lack of understanding that one member of the 'woman class' could mean more than another. Like many Tajik men Malik does not recognise himself as a subject of desire. The very concept of desiring a unique person and thus wishing to marry that person only, rather than experiencing undirected sexual tension that could equally well be satisfied with any member of the appropriate object class, is foreign to the Tajik way of thinking. After all, this would upset some of the chief principles of Tajik society, including the right of parents to decide their children's futures and of men to prove their virility through relations with multiple partners.

Sexuality revisited

I want to return here to the argument with which I started the section on sexuality. I said that sexual relations bore a great deal of the responsibility for the quality of the marital relationship. A survey of the experiences recounted in the stories above will test the truth of this hypothesis.[3] Haydar and Sitora's relationship improved enormously once she started to enjoy sex. Davlatpochcha and Saydali both enjoyed their marriage far more than their previous ones, even if Saydali remained somewhat insensitive towards his wife. Those marriages where the couple do not enjoy each other in bed are rarely satisfactory outside it.

Tahmina's marriage, for instance, is very rocky. Rashid knows how much she hates sex. Although he is gentle with her, approaches her nicely and does his best not to hurt her, even renouncing sex when she becomes pregnant, he still persists in having sexual relations, even if infrequently. It is not that he wants to hurt Tahmina. However, he has sexual needs, which he expects to be able to satisfy with his wife, although he has no conception of how to make her want sex too and probably no idea that it is possible for him to do anything to achieve this. All he seems to think about is how she should satisfy him emotionally and sexually. It does not seem to have occurred to him to consider her needs in this respect and Tahmina makes no attempts to suggest he should. Moreover, although wishing she could enjoy sex, she wanted this to happen somehow magically, of its own accord, not through any conscious effort on her part such as would have been represented by following the sort of sexological exercises used in the west, which was all the help I had to offer her. No doubt she was right to reject them because they only work if a woman wants to be caressed by her partner and

Tahmina could not at that point bear Rashid even to touch her. In such circumstances, trying to get herself to practise enjoying sex with him would have been in the nature of self-rape.

When a man uses a woman sexually without attempting to give her any pleasure, not necessarily out of indifference but simply because, like Rashid and Haydar, he has no idea of the possibility of doing otherwise, is this sexual violence? Sitora liked being with Haydar, even if she only later came to enjoy sex with him. Tahmina did not want to be with Rashid at all, in any way. Could one say that the second is rape but the first is not? Or should one posit a whole new category of sexual abuse? Because there is little doubt in my mind that Tahmina felt abused, while I do not think that Sitora did.

Perhaps the abuse comes less from Rashid as an individual, than from the system that gives men access to women as (sex) objects, but neither provides sex education nor teaches men to respect their wives as human beings. Meanwhile, women are prevented both from learning about their own sexuality and having an outlet for it other than through marriage with a man they are unable to choose, and are ultimately denied the right to refuse in bed. In fact, when parents do not differentiate between class objects in selecting their children's spouses and young couples are forced to have sex at their first meeting the message is clear: women are merely a function of their sex, not persons whose feelings have to be taken into account.

Such abuse does not stem from Islam, which, on the contrary, unlike Christianity, specifically states that women have sexual rights. In the past there must have been considerably more knowledge about sex in Muslim communities than there is today. One of the most important of the mediaeval Islamic jurists, El Ghazali (1058–1111), stated that women had a right to sexual enjoyment. In the early fifteenth century Sheikh Al Nefzawi gave very detailed instructions on how to please a woman in his *Perfumed Garden*, probably written between 1410 and 1434 (Sabbah 1984: 8–9).

Al Nefzawi includes detailed descriptions of foreplay, coitus and post-coital lovemaking, all intended to give the woman pleasure and lead to orgasm, which he saw as essential to the main goal of achieving a tender marital relationship. He explains that coitus should not start until the woman's vagina is wet. Ibn Agiba Aboul Abbas of Tetuwan (1747–1809) says that a 'man who wants coitus should not approach his wife before she is panting, her eyes troubled and she is demanding to be satisfied'. He explains in detail how to produce this effect, as also how to give her pleasure during coitus, and remarks how stimulating and pleasurable this can be *for the man*. Both Ibn Agiba and Al Nefzawi suggest that women need time to reach satisfaction and that men should learn to hold back to facilitate this if they want harmony in their marriages. Such 'sex manuals' were in great demand among Muslim men (Naamane-Guessous 1991: 230–3).

It is a great pity they are not commonly available today and that the rigid gender relations of contemporary life prevent women's sexual needs being taken into account as they appear to have been in the past, at least by the class of men who wrote the treatises and their readers. It is interesting that people label the most backward and woman-unfriendly aspects of Muslim life today 'positively mediaeval', when the evidence suggests that in the Middle Ages Muslim women were treated better, and had superior (sexual) rights than is the case in many Muslim societies nowadays.

According to Pahlen, who was in Central Asia before World War I, in those days sexual instruction was given to boys as young as eight years old, including information on sexually transmitted diseases (1964: 42). It is not clear that this instruction included detailed information on female sexuality, but it seems that Soviet puritanism was responsible for considerable loss of sexual knowledge and therefore possibly for a great deal of marital misery.

The contrast between the knowledge of Haydar's and Rustam's Russian mentors, and the general ignorance in Russia itself (see Geiges and Suvorova 1989), is striking.[4] Sex appears far more important in Tajikistan than in Russia, conceivably because it functions more overtly as a marker of masculine identity. Perhaps it was the combination of their less constrained gender identities with the Tajik influence that encouraged Russians there to explore. After all, there are no great secrets to understanding sex. Outside information can help, but two unrepressed people interested in mutual exploration can surely discover their erogenous zones and how to arouse and satisfy each other for themselves. Unfortunately, in Tajikistan at least, this rarely seems to happen.

In a relationship such as that of Tahmina and Rashid, the tension between the demands of his male sexuality and her lack of response poignantly illustrates the dichotomy at the heart of marriage between two people who remain essentially alien to each other even after several years as husband and wife. The suppression of female sexuality, represented not just by the need to retain virginity until marriage but also by the lack of attention men pay to their wives as sexual (and human) beings, reflects not only male selfishness but also the strong emphasis on correct gender performances that often outweighs all other considerations. Moreover, I find it hard to believe that men's indifference to their wives' sexual needs is not mirrored in the rest of their relationship.

The first few sexual encounters may well set the emotional tone for the entire future of the marriage and thus can be crucial. However, sexual satisfaction without corresponding emotional attachment does not create a good relationship, as Rustam's marriage demonstrates. In other words, a good marriage demands not so much good sex as mutual caring, of which sex is only one, albeit an extremely important, expression.

Of course, as stated earlier, sexual arousal and satisfaction are not necessarily expressions of desire. For most of the couples discussed above, even when their sexual relations are accompanied by positive emotional feelings, these tend to be the companionate rather than the passionate type of love.

Love

As has been stated repeatedly, Tajik parents select their children's spouses less for the young couple's potential compatibility than for the benefit of the family at large. A bride should be a suitable member of a specific subclass – for instance, a cousin, or a domesticated or submissive girl. The individual person appears to be of little consequence.

Nahdiya married Tahmina into a family to whom she owed a debt. She had no idea when she agreed to this which boy would be picked. Jumbul was not on the candidate list when Malik and Dilorom started looking for a bride for Rustam. It was only through her mother's aggression that she became Rustam's wife. She was acceptable because of attributes – virginity, presumed fertility, age and nationality – shared by thousands of girls. This was all that Rustam's parents knew about her before the marriage, but it was sufficient for their purposes.

Afterwards, they clearly thought that their son would soon find himself content with his new relationship and forget about Zhenia. The fact that they believed Jumbul to be an adequate substitute demonstrates how little they understood the emotional world Zhenia and Rustam inhabited.

This is not because the concept of love in itself is alien to Tajik culture. Muslim love-poetry has existed for a thousand years and formed the inspiration for the mediaeval European genre. The Persian language boasts some of the world's finest love poetry.

But in such poetry, passionate love is either an allegory for spiritual union with God or something destructive, tragic, disturbing of the social order and, therefore, undesirable, a reflection of a sort of madness, likely to end in tragedy, as was the case with Romeo and Juliet and Héloïse and Abelard. Such love could never end in the way idealised in the west today, in a stable and enduring marriage.

It is not that the east rejects the idea of love in marriage. It is rather that here love is held to be something that should develop *after* marriage, with propinquity – what has been called companionate love, a warm and tender feeling, essentially a heightened form of affection that bears little relation either to the madness and disorder or to the longing for spiritual and physical union characteristic of passionate love (Hatfield and Rapson 1996: 3).

This last can only be experienced by persons capable of being subjects of desire. This is not to say that an object of desire is always also an object of passionate love. However, an object of passionate love must by definition also be an object of desire.

While in Tajikistan there is no discourse around desire, there is a certain discourse around love in marriage, although it is unclear both how positively this is viewed and what kind of love is under discussion. In any case, emotional ties are supposed to develop *after* marriage, not to be the basis for contracting it. Although marriage for love was discussed by progressive Muslims before the revolution (Kamp 1998: 76), it was the Bolsheviks who introduced it as an important component of modern lifestyles.

In the last few years, young people have increasingly started to mention the word love in connection with marriage. This is partly due to the influence of the media, especially soap operas (Chapter 5) and partly to that of returned migrant workers. Eshmurod and other men who have taken Russian wives have also started to develop new concepts of the meaning of relationships. For the first time they have had the chance to choose their own partners and be chosen by them, based on personal traits. They have lived with women with a very different outlook from that of their Tajik wives, women who demand to be treated as unique individuals with their own special needs and personalities. Thus these men have learned what it is to live with a woman who not only welcomes them into bed but who also expects a partnership outside it, like Tanya (Chapter 5). All the men from Sayot with whom we discussed the subject claimed to enjoy sex with their Russian wives far more than with their Tajik ones, which suggests a level of sexual responsiveness in the former that is presumably not only a function of fewer inhibitions on the women's part but also greater caring on that of the men.

The Russian women are operating from a position of relative power vis-à-vis their Central Asian partners and so can be more demanding than their Tajik counterparts. For many of their husbands, union with a Russian woman is their ticket to a comfortable way of life in Russia, giving them a home and a place in society, rather than having to live as outcasts in barracks, or worse. At the same time this new relationship forces them to adopt different behavioural patterns from those at home. Of major importance here is no doubt the difference in gender norms, especially the fact that, in Russia, brides are not necessarily expected to be virgins nor is male control reified to the same extent as in Tajikistan.

When these men return from Russia they often find themselves dissatisfied with their Tajik relationships compared with those they enjoy in Russia. This does not necessarily mean they have learned to see themselves as subjects of desire. They may simply have learned to choose between different subclasses – Russian (articulate, sexually responsive) women over Tajik (submissive, non-responsive) ones. However, men like Rustam and Haydar do recognise themselves as subjects of desire, and their numbers are growing.

But what of Tajik women? What have the changes meant for them? On the whole, their husbands' changed expectations impose even more problems, yet another obstacle in their marital relationships. While bored with their wives' lack of response, these men refuse to do anything to change the situation, since they believe that if their wives come to enjoy sex they will seek it outside marriage, especially now that their husbands spend most of the year in Russia.

Although few Tajik women are unfaithful, their husbands constantly feel threatened. Even when a man knows his wife loves him, as Karomat loved Khudoydod, this does not preclude jealousy, which seems to be almost universal among Tajik men. Their inevitable reaction is to try to lock their wives away from all possible contact with other men.

While men continually talk about their jealousy, women rarely express such feelings for their husbands.[5] This may be because male jealousy is strongly tied to the performance of masculinity – to control over women – while women's status does not depend on their husband's fidelity. This is just as well since, while most men would appear to have little if any grounds for jealousy, most women would be thoroughly justified in having such feelings. The percentage of faithful Tajik husbands must be very small.

Whatever they actually feel for one another, it is important for both men and women to make a public proclamation that their relationship is functioning correctly. After the first bestowal of her virginity a woman can best display her regard by the only gift she is traditionally required to bestow upon her husband – children. This is no doubt one reason why Rashid and Chahonbek were so insistent that their wives would become pregnant if they really loved them. Men, on the other hand, are expected to demonstrate their regard by means of material gifts, so that a man who lavishes expensive goods on his wife is demonstrating his love to the world (see Al-Khayyat 1990: 63; Wikan 1980: 44–6), which is what

Jumbul demands of Rustam. In other words, here the demands are for public, rather than private, demonstration of marital satisfaction.

This is, of course, exactly what Rustam complains about in his wife. His relationships with Russian women have meant that what he prizes is the private demonstration of love characteristic of Russia and the west, not the public demonstration of material regard traditional in Tajikistan.

Which tendency will come to dominate here will depend on how the socio-political situation develops over the coming years, and whether the major influences continue to come from Russia, from a stricter form of Islam or from a more authoritarian post-Soviet government. The economic situation will also affect this. Should it no longer be necessary for men to go abroad to work, or should Tajiks start to migrate to Muslim countries rather than to Russia, this will also influence the form of personal relationships at home.

CONCLUSION

In this culture, where marriage is the single most significant occurrence in the lives of the vast majority, but where young people rarely have input into the choice of partner, they are particularly vulnerable, dependent for their happiness and futures on the decisions of others, very often made with totally different goals in mind.

While young men see marriage as a way to the legitimate satisfaction of their sexual needs and are therefore likely to welcome it, almost all the unmarried girls I talked to said they saw it as an unavoidable ill, necessary largely to provide them with children and with the prestige of having successfully attained 'adult' status, but especially because without it their position in society would be untenable. Marriage is likely to mean the end of a relatively carefree childhood and the assumption of immediate responsibilities, first to their husbands and mothers-in-law, and later to their children, and the end of any dreams for something different. In addition, it may well expose them to all sorts of ill-treatment.

Girls say they have heard only negative things about marriage. No matter how much I asked, none of them would consider that it might be possible to get happiness from the marital relation itself. They were more concerned with avoiding the negative, such as domestic violence, which they greatly feared. But one of the worst things for most of them is the knowledge that after marriage they will be under the control of husband and parents-in-law, almost always more confining than their natal family, especially during the first few years.

Tajikistan is not alone in being a place where girls have a basically negative attitude to marriage. In Yemen, Makhlouf (1979: 39) found that girls feel very sad when their marriages have been arranged but they know they cannot change their parents' minds. And, like many Tajik girls, Turkish girls in the Netherlands balance the wish to marry as late as possible with the fear of gossip and other problems if they do not marry before they are too old (De Vries 1988: 152).

Moreover, for Tajik girls their future mothers-in-law are likely to play every bit as important a role as their husbands. Karomat's good relationship with her mother-in-law made a very significant contribution to her marital happiness. However, this is an exception. Most women I met expressed very negative feelings about their mothers-in-law.

The only girls I ever heard say they wanted to be married were those who were in love, and had the expectation of being allowed to marry the object of their affections. I did not hear one girl about to be placed in an arranged marriage express anything positive about the institution.

In Morocco younger girls may be seduced into positive feelings towards the idea of marriage by the idea of escape into a freer way of life from that they lead as young girls with their parents, and the promises of the social advancement and material good they will receive from it (Naamane-Guessous 1991: 65). In Tajikistan, however, none of these incentives apply. Most young wives are far more restricted than girls living at home with their parents. Moreover, nowadays, rather than finding themselves materially better off they are more likely to end up like Tahmina, thin through being begrudged food by their in-laws and still financially dependent on their natal families.

Small wonder then that girls here have little wish to marry. Real benefits from this are far off in the future when they in turn become mothers-in-law. But even this may be denied these girls, given the current high divorce rates, which mean they may never attain that cherished position but instead end up as single mothers.

I met hardly any women who claimed to have experienced happiness in their marital relationship. However, the stigma of remaining unmarried after the age of 20 is so strong that it is hardly surprising that the vast majority of girls resign themselves to accepting marriage, especially in rural areas, where they have no real alternative. The main reason appeared to be the absence of any other viable lifestyle in a society where there are immense pressures on single women, and where it is materially, morally and psychologically impossible for most people to live alone.

Once married, these girls and their husbands will find themselves involved in an ongoing negotiation between the ideals of gender performance, which favour male domination, and the reality in which women may be psychologically stronger than their husbands. Nevertheless, since according to tradition, husbands have the upper hand, even the kindest of men, such as Khudoydod, tend to take their right to boss their wives for granted. Certainly, when it comes to the home most husbands assume their wives will wait on them and indeed it is rare that the latter refuse, or even complain to their husbands about this. For the sake of peace women usually at least appear to do as they are told, even when they do not like it. It is not so much that they *are forced* to obey their husbands as that they actively decide to look as if they are doing so in order to make their lives easier, and avoid conflicts.

Urban women who have been exposed to Soviet propaganda on sexual equality may believe in what they call equal weight within marriage, but they know they live in a social order where this is difficult, if not impossible to achieve. In fact, in order to get their own way without arousing their husbands' ire, women generally prefer not to challenge them directly but instead find productive and non-confrontational ways to manipulate them, such as that used by Zulfia (Introduction). All the same, young women married to men of their own age usually seem to feel that it is considerably easier for them to handle their husbands than their parents-in-law, especially their mothers-in-law.

The negative aspects of Tajik marriages are not specifically due to their being arranged, since love matches may be no less unhappy. As long as they do not have their hearts set on someone else, young people in an arranged marriage often do quite well together. It is to the advantage of both to try to do so. Perhaps because they feel their wives do not conform sufficiently to the norms, or because their families usually disapprove of any bride not chosen by themselves, men in love matches may become abusive. This is especially hard on their wives, who expect to continue the good relationship they had before marriage and are bewildered by the change from loving boyfriend to hostile spouse.

Thus it is not the arranged marriage in itself that is an obstacle to happiness, but rather the constricting gender norms that prevent the development of happy relationships. The quality of a marriage tends to be in inverse proportion to the thickness of the gender masks the spouses wear when alone together, the thicker the mask the worse the relationship. In other words, the more closely the couple stick to their stock gender characteristics the less chance there will be that they can treat each other as human beings, rather than as men and women obliged by convention to exhibit gender-appropriate behaviour.

Karomat and Khudoydod, for instance, were happy because, as opposed to most of the characters in this book, they were able to put their feelings for each other before their adherence to gender norms. It is unfortunate that more men are not able to do this and that some are even so insecure in their identity and feel so off balance that they see their only salvation in the performance of brutal and distorted versions of masculinity expressed as violence.

The last few years have been a particularly difficult time for marital relationships. The young are no longer satisfied with their parents' way of life but have been unable to rid themselves of the obligations to follow traditional gender performances that hamper the development of new patterns. Tensions between individualism and the emphasis on communal good are starting to increase. This in turn is creating greater tension between husbands and wives, parents and children.

It is unclear that the new trends are beneficial to women. For many girls, increased pre-marital contact with boys has led more to unhappiness, loss of reputation, illegitimate children or abortion, disgrace and even suicide, rather than to greater emotional satisfaction from more meaningful relationships.

Tajikistan is caught in a clash between very different lifestyles. On the one hand are the old ways with their stable marital relationships, usually life-long, and relatively little emphasis on the personal aspects of the couple relationship. On the other hand are the often confusing new ideas they have been exposed to in the last decade through contact with other cultures. The emphasis on romantic love found in women's favourite television viewing is balanced by easy access to pornography for men that has introduced new ways of objectifying women. The result has been to give both sexes new aspirations, ones that have introduced many complications. One of the chief questions that has arisen from this is how to resolve the conflicts between these new ideas and the current gender identities.

CONCLUSION: CONTROL AND SUBVERSION

Through the stories in this book I have tried to give meaning to the multiple layers of contradictions in which Tajiks find themselves, as they struggle to live their own lives without either totally ceding to sociocultural pressures or exposing themselves to censure by resisting too obviously.

The lives of Karomat's and Rustam's fathers exemplify the type of contradictions produced by the juxtaposition of the Tajik social system with Soviet ideology. Both men were able to rise in the Communist Party while simultaneously, as heads of their families, imposing those same traditions that the Soviet state was spending so much energy combating.

Karomat's father started and ended his life as a deeply religious man, who believed both in Islam and in the traditions of his community. Nevertheless, for the majority of his working life he was a respected Party member, whose task it was to convert his compatriots to an ideology committed to destroying his religion. During this period he allowed his family to adopt many of the outward forms of Sovietisation, including permitting his wife to unveil and his daughters to pursue careers. However, he never failed to enforce strict control, to demand complete obedience to his will, nor to see to it that his family kept the most important of Tajik traditions. By the time of his death, one of his grandsons was a *mullah*, two of his daughters eminent actresses and his eldest granddaughter a respected economist.

While Karomat's father was already a clergyman before the Bolsheviks gained control over Tajikistan, Malik was born during World War II and is an atheist by conviction, not merely by outward show. Yet he imposes his will on his family and enforces traditions banned by Soviet law even more strongly than did the older man. His lack of religious observance has become problematical today, when almost all his neighbours pray and fast, and this may partially account for his continued insistence on his children conforming to the social traditions.

In regard to social control, multiple contradictions also appear between the community at large and its member families. The formal discourse portrays each family as represented before the community by a mature male, who, like Fayziddin (Chapter 1), is charged with ensuring the compliance of the other members. However, daily control is usually in the hands of the senior woman, since it is she who takes charge of the younger generation. The result is ambiguous power relations between mothers and sons, where the generational positioning of the former outweighs the masculine power of the latter, to turn on its head the usual image of Muslim society as a place where submissive women are kept firmly in their places by dominating men.

This apparent paradox derives largely from the fact that the gender stereotypes of the honour-and-shame system are strongly generational. The controlling male is in fact a mature man, and the complementary female a young woman. It is clear that Fayziddin has the right to control Dila, at least until her marriage. However, since regulatory discourse is generally silent on the matter, it is less obvious that Zora's power over Ali does not end with his achieving legal independence, even though stories of mothers coercing their sons into unwanted marriages or forcing them to divorce against their will are commonplace.

Moreover, while parents lose control over daughters at marriage, thus opening the door for them to develop their own agency more fully, sons remain within their parents' jurisdiction for life. This situation may help account for the many adult sons who allow their mothers to dominate them. It was this that Tahmina found so difficult to cope with, and Jahongul and her friends so infuriating, because it erects an often impenetrable emotional and material barrier against girlfriends and even wives.

The one place where men are usually left alone to display their power is in the bedroom, and it is often here that women suffer most from their husband's rights over them or conversely, where the marriage can be strengthened through good psychological and emotional contact. There are many contradictions here also, with husbands demanding their wives respond and love them, while apparently it never occurs to men like Rashid that modifying their own behaviour might go a long way towards achieving their desired goals.

Despite this, Tahmina's story shows how much more she suffers from the domination of her mother-in-law than of her husband. However, she is also aware that this is because Rashid and she are the same age and that she would not have this advantage with an older man. Similarly, as Javhar discovered, when she and her husband moved into a home of their own, she gained enormously in power. Formally, it is the husband who commands but it is quite clear that (older) women often manage to subvert their husbands' power position with regard to the younger family members and become the commanding figure in the household. Hence the frightening image of the mother-in-law compared with that of the father-in-law, who formally possesses the greater power.

Although wives often develop agency earlier than their husbands, official discourse concurs with Tillo's statement, 'We Tajik women must obey our husbands. We have no choice.' In this public acknowledgement of female submission, Tillo is in effect wearing a gender mask to hide her underlying strength. Men may also wear masks to hide their weaknesses behind an image of superiority, since failure to live up to the standards of masculinity carries the penalties of being mocked and jeered at, penalties apparently high enough to keep men as far as possible in outward compliance with the norms. In other words, both sexes may find it convenient to use gender masks to hide non-conformity with prescribed images.

BUTLER, FOUCAULT, SOCIAL CONTROL AND GENDER MASKS

Butler's conceptualisation of gender as performative (1993: x, 13) helped me focus on the fact that it is the public enactment of sex-specific traits, not merely their internalisation, that makes gender identities visible, and thus led me to consider the meaning of the very different ways that Dila, for instance, behaves with her father or her brother (Chapter 1), or that Jahongul behaves with her mother or me (Chapter 5). Analysing these, I came to the conclusion that what was occurring was a deliberate, but not necessarily entirely conscious, manipulation of the situation, through the assumption of specific behavioural patterns in conformity with the audience's gendered expectations. Thus, Dila plays a daughterly role with her father and an elder sisterly role with her brother, and in each her performance depicts a somewhat different character.

Looking at the apparent rationale behind this, I began to understand that this was no mere posturing but a vital strategy, used by both sexes, but especially by women, to preserve their inner selves intact, while enacting roles that, if fully internalised, might prove devastatingly destructive and yet which were crucial for preserving their social status and, as Butler also suggests, even their (social) lives (1993: 182–3). Considering this phenomenon in the light of performativity theory was what brought me to the concept of gender masks as a way of concretising the phenomena I was observing.

The existence of these 'masks' became all the clearer for me when I observed the physical changes that took place in Jahongul and Rustam in front of different audiences, and because the people I became close to would abandon the more stereotypical masks in my presence once they realised that these were unnecessary and I actually preferred their underlying personas (Chapter 5). My participation in their family lives, therefore, gave me the opportunity to witness the many transformations that occurred as masks were assumed and removed.

Foucault's concept of the circulation of power and its possession even by those apparently powerless (1990: 94–6), taken together with his micro-mechanisms of power used by community members to keep order (1980a: 96–102), enabled me to comprehend the way my characters use and react to such weapons as gossip, spying and tale-telling, and the regulatory force they possess. This further permitted me to see the way families are pressured into conformity, and family heads into complicity, with self-appointed community leaders, even in ways that appear harmful to their own children's welfare. Thus, the vulnerability to public censure of Malik and Dilorom, Fayziddin and Sadbarg's parents, forces them to impose strict controls on their children.

Here, gender masks can act as a shield, permitting the public display of conformity to conceal considerable deviation. The effective use of such masks thus permits the subversion of the narrow boundaries of official discourse and protects their wearers from the consequences of their aberrations, while those who do not manage this may be socially condemned. In other words, the masks permit the existence of individuality beneath the surface conformity, albeit within the relatively narrow limits possible in the restricted environment of Tajikistan.

COMMUNALISM VERSUS INDIVIDUALISM

Jahongul's musings on potential life trajectories (Chapter 5) are very different from the inner life her mother and Tillo told me they led at that age. Although this is doubtless in part forgetfulness due to the passage of time, I believe the main reason lies elsewhere. A generation ago few Tajik women had been exposed to more than a very narrow range of lifestyles and behavioural patterns, and there was little stimulation in their environment to think beyond this.

First with the collapse of the Soviet system in the late 1980s and later with independence, war and the encroachment of external cultural forces, including television soap operas, pornography, the availability of hitherto unknown commodities and other types of contact with the outside world, youngsters of Jahongul's generation have been exposed to influences their mothers never dreamed of. Many of these come out of a very different social setting – the individualistic west.

The conflicts that so many of the young people in this book are currently experiencing between their personal hopes and desires, and the expectations of their parents and the community at large that lifestyles will remain very much the same as before, stem from the changes enveloping the region today.

Central Asian societies have long been based on communalistic principles. That is to say, their members are expected to put the good of the community before their personal good, and this demands close adherence to a narrow set of behavioural norms. Thus, much of the apparently cruel behaviour described in this book can be justified in the name of preserving the community.

Soviet society was similarly communally based, the often despotic laws legitimised by an ideology favouring the good of the many over that of the few. When the two ideologies coincided, as they did in Tajikistan, the result was greatly to reinforce the power of the community over the individual. The use of gender masks made the situation tolerable by providing a mechanism for concealing idiosyncrasies from public view.

All this allowed Tajikistan to become one of the most conservative of all the Union Republics, although its geographic isolation and the fact that it was one of the last places to feel the cultural influence of the Russian conquerors, are doubtless also responsible. Moreover, during Soviet times there was little social mingling between Russian-speakers and locals. Even today the two groups live in separate cultural communities, meeting only within official institutions such as schools and the workplace. Thus, Tajiks had relatively little contact with the Russian way of life.

Now, suddenly there has been an explosion of new cultural stimuli, which fascinate the young and horrify their parents. Many of these relate directly to gender identities, including new ways of conceiving the couple relationship. Men like Rustam and Mahmud (Chapter 4) have to a certain extent broken away from Tajik traditions and gained different expectations of marriage from those of their parents, seeking to live with a beloved individual, not merely with a person of the woman class. Male mobility and freedom in sexual matters mean that it is not so difficult for men to achieve this, if necessary by marrying a second wife, although they may have to keep her hidden from their parents.

Women, however, are much more limited in their options. Thus, Jahongul and her friends can only hope and long for the chance to make a marriage that will combine love and mutual respect, but they can do little to make their dreams come true, especially since they are restricted to their one official husband, with severe penalties for taking a lover, and small chance of improvement through divorce. Even though, as a mature woman, Tillo was able to risk what in the past would have been certain social death in order to search for love with Chahonbek, his right to lay down the terms of their relationship eventually prevented her from gaining what she had been seeking from it.

People's desire to experiment with new lifestyles is constrained by the gender identities they have absorbed over the years. This is particularly true for men, for most of whom it appears preferable to go along with tradition than to take the risks associated with change. Women's position makes it hard for them to initiate such changes, so that most find themselves compelled to live first according to their parents' dictates and later in line with those of their marital families, so that very few will be able to realise their own wishes through direct action.

CONCLUSION

The transformation necessary to make it socially possible for women (or even young men) in Tajikistan actively to determine the course of their own lives is unlikely to occur without very significant material upheaval (Marx 1867: 876). Even in the west, despite the decades that have passed since the start of the second women's liberation movement and the stress on individualism in many aspects of life, significant progress in reconceptualising gender identities has not been made. Today, in most families men continue to expect to be regarded as the dominant figure and in general their wives go along with this (Steil 1997). Women are still supposed to conform to a much narrower range of sexual expression than men, and to put their sexuality at the service of their husbands. Those who do not may be able to get away with it more easily than in Tajikistan but regulatory forces, including the medical profession – psychologists and sexologists as well as physicians – almost as powerful in the west as religion in Tajikistan, still manage to a large extent to preserve traditional gender identities (Nicolson 1992; Ussher 1991).

As a result, the underlying norms have changed relatively little. This was brought home to me in May 2002, when I conducted a gender-training seminar with a mixed group of scholars from Europe and the US, Latin America, Africa and Asia. There was remarkable similarity in the gender ideals described by all the participants, and they bore a strong resemblance to those of Tajikistan. For instance, all participants, even those from the west, agreed that male control and female chastity were important components of the gender ideals in their communities. Where they differed was in the degree of emphasis placed on these and the rigorousness with which their communities enforced control.

In a very small way the gender training carried out by the Khatlon Women's Health Project in the villages has shown that it is possible to produce a certain level of social change by working with the whole community and encouraging them to re-examine the stereotypes, or in other words by carrying out consciousness-raising similar to that which occurred in the early days of the second women's movement. The aim here is not to encourage individualism but rather to support the development of a less oppressive form of communalism than those recently experienced, one where members support rather than repress each other.

Unfortunately, in the absence of a solid material basis for developing a new type of society it is unlikely that significant changes in gender identities, and thus in social organisation, could be spread over larger regions without serious opposition by political and religious forces. Meanwhile, the structurally less powerful will continue to be forced to practise subversion in order to mitigate their living circumstances and to use masks to conceal deviation.

At least in so doing they can achieve a certain modicum of power over their own destinies, as we saw at the beginning of this book from the story of Zulfia. I should like to remind the reader how, while remaining within her culturally accepted identity, she was able to manipulate her situation, so that her husband voluntarily acceded to her demands. Thus, by using her ingenuity she was able to improve her life without clashing with either her husband or her community. The other women present were ecstatic at hearing how she had managed this and I am sure they went away strengthened in their own potential to deal with difficult situations. I like to think of Zulfia as an inspiring example of how Tajik women manage their lives and how they refuse to accept that their structurally low position should condemn them to a life of powerlessness and passivity, instead showing their potential for active self-empowerment.

TECHNICAL INFORMATION
AND TERMINOLOGY

TRANSLATION

Where not otherwise indicated, all translations are my own.

TRANSLITERATION

I have transliterated the Tajik words from the Cyrillic, not according to Persian/Arabic standards. In other words, I write Ibn Sino, Donish, *nikoh*, not Ibn Sinâ, Dânish, *nikâh*. I also transliterate Central Asian words used by Russians from their Central Asian, not their Russian spelling – *hujum* not *khudzhum*.

As far as possible I spell place names according to English standards – for instance, Tajik, not Tadzhik (Russian), nor Tojik (Tajik). The names of little-known places, I have transliterated from the Tajik spelling.

USAGES

The following usages have been adopted:

- I use the word *girl* in its Russo-Tajik meaning of an unmarried person of the female sex. To a Tajik, a woman is by definition a non-virgin, who therefore should have been married at least once.
- I use the word *God* rather than Allah in most places as a translation of the Tajik word *khudo*. Tajiks rarely use the Arabic word.
- Besides ethnic Russians, many other people from outside Central Asia have lived in Tajikistan. These are locally known as *Russian-speakers*, since this was the language they communicated in. I have followed this custom.
- Following usage in Tajikistan I use the word *local* to describe people of Central-Asian ethnicities.

ABBREVIATIONS

CIS – Commonwealth of Independent States (comprising 12 of the 15 Union republics of the FSU, that is, all except the three Baltic republics).

FSU – former Soviet Union.

IUD – inter-uterine device, or coil. Female contraceptive inserted into the womb, the most popular method of birth control in Tajikistan and many developing countries.

ZAGS – Soviet civil registry office of births, marriages and deaths.

GLOSSARY

To control – to exercise restraint or direction over; to dominate, command.
To subvert – to undermine the principles of, corrupt.
(*Random House Dictionary of the English Language*, 2nd edn 1987)

SOVIET TERMS

hujum – literally 'attack' in Tajik/Uzbek. Used for the Soviet attack on
    female seclusion and veiling in the late 1920s.
kolkhoz – collective farm.
Komsomol – Young Communist League.
oblast – corresponds to the English state or province.

LOCAL WORDS

Unless otherwise indicated, these words are Tajik (or Arabic that has
    been accepted into normal usage).
aryk – irrigation canal, or ditch.
ayb – shame – the opposite of *nomus.*
babka – old woman (Russian), sometimes used to designate traditional
    birth attendants.
bai – the rich.
basmachi – anti-Soviet Islamic rebels of the 1920s and 1930s in Central
    Asia and especially Tajikistan.
bibiotun (Uzbek otin) – female religious leader.
chachvan – horsehair veil worn by some groups of Central Asian women
    before the Revolution together with the *faranja.*
dastarkhon – tablecloth laid on the ground, on which the food is placed at
    meal times.
dechkan – Central-Asian peasant.
ezor – women's loose trousers, worn under a dress instead of underwear
    and to conceal their legs.

faranja (Russian *paranja*, Uzbek *paranji*) – all-enveloping cloak worn together with the *chachvan*.

Fiqhs – writings on Islamic jurisprudence.

haram – unclean, bad, sinful – an Islamic term.

Jadidism – a progressive political movement that started in the late nineteenth century among the Crimean Tatars, for the defence of their culture against Russification, which was especially concerned with the modernisation of their educational system so that they could become competitive in the modern world. They established what were called 'new method' schools in Central Asia, in which more secular subjects were taught than in the traditional Muslim schools of the time.

kalym – bride price. Paid to the bride's family, usually her parents, by the groom or his family.

kelin – daughter-in-law or bride. From the Uzbek word to come (in), thus literally incomer. It carries the implication that the new member is not an accepted family member. Furthermore, the term does not specifically attach her to her husband but suggests she belongs to the entire family. There is no fixed point at which a woman stops being a *kelin* and becomes a member of a family, although usually this happens some time before the time she is ready to welcome her own first *kelin*.

kofir – barbarian. Person who does not adhere to one of the religions of the book – Islam, Christianity, or Judaism. Russians not explicitly Christians are considered *kofirs* because of Soviet atheist ideology, while westerners are assumed to be Christians.

mahalla – region or locality. The cult of locality is so strong that it is a major factor in all aspects of life in Tajikistan. It carries many of the same connotations as ethnicity does in the Great Lakes area of Africa, or in the former Yugoslavia. In Tajikistan *mahalla* can also denote a separate area of a town, or even a village, with its own mosque and committee of elders.

mahr – a payment to a wife by her husband in order for her to be able to maintain herself if the marriage ends. Equivalent to alimony but either paid or promised at the time of marriage and distinct from *kalym*, which is paid to the wife's family.

maktab – (Muslim) school.

medressa – Muslim college.

mujahaddin – Muslim freedom fighters, such as the members of the Afghan Northern Alliance.

mullah – self-styled local male religious leader. He may have received some formal religious education but more usually has not. He may not even have read the Qur'an. In theory any man can call himself a *mullah* and then dictate to others how to live.

nikoh – Muslim marriage ceremony.

nomus – type of honour dependent on the correct performance of gender identities.

non – flat round local bread.

pilau – local dish of rice, meat and vegetables.

qadi/qazi – Islamic judge.

rumol – woman's headscarf. Not the equivalent of a 'veil' but worn tied at the back of the head, exposing neck, shoulders and considerable amounts of hair.

Sart – Tsarist period name for inhabitants of South Eastern Uzbekistan and the Tajik plains.

sharaf – honour gained through one's own attributes or actions.

sharia (Russian *shariat*) – Islamic legal code, especially important in regard to family law.

taloq – repudiation (divorce). Three *taloqs* make a divorce final.

tui – party to celebrate a rite of passage, such as a wedding or male circumcision.

Young Bukharan – a progressive political movement started in 1909 in Bukhara with similar aims to Jadidism.

waqf – a system of charitable land grants given by the wealthy for the poor and administered by the Muslim clergy, who gained both power and wealth by it. It provided income for maintaining mosques, schools, and hospitals (Keller 2001: 37).

NOTES

INTRODUCTION

1. See glossary for a definition of *subversion* in the context of this book.
2. More detailed information on this project can be found in Harris (1998b, 1999).
3. With increased support from Christian Aid, through its Central Asian affiliate ACT Central Asia, and a grant from the TACIS LIEN Fund of the European Union (1999–2000).
4. During my time with the centre it was funded by the Swiss Development Corporation and the Lombard Odier Bank.
5. Within speech act theory, a performative is that discursive practice that enacts or produces that which it names (Butler 1993: 13, 1995b: 134).
6. During the *glasnost'* period in the mid-1980s stories of suicides for such reasons were frequently published in the newspapers (Khushkadamova 1993), and discussed on television. They continue to be discussed in the pages of popular newspapers, such as *Chakri Gardun*.
7. While Tajiks usually took me for a Russian. In fact, lacking experience of foreigners, most of my Tajik acquaintances, including the subjects of this book, treated me more or less as an honorary Russian.
8. Although Karomat and her family were originally from the north, she moved to the south as a young child and spent the rest of her life there.
9. I use the terms west/western in this book as a synonym for northwestern Europe and the white English-speaking countries. However, most of my examples are drawn from the two countries I know best, Britain and the United States.
10. According to a BBC2 television programme broadcast on 14 June 1999, produced by the Community Programme Unit.
11. Broadcast as part of the BBC learning zone on 8 September 1999.

1 CONCEPTUAL BACKGROUND

1. Performativity must be understood not as a singular or deliberate 'act', nor as a mechanical repetition of the norms (Butler 1997b: 16), but rather as 'the reiterative and citational practice' (1993: x) 'which brings into being or enacts that which it names, and so marks the constitutive or productive power of discourse' (1995b: 134). According to Butler performance cannot be assumed at will but is an integral part of the gendered subject, transformable only by way of minute variations (1993: x). But gender is not reducible merely to the performable. Performance can only reproduce an already existing ideal. 'The effect of gender is produced through the stylization of the body and, hence, must be understood as the mundane way in which bodily gestures, movements, and styles of various kinds constitute the illusion of an abiding gendered self' (Butler 1990: 140).

2. Parallels can be drawn between this and the reactions of minority Muslim communities in the west, such as Turks in the Netherlands (see Brouwer 1998; De Vries 1987) or Pakistanis in the UK (see Jacobson 1998).

3. Compare Kandiyoti's findings that the male child (in Anatolia, Turkey) takes on a subservient attitude vis-à-vis adult males similar to that expected of women (1994: 207).

4. Although even here it seems to me that more fine-grained research into how the members of different groups of heterosexual males experience their sexuality will very likely disprove this, as also, of course, the concept of a universal female heterosexuality.

5. There appear to be some societies, however, where this may be less straightforward (Moore 1994b: 36ff).

6. See Turner (1999) for a detailed account of how this is done.

7. Some babies are born with indeterminate genitalia, which makes it difficult to assign them categorically to one sex or the other. In modern terminology they are called intersexed. In the past this condition was known as hermaphroditism. Western doctors tend to operate to give such babies clearly sexed bodies, usually female, irrespective of their actual genetic makeup. For an inside look at the psychological problems this can produce see Turner (1999); see also Foucault on the subject of hermaphroditism (1980b) and Butler's commentary on it (1990: 93ff). There is even an American Intersex Society. In countries like Tajikistan, such people are also usually raised female but, without the corresponding operation, may not have the appropriate sexual organs, such as a serviceable vagina. This can cause real problems when it comes to marriage.

8. Or, as Foucault puts it, 'the individual which power has constituted is at the same time its vehicle' (1980a: 98).

9. Since agency is exerted through the ego which is 'first and foremost a bodily ego' (Freud 1960: 16, in Butler 1993: 13) and since gender is also inscribed on that body, it follows that both the formation of the ego and the subsequent development of agency must be gendered.

10. Zora is unusual in not demanding total obedience from her daughter.

11. Although Scott himself deliberately refuses to consider gender as a factor in dominant power relations (1990: 22) his premises are nonetheless useful for those of us who wish to employ them in this way (see Cornwall and Lindisfarne 1994b: 46).

12. I wish to thank Lorraine Nencel for bringing this passage to my attention.

13. Developed at the Group Theatre and later at the Actor's Studio in New York as a result of an idiosyncratic interpretation of the techniques of the Russian director Konstantin Stanislavski, method acting is based on the actors' ability to identify psychologically with the characters they are playing.

14. Useful histories dealing with Central Asia as a whole are Adshead (1993), Caroe (1967), Massell (1974), Park (1957), Pierce (1960), Pipes (1964), Sharma (1979), Vaidyanath (1967) and Wheeler (1964). Atkin (1989) and Rakowska-Harmstone (1970) deal specifically with Tajikistan.

15. Except where otherwise indicated, the current work does not deal at all with the peoples of this region.

16. For an in-depth discussion of these differences see Akiner (2001).

17. See for instance, Akiner (2001), Atkin (1997), Hyman (1994), Niyazi (1994), Roy (1993).

18. Although after the peace agreement was signed in 1997, opposition leaders were allotted some of the ministries and thus had a chance to include their own people. By and large, however, the Kulobis continue to hold a majority of government posts.

19. According to estimates of the United Nations High Commissioner for Refugees (UNHCR) and the International Committee of the Red Cross.

20. A useful summary of the central tenets of Islam can be found in Jacobson (1998: 26ff).

21. At that time, for example, the opposition to religious marriage services was weakened, so that Karomat could be openly married by a *mullah*, something normally severely castigated.

22. While excoriated for his role in breaking up the Soviet Union and hence indirectly causing the economic hardships and the civil war.

23. See *Sura* 24: 32: 'marry the single among you'.

24. See *Sura* 30: 31: 'And one of [Allah's] signs is, that He has created for you mates from yourselves, that you may dwell in tranquillity with them, and has ordained between you Love and Mercy'. *Sura* 7: 189: 'It is He who created you from a single soul (*nafs*) and therefrom did make his mate, that he might dwell in tranquillity with her' (Omran 1992: 14).

25. Such marriages are traditional in Maghreb families (Bouamama and Sad Saoud 1996: 40). In Egypt marriages among peasants and lower-class urban families are almost always between cousins. Only educated girls can marry exogamously (Rugh 1984: 11, 133; Zénié-Ziegler 1988: 23). Cousin marriage is also common in Iran and throughout Central Asia.

26. According to al-Bukhari the Prophet said: 'Learning is a duty for every Muslim [male and female]' (Omran 1992: 46).

27. Although this is slowly changing, witness the recent introduction of *sharia* law into Nigeria.

28. This again is neither specific to Tajikistan nor to Muslim societies. During gender-training workshops in Catholic Ecuador even young educated men have made the same claims. But this culture, like others in Latin America, has been heavily influenced by the Mediterranean honour-and-shame system imported from Spain.

29. I use the word mature to apply to persons whose (eldest) children have reached marriageable age.

30. But even today I have seen 30 or more people living in one compound in parts of Khatlon.

31. Aside from the earnings of women, for instance, from breeding silk worms or embroidering hats, etc. These earnings were considered to be private and thus not to be absorbed into general family finances (Meakin 1903: 100–1). Under Islamic law the husband is supposed to be the sole financial supporter of the family. However, in Turkestan in cases of great poverty, disability, widows without male relatives, etc. a woman's earnings might have to go towards the provision of basic family needs (Harris 1996: 91).

32. Here the women might sit in but often had no active voice. However, if they got on well with their husbands they might be able to influence them in private discussions outside the family meetings.

33. Compare the attitudes of the Tajik men returning from Russia today (Chapter 5).

34. The same was true in Europe until child mortality rates started to fall sharply in the eighteenth century (Stone 1977: 68).

35. For this reason official marriage statistics correspond only very partially to reality. Even today many marriages are not registered and such couples also frequently fail to register the births of their children.

36. China, Iran and Afghanistan to name a few, have long histories of young people's and especially young women's suicides, for much the same reasons as in Tajikistan (see Afshar 1987: 76; Lajoinie 1980: 82).

37. According to Monogarova 53.5 per cent of marriages in Dushanbe are arranged by parents but there are fairly substantial differences among people originally from different localities (1982: II, 90, 140).
38. Older brother is *aka*, younger *dodar*. Older sister is *apa*, younger *khohar*.

2 THE BOLSHEVIKS ATTACK BUT THE TAJIKS RESIST

1. Much of the historical discussion in this chapter focuses on that part of Central Asia culturally similar to Tajikistan, essentially comprising modern Tajikistan and the south-eastern part of Uzbekistan, including Samarkand, Bukhara, Tashkent and the Ferghana Valley. The Bolshevik policies, as well as the local responses, were very much the same over all this area, except for the southern and eastern parts of Tajikistan, which were the last to be fully brought under Soviet rule.
   Many of the historical segments in fact deal with the *Sarts*. As stated in Chapter 1, this was a cultural group whose members later identified themselves either as Uzbeks or Tajiks in Soviet censuses, their traditions and lifestyles being virtually indistinguishable (see Kamp 1998: 9)
2. More detailed descriptions of the region's pre-revolutionary lifestyles can be found in Constantine (2001: 48–82), Harris (1996) and Kamp (1998: 26–46).
3. Infant mortality rates were extremely high (Harris 2002). All of Karomat's mother's nine siblings and all but one of those of Karomat's father, as well as five of Karomat's own siblings – including all four brothers – died in childhood.
4. For more details on such establishments see Kamp (1998: 118–30).
5. For more details on the political, economic and religious history of the Tsarist period in Turkestan see Keller (2001: 5–29).
6. A succinct political history of the early Soviet period in Central Asia can be found in Keller (2001: 31–67).
7. Although the following passages date from well after the initial period of emancipation they present the ideological basis for the Bolsheviks' 1920s campaigns.
8. See Chapter 1. The word *faranja* was usually used for both garments.
9. According to Keller, in the mid-1930s when Soviet pressures relaxed there was a spate of re-veiling in Uzbekistan (1998: 31), and the veil was still being worn by some women in Namangan in the 1950s (Kamp 1998: 295).
10. These were largely from the group formerly referred to as *Sarts*. Most of them called themselves Uzbeks, although a few claimed to be Tajiks.
11. For a more detailed account of this scene in Karomat's own words see Harris (1998a).
12. The vast majority of skilled factory workers in Tajikistan were Russian-speakers, although this fact is rarely mentioned in Soviet accounts; statistics on the workforce are broken down by sex but not nationality.
13. Personal communication from Guljakhon Bobosadikova, who carried out such work during the 1960s and 1970s.

3 COMMUNITY CONTROL

1. See Chapter 5 for more details of Jahongul's background.
2. This does not mean he is from the Middle East but from a group of indigenous Arabs who have lived in southern Tajikistan for generations. There is a large contingent of them in the Shaartuz region, where Chahonbek comes from.
3. See Chapter 6 for the sequel to Tillo's story.
4. Tillo is one of the few non-elite women I met in Tajikistan who has ever been outside the borders of the former Soviet Union.

5. This story was told me by Bahodur Toshmatov, the staff member in question.
6. At the stage before heroin depresses the male libido it appears to have the opposite effect, but at the same time to make it difficult for men to reach the point of ejaculation – see Chahonbek's story in Chapter 6.
7. This story was told me by Ayesha Homed.
8. This story was told me by Monawar Kalandar.
9. As I point out in the introduction, it is not so long since the same attitude existed in England.
10. This is, of course, not limited to societies where the honour-and-shame system is important. In the Netherlands and many small towns in the US, for instance, pressures towards social conformity are intense.
11. Russians find it hard to handle Tajik names, so they often give people Russian names. Karomat was always called Clara at work.
12. The Spaniards exported their honour-and-shame system to their colonies.

4   INTERGENERATIONAL FAMILY CONTROL

1. This story was told me by Hurshed Babaev.
2. There are close similarities here between rural Tajik women's criteria for selection of daughters-in-law and those of women in extended families in, for example, the countries of the Maghreb (Bouamama and Sad Saoud 1996: 24).
3. Compare accounts of Indian families (for example, Patel 1994).
4. However, since most people in Tajikistan do not connect nutrition with health, this is perhaps not so surprising.
5. A woman's life cycle in such families is such that, while young brides are likely to experience deprivation and hardship, they know that this will eventually give way to a time when they will exercise control and authority over their children and eventually *kelins*. This encourages their tacit acceptance of their situation as brides, their willingness to wear a mask of subordination while waiting for their turn to assume power (see Kandiyoti 1991: 32–3).
6. This story was told me by Hurshed Babaev, who was teaching the class Mahmud attended.

5   THE INDIVIDUAL UNMASKED

1. Compare this with a comment from before the revolution: 'Every first wife prays God that her husband may never become rich, so that she may be his only wife always. We are happy if there is just enough money to buy food and drink. If there is a little over there comes a new wife, and our happiness is gone.' Thus spoke a woman in Tajik-cultured Samarkand to Annette Meakin around a century ago (1903: 140).
2. This is a reference to the Islamic head-veil, a scarf that conceals both hair and neck, as opposed to the small headscarves customarily worn by Tajik women with their national dress, which are tied at the back of the head, leaving both hair and neck visible.
3. Although how she managed this I do not know. She barely knows where the letters are on the keyboard and her speed is tortoise-like.
4. Rosa is the only *mestiza*, and therefore poor person, in a cast of blondes. She acquires wealth at the end of the series through finding her 'real' (blonde) mother. (Also see note 6.)
5. This is not true for all Tajik women. Jahongul's father, for instance, took Nahdiya and the young Tahmina on holiday to Leningrad once and, had he lived, they would

probably all have travelled outside Tajikistan. Tillo, Sadbarg's near neighbour, travelled abroad on business (Chapter 3).

6. The type of influences that soap operas can have on the more sophisticated of Central Asian youth is described in Kuehnast's article on Kyrgyzstan (1998). Her main protagonist wishes to become a writer of soap operas and likes to see herself as resembling the most glamorous of the businesswomen portrayed in the advertisements from Moscow. In Tajikistan, as in Kyrgyzstan 'soap operas [provide the youth] with a set of images of the world beyond the former Soviet Union, a set of images they sometimes [mistake] for reality' (Kuehnast 1998: 645). However, in Tajikistan the uneducated youth with whom the present book deals are unable to appreciate the favourite soap operas of the Kyrgyz, and for that matter of the Russians and other European members of the CIS, partly because their Russian is so poor. As Sadbarg says, the American *Santa Barbara* is too complicated for her to understand. The only Tajiks I ever saw watching it on a regular basis were academics. Tajik girls can usually only cope with the less complicated plots of the Latin American soaps. Girls from the social background I deal with in this book find themselves culturally, as well as educationally, too distant to be able to relate in the same way to these images as the Kyrgyz woman described by Kuehnast.

7. See for instance, the works of Robert Connell (1988, 1993, 1996), Cornwall and Lindisfarne (1994a, 1994b), Matthew Gutmann (1997), Jeff Hearn (1992), Deniz Kandiyoti (1994), Michael Kaufman (1993, 1995), Michael Kimmel (1987, 1996), Nancy Lindisfarne (1994), David Morgan (1992), Michael Roper (1990, 1994), Victor Seidler (1994) and Chenjerai Shire (1994).

8. See, for instance, Brittan (1989: 189, 192).

9. This story was told me by Kalongul Magzumova.

10. See Harris (1998a) for a fuller account of her life.

6 THE COUPLE RELATIONSHIP: LOVE, SEX AND MARRIAGE

1. In Central Asia a girl is a virgin and a woman is not.

2. Hissor, where Rashid lives, is practically a suburb of Dushanbe and as such is much more modern and Sovietised than Sayot and the other villages of the health project. Hissori women have higher educational levels and considerably greater mobility than women from Sayot.

3. Also see Harris (forthcoming) for a detailed exploration of this theme.

4. Although in some areas of the Soviet Union, where there was at times a little more freedom, secretly published sex manuals were available, for instance in Akademgorodok of Novysibirsk in Siberia in the late 1960s. The men I know who studied there at that time were practically the only Russian men with whom I discussed the subject who understood anything about female sexuality.

5. The relative strength of many women's feelings for their husbands and their sons is shown by the fact that women's jealousy tends to be aimed not at their own marital relationships but at those between their sons and their *kelins*.

BIBLIOGRAPHY

WESTERN EUROPEAN LANGUAGES

Abrahams, Roger D. (1970) 'A Performance-centred Approach to Gossip', *Man Quarterly* 5(June): 290–301.

Abu-Odeh, Lama (1996) 'Crimes of Honour and the Construction of Gender in Arab Societies', in Mai Yamani (ed.) *Feminism and Islam: Legal and Literary Perspectives*, London: Ithaca Press, pp. 141–94.

Adshead, S.A.M. (1993) *Central Asia in World History*, London: Macmillan.

Afshar, Haleh (1987) 'Women, Marriage, and the State in Iran', in Haleh Afshar (ed.) *Women, State and Ideology: Studies from Africa and Asia*, Basingstoke: Macmillan, pp. 70–86.

Akiner, Shirin (2001) *Tajikistan: Disintegration or Reconciliation?* London: Royal Institute of International Affairs.

Al-Khayyat, Sana (1990) *Honour and Shame: Women in Modern Iraq*, London: Saqi Books.

Anonymous (1997) *For Ourselves: Women Reading the Quran*, Women Living Under Muslim Laws.

Anthias, Floya and Yuval-Davis, Nira, with Cain, Harriet (1992) *Racialized Boundaries: Race, Nation, Gender, Colour and Class and the Anti-racist Struggle*, London and New York: Routledge.

Atkin, Muriel (1989) *The Subtlest Battle: Islam in Soviet Tajikistan*, Philadelphia: Foreign Policy Research Institute.

—— (1997) 'Tajikistan: Reform, Reaction and Civil War', in Ian Bremmer and Ray Taras (eds) *New States, New Politics: Building the Post-Soviet Nations*, Cambridge: Cambridge University Press, pp. 603–34.

Bacon, Elizabeth E. (1966) *Central Asians under Russian Rule: A Study in Cultural Change*, Ithaca, NY: Cornell University Press.

Bobroff, Anne (1974) 'The Bolsheviks and Working Women, 1905–20', *Soviet Studies* 26(4): 540–67.

Bouamama, Saïd and Sad Saoud, Hadjila (1996) *Familles Maghrébines de France*, Paris: Desclée de Brouwer.

Bouhdiba, Abdelwahab (1975) *La Sexualité en Islam*, Paris: Quadrige/Presses Universitaires de France.

Bourdon, Marie Ufalvyne (1880) *De Paris à Samarkand: Impressions d'un voyage d'une Parisiènne*, Paris.

Brittan, Arthur (1989) *Masculinity and Power*, Oxford: Basil Blackwell.

Brouwer, Lenie (1998) 'Good Girls, Bad Girls: Moroccan and Turkish Runaway Girls in the Netherlands', in Steven Vertovec and Alisdair Rogers (eds) *Muslim European Youth: Reproducing Ethnicity, Religion, Culture*, Aldershot: Ashgate, pp. 145–66.

Butler, Judith (1990) *Gender Trouble: Feminism and the Subversion of Identity*, New York and London: Routledge.

—— (1993) *Bodies that Matter: On the Discursive Limits of Sex*, New York and London: Routledge.

—— (1995a) 'Melancholy Gender/Refused Identification', in Maurice Berger, Brian Wallis, Simon Watson and Carrie Mae Weems (eds) *Constructing Masculinity*, London: Routledge, pp. 21–36.

—— (1995b) 'For a Careful Reading', in Linda Nicholson (ed.) *Feminist Contentions: A Philosophical Exchange*, London: Routledge, pp. 127–44.

—— (1997a) *Excitable Speech: A Politics of the Performative*, New York and London: Routledge.

—— (1997b) *The Psychic Life of Power: Theories in Subjection*, Stanford, CA: Stanford University Press.

—— (1999) 'Revisiting Bodies and Pleasures', in Vikki Bell (ed.) *Theory, Culture & Society* (Special Issue on Performativity and Belonging) 16(2): 11–20.

Caroe, Sir Olaf Kirkpatrick (1967) *Soviet Empire: The Turks of Central Asia and Stalinism*, 2nd edn, London: Macmillan.

Carrigan, Tom, Connell, Robert and Lee, John (1987) 'Toward a New Sociology of Masculinity', in Harry Brod (ed.) *The Making of Masculinities*, Boston: Allen and Unwin, pp. 63–102.

Chhachhi, Amrita and Pittin, Renée (1996) 'Multiple Identities, Multiple Strategies', in Amrita Chhachhi and Renée Pittin (eds) *Confronting State, Capital and Patriarchy: Women Organizing in the Process of Industrialization*, Basingstoke: Macmillan/New York: St Martin's Press, pp. 93–132.

Connell, Robert W. (1988) *Gender and Power*, Stanford, CA: Stanford University Press.

—— (1993) 'The Big Picture: Masculinities in Recent World History', *Theory and Society* 22: 597–623.

—— (1996) *Masculinities*, Cambridge: Polity Press.

Constantine, Elizabeth (2001) 'Public Discourse and Private Lives: Uzbek Women under Soviet Rule, 1917–1991', PhD Dissertation, Indiana University.

Cornwall, Andrea and Lindisfarne (Tapper), Nancy (1994a) 'Introduction', in Andrea Cornwall and Nancy Lindisfarne (Tapper) (eds) *Dislocating Masculinities, Comparative Ethnographies*, London: Routledge, pp. 1–10.

—— (1994b) 'Dislocating Masculinity: Gender, Power and Anthropology', in Andrea Cornwall and Nancy Lindisfarne (Tapper) (eds) *Dislocating Masculinities, Comparative Ethnographies*, London: Routledge, pp. 11–47.

Dahl, Tove Stang (1997) *The Muslim Family: A Study of Women's Rights in Islam*, Oslo: Scandinavian University Press.

De Vries, Marlene (1987) *Ogen in je rug: Turkse meisjes en jonge vrouwen in Nederland*, Alphen aan den Rijn and Brussels: Samsom Uitgeverij.

El Dawla, Aida Seif, Abdel Hadi, Amal and Abdel Wahab, Nadia (1998) 'Women's Wit over Men's: Trade-offs and Strategic Accommodations in Egyptian Women's Reproductive Lives', in Rosalind P. Petchesky and Karen Judd (eds) *Negotiating Reproductive Rights: Women's Perspectives across Countries and Cultures*, London and New York: Zed Books, pp. 69–107.

Engels, Friedrich (1972) *The Origins of the Family, Private Property and the State*, ed. Eleanor Burke Leacock, trans. Alec West, London: Lawrence and Wishart.

Fierman, William (1991) *Language Planning and National Development: The Uzbek Experience*, Berlin: Mouton.

Firestone, Shulamith (1971) *The Dialectic of Sex*, London: Cape.

Foucault, Michel (1980a) *Power/Knowledge: Selected Interviews and Other Writings, 1972–1977*, ed. and trans. Colin Gordon, New York: Pantheon Books.

—— (1980b) *Herculine Barbin: Being the Recently Discovered Memoirs of a Nineteenth-century Hermaphrodite*, trans. Richard McDougall, Brighton: Harvester Press.

—— (1990) *The History of Sexuality, Vol. 1: An Introduction*, trans. Robert Hurley, London: Penguin Books.

—— (1992) *The History of Sexuality, Vol. 2: The Use of Pleasure*, trans. Robert Hurley, London: Penguin Books.

Fox, Geoffrey E. (1973) 'Honor, Shame, and Women's Liberation in Cuba: Views of Working-class Émigré Men', in Ann Pescatello (ed.) *Female and Male in Latin America: Essays*, Pittsburgh: University of Pittsburgh Press, pp. 273–90.

Fraser, Nancy (1995) 'Pragmatism, Feminism, and the Linguistic Turn', in Linda Nicholson (ed.) *Feminist Contentions: A Philosophical Exchange*, London: Routledge, pp. 157–72.

Freud, Sigmund (1960) *The Ego and the Id*, trans. Joan Riviere, revised and ed. James Strachey, New York: Norton.

Friedl, Erika (1989) *Women of Deh Koh: Lives in an Iranian Village*, Washington and London: Smithsonian Institution Press.

Gardner, Jennifer (1970) 'False Consciousness', in Shulamith Firestone and Anne Koedt (eds) *Notes from the Second Year Women's Liberation: Major Writings of the Radical Feminists*, New York: Radical Feminism, p. 82.

Geiges, Adrian and Suvorova, Tat'iana (1989) *Liebe steht nicht auf dem Plan: Sexualität in der Sowjetunion heute*, Frankfurt am Main: Wolfgang Krüger Verlag.

Gilmore, David (1987) 'Introduction: The Shame of Dishonor', in David Gilmore (ed.) *Honor and Shame and the Unity of the Mediterranean*, Washington, DC: American Anthropological Association, pp. 2–21.

Ginat, Joseph (1982) *Women in Muslim Rural Society: Status and Role in Family and Community*, New Brunswick, NJ: Transaction.

Giovannini, Maureen J. (1987) 'Female Chastity Codes in the Circum-Mediterranean: Comparative Perspectives', in David Gilmore (ed.) *Honor and Shame and the Unity of the Mediterranean*, Washington, DC: American Anthropological Association, pp. 61–74.

Gramsci, Antonio (1971) *Selections from the Prison Notebooks*, ed. and trans. Quintin Hoare and Geoffrey Nowell Smith, London: Lawrence and Wishart.

Gray, Francine du Plessix (1991) *Soviet Women Walking the Tightrope*, London: Virago Press.

Gutmann, Matthew C. (1997) 'Trafficking in Men: the Anthropology of Masculinity', *Annual Review of Anthropology* 26: 385–409.

Halle, Fannina W. (1938) *Women of the Soviet East*, New York: E.P. Dutton.

Harris, Colette (1996) 'Women of the Sedentary Population of Russian Turkestan through the Eyes of Western Travellers', *Central Asian Survey* 15(1): 75–95.

—— (1998a) 'Karomat Isaeva's Tale', *Soundings: A Journal of Politics and Culture* 8: 67–82.

—— (1998b) 'Bokhtar Women's Health Project, Year End Report, April 1997–March 31, 1998', unpublished manuscript.

—— (1999) 'Health Education for Women as Liberatory Process? An Example from Tajikistan', in Haleh Afshar and Stephanie Barrientos (eds) *Globalisation and Fragmentation*, Basingstoke: Macmillan, pp. 196–214.

—— (2002) 'Muslim Views on Population: The case of Tajikistan', in J. Meuleman (ed.) *Islam in the Era of Globalization: Muslim Attitudes towards Modernity and Identity*, London: Routledge/Curzon, pp. 211–22.

—— (forthcoming) 'Approaches to Tackling Sexual Distress: Two Case Studies from a Muslim Central Asian Republic', in Anita Hardon and Diana Gibson (eds) *Rethinking Gender and Masculinities: Confronting Issues of Health*, Amsterdam: Aksant.

Hatfield Elaine and Rapson, Richard L. (1996) *Love and Sex: Cross-cultural Perspectives*, Boston: Allyn and Bacon.

Hearn, Jeff (1992) *Men in the Public Eye: The Construction and Deconstruction of Public Men and Public Patriarchies*, London: Routledge.

Hegland, Mary (1992) 'Wife Abuse and the Political System: A Middle-Eastern Case Study' in Dorothy A. Counts, Judith K. Brown and Jacquelyn C. Campbell (eds) *Sanctions and*

Sanctuary: Cultural Perspectives on the Beating of Wives, Boulder, CO: Westview Press, pp. 203–18.

Heller, Mikhail (1988) *Cogs in the Wheel: The Formation of Soviet Man*, New York: Alfred A. Knopf.

Hite, Shere (1976) *The Hite Report: A Nationwide Study on Female Sexuality*, New York and London: Macmillan Publishing Co.

Human Development Report (1995) *Republic of Tajikistan: Human Development Report*, Dushanbe, UNDP/Government of Tajikistan.

—— (1997) *Republic of Tajikistan: Human Development Report*, Dushanbe, UNDP/ Government of Tajikistan.

Humphrey, Caroline (1983) *Karl Marx Collective: Economy, Society and Religion in a Siberian Collective Farm*, Cambridge: Cambridge University Press.

Hyman, Anthony (1994) 'Power and Politics in Central Asia's New Republics', London: Research Institute for the Study of Conflict and Terrorism.

IMF (1992) 'Economic Review: Tajikistan', Washington, DC: International Monetary Fund. (prepared under the direction of John Odling-Smee et al.).

Jacobson, Jessica (1998) *Islam in Transition: Religion and Identity among British Pakistani Youth*, London: Routledge.

Kamp, Marianne (1998) 'Unveiling Uzbek Women: Liberation, Representation and Discourse, 1906–1929', PhD Dissertation, University of Chicago.

Kandiyoti Deniz (1991) 'Islam and Patriarchy: A Comparative Perspective', in Nikki R. Keddie and Beth Baron (eds) *Women in Middle Eastern History: Shifting Boundaries in Sex and Gender*, New Haven, CT: Yale University Press, pp. 23–42.

—— (1994) 'The Paradoxes of Masculinity: Some Thoughts on Segregated Societies', in Andrea Cornwall and Nancy Lindisfarne (Tapper) (eds) *Dislocating Masculinities, Comparative Ethnographies*, London: Routledge, pp. 197–213.

—— (1998) 'Rural Livelihoods and Social Networks in Uzbekistan: Perspectives from Andijan', *Central Asian Survey* 17(4): 539–60.

Kaufman, Michael (1993) *Cracking the Armour: Power, Pain and the Lives of Men*, Toronto and New York: Viking Press.

—— (ed.) (1995) *Beyond Patriarchy: Essays by Men on Pleasure, Power and Change*, Toronto and New York: Oxford University Press.

Keddie, Nikkie R. (1992) 'Material Culture, Technology, and Geography: Toward a Holistic Comparative Study of the Middle East', in Juan Cole (ed.) *Comparing Muslim Societies: Knowledge and the State in a World Civilisation*, Ann Arbor: University of Michigan Press, pp. 31–62.

Keller, Shoshana (1998), 'Trapped Between State and Society – Women's Liberation and Islam in Soviet Uzbekistan, 1926–1941', *Journal of Women's History* 10(1): 20–44.

—— (2001) *To Moscow, Not Mecca: The Soviet Campaign Against Islam in Central Asia, 1917–1941*, Westport, CT and London: Praeger.

Kimmel, Michael (ed.) (1987) *Changing Men: New Directions in Research on Men and Masculinity*, Newbury Park, CA: Sage Publications.

—— (1996) *Manhood in America: A Cultural History*, New York: The Free Press.

Kisch, Egon Erwin (1932) *Asien Gründlich Verändert* in Bodo Uhse and Gisela Kisch (eds) *Gesammelte Werke in Einzelnausgaben*, Berlin and Weimar: Aufbau-Verlag (1980), Vol. 3.

Kon, Igor (1995) *The Sexual Revolution in Russia, from the Age of the Czars to Today*, trans. James Riordan, New York and London: The Free Press.

Kuehnast, Kathleen (1998) 'From Pioneers to Entrepreneurs: Young Women, Consumerism, and the "World Picture" in Kyrgyzstan', *Central Asian Survey* 17(4): 639–54.

Kunitz, Joshua (1936) *Dawn Over Samarkand*, London: Lawrence and Wishart.

Lajoinie, Simone B. (1980) *Conditions de femmes en Afghanistan*, Paris: Éditions Sociales.

Langton, Rae (1993) 'Speech Acts and Unspeakable Acts', *Philosophy and Public Affairs* 22(4): 293–330.

Lenin, Vladimir I. (1972) *The Emancipation of Women*, New York: International Publishers.

Liebowitz, Ronald D. (1992) 'Soviet Geographical Imbalances and Soviet Central Asia', in Robert A. Lewis (ed.) *Geographic Perspectives on Soviet Central Asia*, London and New York: Routledge, pp. 101–31.

Lindisfarne (Tapper), Nancy (1994) 'Variant Masculinities, Variant Virginities: Rethinking "Honor and Shame"', in Andrea Cornwall and Nancy Lindisfarne (Tapper) (eds) *Dislocating Masculinities, Comparative Ethnographies*, London: Routledge, pp. 82–96.

Lubin, Nancy (1984) *Labour and Nationality in Soviet Central Asia*, London: Macmillan.

Macleod, Arlene E. (1991) *Accommodating Protest: Working Women, the New Veiling, and Change in Cairo*, New York: Columbia University Press.

Makhlouf, Carla (1979) *Changing Veils: Women and Modernisation in North Yemen*, London: Croom Helm.

Mamonova, Tat'yana (ed.) (1984) *Women and Russia: Feminist Writings from the Soviet Union*, trans. Rebecca Park and Catherine A. Fitzpatrick, Boston, MA: Beacon Press.

Marx, Karl (1846a) *The German Ideology*, ed. C.J. Arthur, New York: International Publishers (1989).

—— (1846b) 'Letter from Marx to P.V. Annenkov (Brussels 28 December 1846)', in Neil J. Smelser (ed.) *Marx on Society and Social Change*, Chicago: University of Chicago Press (1973), pp. 3–5.

—— (1867) *Capital, Vol. 1*, trans. Ben Fowkes, New York: Vintage Books (1977).

Massell, Gregory (1974) *The Surrogate Proletariat: Muslim Women and Revolutionary Strategies in Soviet Central Asia 1919–1929*, Princeton, NJ: Princeton University Press.

Meakin, Annette (1903) *In Russian Turkestan*, London: George Allen.

Meek, Dorothea L. (1957) *Soviet Youth: Some Achievements and Problems (Excerpts from the Soviet Press, edited and translated by DM)*, London: Routledge and Kegan Paul.

Mernissi, Fatima (1987) *Beyond the Veil: Male–Female Dynamics in Modern Muslim Society*, revised edn, Bloomington: Indiana University Press.

Meyendorff, Baron Georg Von (1870) *A Journey from Orenburg to Bokhara in the Year 1820*, Calcutta: Foreign Department Press.

Ministry of Health of the USSR (1967) *The System of Public Health Services in the USSR*, Moscow.

Moore, Henrietta (1994a) 'The Problem of Explaining Violence in the Social Sciences', in Penelope Harvey and Peter Gow (eds) *Sex and Violence: Issues in Representation and Expression*, London: Routledge, pp. 139–54.

—— (1994b) *A Passion for Difference: Essays in Anthropology and Gender*, Bloomington, IN and Cambridge: Indiana University Press.

Morgan, David (1992) *Discovering Men*, London: Routledge.

Musallam, B.F. (1983) *Sex and Society in Islam: Birth Control Before the Nineteenth Century*, Cambridge: Cambridge University Press.

Naamane-Guessous, Soumaya (1991) *Au-delà de toute pudeur*, revised edn, Casablanca, Morocco: EDDIF.

Nazaroff, Paul (1980) *Kapchigai Defile: The Journal of Paul Nazaroff*, London: Athenaeum.

—— (1993) *Hunted through Central Asia*, Oxford: Oxford University Press.

Nicolson, Paula (1992) 'Towards a Psychology of Women's Health and Health Care', in Paula Nicolson and Jane Ussher (eds) *The Psychology of Women's Health and Health Care*, Basingstoke: Macmillan, pp. 7–30.

Niyazi, Aziz (1994) 'Tajikistan', in Mohiaddin Mesbahi (ed.) *Central Asia and the Caucasus after the Soviet Union: Domestic and International Dynamics*, Gainesville: University Press of Florida, pp. 164–90.

Northrop, Douglas (2001) 'Subaltern Dialogues: Subversion and Resistance in Soviet Uzbek Family Law', *Slavic Review* 60(1): 115–39.

Omran, Abdel Rahim (1992) *Family Planning in the Legacy of Islam*, London and New York: Routledge/UNFPA.

Pahlen, Count K.K. (1964) *Mission to Turkestan*, London: Oxford University Press.

Park, A.G. (1957) *Bolshevism in Turkestan, 1917–1927*, New York: Columbia University Press.

Patel, Tulsi (1994) *Fertility Behaviour: Population and Society in a Rajasthan Village*, Delhi and New York: Oxford University Press.

Peristiany, J.G. (ed.) (1966) *Honour and Shame: The Values of Mediterranean Society*, London: Weidenfeld and Nicolson.

Peslikis, Irene (1970) 'Resistances to Consciousness', in Shulamith Firestone and Anne Koedt (eds) *Notes from the Second Year Women's Liberation: Major Writings of the Radical Feminists*, New York: Radical Feminism, p. 81.

Pierce, Richard A. (1960) *Russian Central Asia, 1867–1917*, Berkeley, Los Angeles: University of California Press.

Pipes, R. (1964) *The Formation of the Soviet Union, Communism and Nationalism, 1917–1923*, revised edn, Cambridge, MA: Harvard University Press,.

Rakowska-Harmstone, Teresa (1970) *Russia and Nationalism in Central Asia: The Case of Tadzhikistan*, Baltimore, MD: Johns Hopkins University Press.

Riley, Denise (1988) *'Am I that Name?' Feminism and the Category of 'Women' in History*, Basingstoke: Macmillan.

Roper, Michael (1990) 'Recent Books on Masculinity: Introduction', *History Workshop* 29(spring): 184–7.

—— (1994) *Masculinity and the British Organisation Man since 1945*, Oxford: Oxford University Press.

Ross, Eileen and Rapp, Rayna (1997) 'Sex and Society: A Research Note from Social History and Anthropology', in Roger N. Lancaster and Micaela di Leonardo (eds) *The Gender and Sexuality Reader*, New York and London: Routledge, pp. 154–69.

Roy, Olivier (1993) 'The Civil War in Tajikistan: Causes and Implications', Washington, DC: United States Institute of Peace.

Rugh, Andrea B. (1984) *Family in Contemporary Egypt*, Syracuse: State University of New York Press.

Sabbah, Fatna (1984) *Woman in the Muslim Unconscious*, New York and London: Pergamon Press.

Sanders, Paula (1991) 'Gendering the Ungendered Body: Hermaphrodites in Medieval Islamic Law', in Beth Baron and Nikki R. Keddie (eds) *Women in Middle Eastern History: Shifting Boundaries in Sex and Gender*, New Haven and London: Yale University Press, pp. 74–94.

Schrijvers, Joke (1993) *The Violence of Development*, Amsterdam: Spinhuis.

—— (1999) 'Fighters, Victims and Survivors: Constructions of Ethnicity, Gender and Refugeeness among Tamils in Sri Lanka', *Journal of Refugee Studies* 12(3): 307–33.

Schwarz, Franz von (1900) *Turkestan, Die Wiege Der Indogermanischen Völker*, Freiburg in Breisgau: Herder.

Scott, James (1985) *Everyday Forms of Peasant Resistance*, New Haven, CT: Yale University Press.

—— (1990) *Domination and the Arts of Resistance: Hidden Transcripts*, New Haven, CT: Yale University Press.

Segal, Lynne (1994) *Straight Sex: The Politics of Pleasure*, London: Virago.

Seidler, Victor (1991) *Recreating Sexual Politics: Men, Feminism, and Politics*, London, New York: Routledge.

—— (1994) *Unreasonable Men: Masculinity and Social Theory*, London: Routledge.

Shaffer, Jerome (1997) 'Sexual Desire', in Alan Soble (ed.) *Sex, Love, and Friendship: Studies of the Society for the Philosophy of Sex and Love, 1977–1992*, Amsterdam and Atlanta, GE: Editions Rudopi, pp. 1–14.

Sharma, R.R. (1979) *A Marxist Model of Social Change: Soviet Central Asia 1917–1940*, Delhi: Macmillan Co. India.

Shire, Chenjerai (1994) 'Men Don't Go to the Moon: Language, Space and Masculinities in Zimbabwe', in Andrea Cornwall and Nancy Lindisfarne (Tapper) (eds) *Dislocating Masculinities, Comparative Ethnographies*, London: Routledge, pp. 147–58.

Shlapentokh, Vladimir E. (1984) *Love, Marriage and Friendship in the Soviet Union: Ideals and Practices*, New York and Eastbourne: Praeger.

—— (1989) *Public and Private Life of the Soviet People: Changing Values in Post-Stalin Russia*, New York: Oxford University Press.

Siddiqui, Mona (1996) 'Law and the Desire for Social Control', in Mai Yamani (ed.) *Feminism and Islam: Legal and Literary Perspectives*, London: Ithaca Press, pp. 49–68.

Singerman, Diane (1995) *Avenues of Participation: Family, Politics and Networks in Urban Quarters of Cairo*, Princeton, NJ: Princeton University Press.

Stalin, Joseph (1971) *Selected Works*, Davis, CA: Cardinal Publishers.

Steil, Janice. M. (1997) *Marital Equality: Its Relationship to the Well-Being of Husbands and Wives*, Thousand Oaks, CA and New Delhi: Sage.

Stone, Lawrence (1977) *The Family, Sex and Marriage in England 1500–1800*, London: Weidenfeld and Nicolson.

Strong, Anna Louise (1930) *Red Star in Samarkand*, London: Williams and Norgate.

Tadjbakhsh, Shahrbanou (1996) 'National Reconciliation: The Perfect Whim', *Central Asian Survey* 15(3): 325–48.

Tebbutt, Melanie (1995) *Women's Talk? A Social History of 'Gossip' in Working-class Neighbourhoods, 1880–1960*, Aldershot, Hants and Brookfield, VT: Scolar Press.

Tett, Gillian (1994) '"Guardians of the Faith?" Gender and Religion in an (Ex-) Soviet Tajik Village', in Camillia Fawzi El-Solh and Judy Mabro (eds) *Muslim Women's Choice: Religious Belief and Social Reality*, Oxford: Berg Publishers, pp. 128–51.

—— (1995) 'Ambiguous Alliances: Marriage and Identity in a Muslim Village in Soviet Tajikistan', PhD Dissertation, University of Cambridge, UK.

Tohidi, Nayereh (1996) 'Soviet in Public, Azeri in Private: Gender, Islam, and Nationality in Soviet and Post-Soviet Azerbaijan', *Women's Studies International Forum* 19(1–2) 111–23.

—— (1997) 'The Intersection of Gender, Ethnicity and Islam in Soviet and Post-Soviet Azerbaijan', *Nationalities Papers* 25(1): 147–67.

Turner, Stephanie S. (1999) 'Intersex Identities: Locating New Intersections of Sex and Gender', *Gender & Society* 13(4): 457–79.

Ussher, Jane (1991) *Women's Madness: Misogyny or Mental Illness?* Amherst: University of Massachusetts Press.

Vaidyanath, R. (1967) *The Formation of the Soviet Central Asian Republics: A Study in Soviet Nationalities Policy 1917–1936*, New Delhi: People's Publishing House.

Warnock, Kitty (1990) *Land before Honour: Palestinian Women in the Occupied Territories*, New York: Monthly Review Press.

Weyland, Petra (1994) *Inside the Third World Village*, London and New York: Routledge.

Wheeler, Geoffrey (1964) *The Modern History of Soviet Central Asia*, London: Weidenfeld and Nicolson.

WHO (2000) 'Violence against Women: WHO 1999 Pilot Survey in Tajikistan – Working Document, Workshop on Violence against Women in Tajikistan, Dushanbe 29–30 March, 2000', Copenhagen: World Health Organisation Regional Office for Europe.

Wikan, Unni (1980) *Life among the Poor in Cairo*, London: Tavistock.

—— (1984) 'Shame and Honour, a Contestable Pair', *Man Quarterly* 19(4): 635–52.

World Bank (1994) *Tajikistan: A World Bank Country Study*, Washington, DC: World Bank.

Zénié-Ziegler, Wédad (1988) *In Search of Shadows: Conversations with Egyptian Women*, London: Zed Books.

RUSSIAN LANGUAGE

Donish, Ahmed (1960) 'Redkosti Sobytie', in *Puteshestvie iz Bukhary v Peterburg*, Dushanbe: Tadzhikgosizdat.

Ergina, T.P. and Rustamova, M.S. (1983) 'Rasprostranennost' skrytogo defitsita zheleza i anemii sredi beremennykh v Tadzhikskoy SSR', Dushanbe: Nauchno-Issledovatel'ski Institut Okhrany Materinstva i Detstva, supervisor S.H. Hakimova.

Gafarova, M.G. (1969) *Dukhovny oblik zhenshchiny Sovetskogo vostoka*. Dushanbe: Irfon.

Khushkadamova, Khalimakhon O. (1993) 'Otrazhenie sotsial'nogo polozheniya zhenshchin v periodicheskoy pechati Tadzhikistana', kanditat sotsialnikh nauk, Rossiskaya Akademiya Nauka, Sotsiologichesky i Sotsial-psikhologichesky Tsentr, Moscow.

Kislyakov, N.A. (1935) 'Izuchenie patriakhal'noy bol'shoy sem'i v doline r. Vandzh (Tadzhikistan), *Sovetskaya Etnografia* 1: 119–21.

—— (1959) *Sem'ya i brak u Tadzhikov, po materialam kontsa XIX– nachala XX*, Moscow and Leningrad: Izdatel'stvo Akademiya Nauka SSSR.

Kislyakov, N.A. and Pisarchik, A.K. (1970) *Tadzhiki KQategina i Darvaza*, Dushanbe: Donish, Vol. 1.

—— (1976) *Tadzhiki Karategina i Darvaza*, Dushanbe: Donish, Vol. 3.

Monogarova L.F. (1982) 'Struktura sovremmennoy gorodskoy sem'i Tadzhikov (po materialam gorodov UraTyube i Isfary)', *Sovetskaya Etnografia* 3.

Nalivkin, V. and Nalivkina, M. (1886) *Ocherk byta zhenshchiny osedlago tuzemnago naseleniya Fergany*, Kazan': Tipografiia Iperatorskago Universiteta.

Nukhrat, Antonina Ivanovna (1930) *Bytovaya rabota*, Moscow: Tsentrosoyuz.

Pal'vanova, Bibi (1982) *Emantsipatsiya Musulman'ki*, Moscow: Izdatel'stvo Nauka, Glavnaya Redaktsiya Vostochnoy Literatury.

Peshchereva, Elena Mikhaylovna (1976) *Yagnobskie etnograficheskie materialy*, Dushanbe: Institut Istorii Akademii Nauka.

Raskreproshchenie (1971) *Veliki oktyabr i raskreposhchenie zhenshchin Sredney Azii i Kazakhstana (1917–1936gg): Sbornik dokumentov*, Moscow: Izdatel'stvo Mysl.

Shishov, A. (1904) *Sarty*. Tashkent: Turkest.

—— (1910) *Tadzhiki*. Tashkent: Turkest.

Tyurin, Konstantin D. (1962) *Formirovanie Sovetskoy sem'i v Uzbekistane: Pravovye Problemy, 1917–1938gg*, Tashkent.

Yusufbekova, Z. (1989) 'Nekotorye predsvadebnye obychiya i obryady Shugantsev', v Sbornike *Etnografiya v Tadzhikistane*, Dushanbe: Donish.

INDEX